THE CAMBRIDGE COMPANION TO
J. M. SYNGE

John Millington Synge was a leading literary figure of the Irish Revival who played a significant role in the founding of Dublin's Abbey Theatre in 1904. This Companion offers a comprehensive introduction to the whole range of Synge's work, from well-known plays like *Rider to the Sea*, *The Well of the Saints* and *The Playboy of the Western World*, to his influential prose work *The Aran Islands*. The essays provide detailed and insightful analyses of individual texts, as well as perceptive reflections on his engagements with the Irish language, processes of decolonisation, gender, modernism and European culture. Critical accounts of landmark productions in Ireland and America are also included. With a guide to further reading and a chronology, this book will introduce students of drama, postcolonial studies and Irish studies, as well as theatre-goers, to one of the most influential and controversial dramatists of the twentieth century.

P. J. MATHEWS lectures in the School of English, Drama and Film at University College Dublin.

A complete list of books in the series is at the back of this book

D0303360

THE CAMBRIDGE
COMPANION TO
J. M. SYNGE

EDITED BY
P. J. MATHEWS
University College Dublin

CAMBRIDGE
UNIVERSITY PRESS

CAMBRIDGE UNIVERSITY PRESS
Cambridge, New York, Melbourne, Madrid, Cape Town, Singapore,
São Paulo, Delhi, Dubai, Tokyo

Cambridge University Press
The Edinburgh Building, Cambridge CB2 8RU, UK

Published in the United States of America by Cambridge University Press, New York

www.cambridge.org
Information on this title: www.cambridge.org/9780521125161

© Cambridge University Press 2009

First published 2009

Printed in the United Kingdom at the University Press, Cambridge

A catalogue record for this publication is available from the British Library

ISBN 978-0-521-11010-5 Hardback
ISBN 978-0-521-12516-1 Paperback

CONTENTS

CONTENTS

vi

CONTRIBUTORS

MARY BURKE is a graduate of Trinity College Dublin and Queen's University Belfast, and was NEH Keough Fellow at the Keough Institute at the University of Notre Dame in 2003–04. Her QUB doctoral thesis examined the 'tinker' figure in Irish writing, and her book *'Tinkers': Synge and the Cultural History of the Irish Traveller* was published in 2009. Mary joined the University of Connecticut in 2004, where she teaches twentieth-century Irish literature.

GREGORY DOBBINS is an assistant professor of English at the University of California, Davis. He has published essays on Flann O'Brien and James Connolly and is currently working on a book entitled 'Lazy Idle Schemers: Irish Modernism and the Cultural Politics of Idleness'.

OONA FRAWLEY is a post-doctoral research associate at Trinity College Dublin. She received her doctorate from the Graduate School and University Center, the City University of New York. She is the author of *Irish Pastoral* (2005), and the editor of several books, including *Selected Essays of Nuala Ní Dhomhnaill* (2005). She is currently editing a four-volume project on 'Irish Cultural Memory' and completing a study of Edmund Spenser, 'Spenser's Trace'.

NICHOLAS GRENE is Professor of English Literature at Trinity College Dublin, a fellow of the College and a member of the Royal Irish Academy. He has published widely on Irish literature and on Shakespeare. His books include *The Politics of Irish Drama* (Cambridge University Press 1999), *Shakespeare's Serial History Plays* (Cambridge University Press 2002), and *Yeats's Poetic Codes* (2008). His edited collection of Synge's travel essays, *Travelling Ireland*, was published in 2009.

SUSAN CANNON HARRIS is an associate professor of English at the University of Notre Dame. Her book *Gender and Modern Irish Drama* was published in 2002. Her work on gender and eighteenth-century Irish theatre has appeared in *PMLA*, *Theatre Journal*, and *Éire-Ireland*. Recent publications include, 'Red Star vs. Green Goddess: Sean O'Casey's *The Star Turns Red* and the Politics of Form', and 'Mixed Marriage: Sheridan, Macklin, and the Hybrid Audience'.

C. L. INNES is Emeritus Professor of Postcolonial Literatures, University of Kent, Canterbury, UK. She is the author of books and essays on Irish, African, Black British, and Australian writing. Her *Introduction to Postcolonial Literatures in English* was published by Cambridge University Press in 2007.

DECLAN KIBERD is Professor of Anglo-Irish Literature and Drama at University College Dublin. His publications include: *Synge and the Irish Language* (1979, 1993); *Idir Dhá Chultúr* (1993, 2002); *Inventing Ireland* (1995); *Irish Classics* (2000); and *The Irish Writer and the World* (Cambridge University Press 2006). He is a member of the Board of Directors of the Abbey Theatre and a frequent speaker at the Synge Summer School.

BEN LEVITAS is a senior lecturer in Drama at Goldsmiths College, London. He is author of *The Theatre of Nation: Irish Drama and Cultural Nationalism 1890–1916* (2002) and editor (with David Holdeman) of *W. B. Yeats in Context* (Cambridge University Press 2009).

P. J. MATHEWS lectures in the School of English, Drama and Film at University College Dublin. He is the author of *Revival: The Abbey Theatre, Sinn Féin, the Gaelic League and the Co-operative Movement* (2003) and editor of the *UCDscholarcast* series, *The Art of Popular Culture: From 'The Meeting of the Waters' to* Riverdance (2008). He was the Naughton Fellow and Visiting Associate Professor of English at the University of Notre Dame in 2007–08.

BRENDA MURPHY is Board of Trustees Distinguished Professor of English at the University of Connecticut. She is the author of numerous articles on drama and theatre, and eleven books, including *The Provincetown Players and the Culture of Modernity* (2005), *Congressional Theatre: Dramatizing McCarthyism on Stage, Film, and Television* (1999), *O'Neill: Long Day's Journey into Night* (2001), *Tennessee Williams and Elia Kazan: A Collaboration in the Theatre* (1992), and *The Cambridge Companion to American Women Playwrights* (1999).

SHAUN RICHARDS is Professor of Irish Studies at Staffordshire University. He is the co-author (with David Cairns) of *Writing Ireland: Nationalism, Colonialism and Culture* (1988) and editor of *The Cambridge Companion to Twentieth-Century Irish Drama* (2004), and has published widely on Irish drama in major journals and edited collections.

ANTHONY ROCHE is Associate Professor in the School of English, Drama and Film at University College Dublin. Recent publications include *The Cambridge Companion to Brian Friel* (2006) and the chapter on 'Contemporary Irish Drama: 1940–2000' in *The Cambridge History of Irish Literature* (2006). In 2009 Palgrave Macmillan published a revised edition of *Contemporary Irish Drama: From Beckett to McGuinness*. His book *Brian Friel: Theatre and Politics* will be published in 2010.

ELAINE SISSON is a research fellow at the Graduate School of Creative Arts and Media, Dublin. She was previously Senior Lecturer in Visual Culture at the Institute of Art, Design and Technology, Dún Laoghaire. The author of *Pearse's Patriots: St Enda's and the Cult of Boyhood* (2004), she is currently co-editing a collection of essays on Irish design and material culture called *Made in Ireland? Visualising Modernity 1922–1992*.

ALAN TITLEY is Professor of Modern Irish in University College Cork. He is the author of four novels, hundreds of stories and many plays, including *Tagann Godot*, a sequel to Beckett's play which was produced in the Abbey Peacock. It has been translated from the original into Italian, Russian and French, and his stories have appeared in many other languages, including Croatian, Bulgarian, Albanian, Polish, English and Scottish. He writes a weekly column for the *Irish Times* on current and cultural matters and presents a programme on literature for RTÉ Radio 1. His scholarly works include studies of the Irish novel and contemporary Scottish Gaelic literature.

ACKNOWLEDGEMENTS

Sincere thanks to Ray Ryan for commissioning this book and for sound advice at every stage of the project, and to all the contributors for their insight and professionalism. I am grateful to Sean Corcoran, Padhraic Egan, Andrea Gallagher, Derek Hand, Maurice Mathews and Colin Rothery for their invaluable comments. I would like to acknowledge the Keough-Naughton Institute for Irish Studies at the University of Notre Dame for the award of the Naughton Fellowship for 2007–08 which allowed me to develop this project. Special thanks to Chris Fox, and to the Notre Dame graduate students for their invaluable contributions to my J. M. Synge class. I am greatly indebted to the students of the MA in Anglo-Irish literature at University College Dublin and to Jennika Baines, Giulia Bruna, Alan Graham, Yulia Pushkarevskya and Louise Walsh for astute perspectives and insightful dialogue. Thanks also to Maartje Scheltens, Tom O'Reilly, Eimear O'Connor, Patricia Harkin, Philip Harvey, Buddy and Marie Mathews and John and Moira Murtagh for kind assistance along the way. My deepest debt is to Audrey for wise counsel and unending support from beginning to end, and to Macdara and Theo – my own two playboys of the western world.

ABBREVIATIONS AND SHORT TITLES

Generally, references to Synge's works are given parenthetically in the text (by abbreviated title, followed by volume and page reference). A list of the abbreviations follows.

CW   *Collected Works*, gen. ed. Robin Skelton., 4 vols.

CW I   Vol I, *Poems*, ed. Robin Skelton (London: Oxford University Press, 1962).

CW II   Vol II, *Prose*, ed. Alan Price (London: Oxford University Press, 1966).

CW III Vol III, *Plays: Book 1*, ed. Ann Saddlemyer (London: Oxford University Press, 1968).

CW IV   Vol IV, *Plays: Book 2*, ed. Ann Saddlemyer (London: Oxford University Press, 1968).

CL   *Collected Letters* [followed by volume number], ed. Ann Saddlemyer, 2 vols. Oxford: Clarendon Press, 1983–84.
        I, 1871–1907
        II, 1907–1909.

1871   John Millington Synge born in Rathfarnham in Dublin on 16 April to John Hatch Synge and Kathleen Traill, last of five children; Charles Darwin's, *The Descent of Man* published.

1872   Death of Synge's father from smallpox. He is buried on John's first birthday.

1879   The Land League founded, beginning of a sustained period of agrarian unrest in rural Ireland; Ibsen's *A Doll's House* first performed.

1884   The Gaelic Athletic Association founded to promote traditional Irish sports such as hurling and Gaelic football; Huysmans' *Against Nature* published.

1885   Joins Dublin Naturalists' Field Club.

1889   Begins studies at Trinity College Dublin; also studies violin at Royal Irish Academy of Music.

1891   Death of Charles Stewart Parnell.

1892   Graduation from Trinity College Dublin having specialised in Irish and Hebrew; Douglas Hyde's address, 'The Necessity for De-Anglicising Ireland'.

1893   Spends a year in Germany (Koblenz and Würzburg) studying music. Founding of the Gaelic League to promote the use of the Irish language.

1895   In Paris takes courses in French literature with A. E. Faguet, medieval literature with Petit de Julleville (Sorbonne), and comparative phonetics with Paul Passy (École Pratique des Hautes-Études).

1896   Spends four months in Rome and Florence studying Italian language and art. Marriage proposal to Cherrie Matheson is rejected; continues studies in French literature at Sorbonne; meets W. B. Yeats in Paris.

1897   Attends inaugural meeting of Maud Gonne's *Association Irlandaise*, resigns three months later; operation on swollen gland in his neck, early manifestation of Hodgkin's disease.

1898   Studies Irish and Homeric civilisations with d'Arbois de Jubainville; first summer visit to Aran Islands (10 May–25 June).

1899   Attends opening production of Irish Literary Theatre, *The Countess Cathleen* by W. B. Yeats; second visit to Aran (12 Sept–7 Oct); outbreak of Boer War.

1900   Third visit to Aran (15 Sept–3 Oct).

1901   Fourth visit to Aran (21 Sept–19 Oct); attends first professional production of an Irish language play, *Casadh an tSugáin* by Douglas Hyde.

1902   Takes course in Old Irish with d'Arbois de Jubainville. Writes *Riders to the Sea*, *The Shadow of the Glen* and a draft of *The Tinker's Wedding*.

1903   Meets James Joyce in Paris; first play, *The Shadow of the Glen*, staged by the Irish National Theatre Society in Dublin.

1904   *Riders to the Sea* produced; Abbey Theatre opens.

1905   *The Well of the Saints* produced at the Abbey Theatre; commissioned (with artist Jack B. Yeats) by the *Manchester Guardian* to write a series of twelve articles on the congested districts of the west of Ireland.

1906   *The Well of the Saints* staged at Deutsches Theatre in Berlin (translated by Max Meyerfeld); *The Shadow of the Glen* produced at the Inchover Theatre, Prague (translated by Karel Mušek).

1907   First production of *The Playboy of the Western World* at the Abbey Theatre, disturbances in the theatre during production; *The Aran Islands* published; *The Shadow of the Glen* produced at National Theatre, Prague; *The Tinker's Wedding* published.

1908   Directs Sudermann's *Teja* and Molière's *The Rogueries of Scapin*, both translated by Lady Gregory; death of Synge's mother.

1909   Dies 24 March; *The Playboy, Well, Shadow* and *Riders* at Court Theatre, London; first production of *The Tinker's Wedding*, His Majesty's Theatre, London.

1910   *Deirdre of the Sorrows* at the Abbey Theatre with Molly Allgood as Deirdre; W. B. Yeats publishes 'J. M. Synge and the Ireland of his Time'; publication of *The Works of John M. Synge* by Maunsel.

1911   On a US tour Abbey Theatre production of *The Playboy* causes disturbances in Boston, New York and Philadelphia. Eugene O'Neill attends and is deeply impressed by Synge's plays.

1913   Maurice Bourgeois's translation of *The Playboy* (*Le Baladin du monde occidental*) produced at Théâtre de L'Oeuvre, Paris.

1914   Shoyo Tsubouchi's version of *Well*, *Reigen* (A Miracle), performed in Toyko.

1917   Djuna Barnes's article on Synge published in the New York *Morning Telegraph* (18 Feb).

1922   James Weldon Thornton acknowledges the influence of Synge in the Preface to *The Book of American Negro Poetry*.

1933   *Riders* influences Federico García Lorca's *Blood Wedding*.

1934   Robert Flaherty directs his Synge-inspired film *Man of Aran*.

1935   Film version of *Riders* directed by Brian Desmond Hurst.

1937   Bertolt Brecht and Margarete Steffin adaptation of *Riders*, *Señora Carrar's Rifles*; Antonin Artaud visits the Aran Islands to retrace the footsteps of Synge.

1941   Marcel Herrand stages *The Playboy* at the Théâtre des Mathurins; *The Aran Islands* translated into Japanese by Masami Anezaki.

1955   Japan's famous 'Gekidan Mingei' (People's Theatre Art Players) production of *The Playboy*.

1962   Film version of *The Playboy* directed by Brian Desmond Hurst.

1963   Arabic version of *Riders* produced by Syrian Arab Television.

1969   Unsi El Haj's translation of *Well* performed at the Beit Meri Roman Temple, Lebanon.

1971   First performance of *The Tinker's Wedding* at the Abbey Theatre.

1975   British National Theatre production of *The Playboy*.

1979   Derek Walcott acknowledges *Riders* as a model for *The Sea at Dauphin*.

1982   Druid Theatre's landmark production of *The Playboy* directed by Gary Hynes.

1984   Mustafa Matura's *Playboy of the West Indies* based on Synge's *The Playboy* performed at the Oxford Playhouse.

1994   Abbey Theatre revival of *The Well of the Saints*, directed by Patrick Mason.

1997   National Theatre in Prague stages *The Playboy* translated by Martin Hilský.

2005   Druid Theatre Company, Galway, produces DruidSynge: a performance of the entire canon of Synge's plays which tours in Ireland, UK and USA.

2006   Chinese version of *The Playboy* staged in Beijing and Dublin by Pan Pan theatre company.

2007   In centenary year of its original production, the Abbey Theatre stages adaptation of *The Playboy* by Bisi Adigun and Roddy Doyle.

PART I

The Synge Texts

I

P. J. MATHEWS

Re-thinking Synge

John Millington Synge, widely regarded as the most influential Irish dramatist of the twentieth century, burst on to the scene in 1903 when his first play, *The Shadow of the Glen*, caused a stir among audiences and critics alike during its opening run in Dublin. Over the next two years Synge produced another two plays: *Riders to the Sea* (1904), which is considered to be one of the greatest one-act plays in the history of modern drama; and *The Well of the Saints* (1905) which celebrates the imagination and heroism of the dissident who refuses to be coerced into conformity at the behest of the moral majority. Synge may well have drawn on the lessons of the latter play when, in 1907, he became notorious as the author of *The Playboy of the Western World*, which caused riots in the Abbey Theatre and brought his work to the attention of the wider world for the first time. Two other plays, *The Tinker's Wedding* written in 1907 and *Deirdre of the Sorrows* staged posthumously in 1910, complete the canon of Synge's plays. Yet before his early death in 1909 he also left a small body of prose of considerable significance which includes *The Aran Islands* (1907) and an extraordinarily rich compendium of travel essays, now collected under the title *In Wicklow, West Kerry and Connemara* (CW II, 187–343), as well as a robust collection of poetry (1909).

Despite the relatively small corpus of work he left behind, Synge's stature has continued to grow steadily among audiences, readers and critics since his early death over a century ago. From that time onwards his plays have been performed frequently and consistently on stages in Ireland and abroad, with much of his work being paid the compliment of translation into many other languages. His major prose work, *The Aran Islands*, has taken its place as the acknowledged progenitor of the sub-genre of Irish island memoirs and, accordingly, has had a seminal influence on visual representations of the west of Ireland – from the paintings of Paul Henry to Robert Flaherty's film, *Man of Aran* (1934). His travel essays also endure as superb, if somewhat neglected, reflections on the lesser-documented social and cultural dynamics of rural Ireland at the close of the nineteenth century. One of the most palpable measures of his enduring appeal is Synge's obvious and lasting imprint on the work of succeeding generations of Irish playwrights. This is widely acknowledged and readily apparent in every decade since his death, but is particularly noteworthy in the work of major contemporary writers such as Brian Friel, Tom Murphy and Frank McGuinness, and acutely obvious among an emerging cohort of playwrights which includes Marina Carr, Conor McPherson and Martin McDonagh.

Synge's stature as a dramatist of international importance was assured early on and continues to grow. As many of the essays in this volume attest, his global influence extends far and wide to the work of Eugene O'Neill, Djuna Barnes and James Weldon Johnson in America; to Louis Esson in Australia; to Bertolt Brecht and Federico García Lorca in Europe; and to Derek Walcott and Mustapha Matura in the West Indies. In terms of academic scrutiny his texts have borne the weight and survived the vagaries of successive waves of critical inquiry. Over the course of a century, Synge's works have been mobilised in the pursuit of nationalist, liberal humanist, formalist, feminist, Marxist, historical revisionist and postcolonial critical agendas. Yet in all of this, inevitably, certain patterns of response and orthodoxies of approach to his texts have become entrenched in the theatre and in the criticism.

Not surprisingly, *The Playboy of the Western World* is regarded as his crowning achievement: in most cases it is the one text by Synge that those coming to him for the first time will have heard of before. Although it is hard to argue against the iconic status that the play has earned, arising out of its infamous first production and as a work of dramatic excellence in its own right, the disproportionate attention that it routinely receives often forecloses deeper and more engaged considerations of Synge's 'minor' works – many of which remain lesser known and under-analysed. The pecking order of acclaimed texts is now well established: *The Playboy* is Synge's pinnacle achievement, *The Shadow* and *Rider's* are exceptional trial pieces, *The Well of the Saints* is a lesser *Playboy*, *The Tinker's Wedding* and *Deirdre of the Sorrows* are incidental curiosities. Extending this prescribed hierarchy of merit to the non-dramatic work: *The Aran Islands* becomes a useful source-book for the play's scenarios, the travel essays are off-cuts from *The Aran Islands*, and the poetry of minor significance only.

The publication of this *Companion* offers a timely opportunity to reflect on some of the established critical thinking that has cohered around the Synge oeuvre. With the staging of the ambitious and highly acclaimed DruidSynge initiative by Galway's Druid Theatre Company in 2005, the corpus of Synge's dramatic works was performed in one impressive production which played to packed houses all over Ireland and around the world. Plays not normally seen were given their debut in many cities, and the more familiar works were viewed in a new light. Apart from providing an obvious demonstration of the enduring international appeal of Synge's drama, the DruidSynge project was an important catalyst in prompting critical discussion to move beyond the select number of plays that readily spring to mind whenever Synge's name is mentioned. Arising out of this, Part I of this volume is given over to discrete critiques of Synge's texts. The intention is to cater to readers coming to the work for the first time by laying out key issues and backgrounds that will enable more informed engagements with individual texts. However, the contributors to the opening section also open up new avenues of interpretation and new modes of theorisation in relation to the greater- and lesser-known texts. These essays challenge the limits of inherited critical categorisations and make compelling claims in relation to individual works by Synge that command further critical and theatrical treatment.

The essays in Part II of this volume represent a more broadly thematic engagement with Synge's work from a range of critical and disciplinary perspectives. As W. J. Mc Cormack's illuminating biography[1] has demonstrated, Synge's intellect was remarkably agile. He was an omnivorous reader whose intellectual curiosity extended across an extraordinarily rich spectrum of subjects including literature, folklore, philology, natural science, anthropology, music, philosophy and social theory; and over an impressive range of languages that included English, Irish, French, German and Italian. The essays in Part II of the *Companion* reflect the fact that Synge's work has attracted the scrutiny of a more diverse academic community with the passage of time. Now that more than a century has passed since all of Synge's texts were originally published or first performed, it is possible to reflect anew, with some historical distance and new theoretical insights, on the significance and critical treatment of one of Ireland's most important literary figures. The essays in the second section, therefore, map the contours of the major theoretical debates surrounding Synge and suggest potential lines of inquiry for the future.

Much intellectual energy has been invested since Synge's own time in recording and analysing the details of his plays in production. Indeed, the original staging of *The Playboy of the Western World* and the controversy which surrounded it must rank as one of the best-documented events in theatre history. Synge's plays provide fertile ground for those keen to investigate the dynamics of audience response and the function of theatre at particular historical moments. Yet the range of productions that Synge's work has inspired also demands critical attention. It is appropriate, therefore, that Part III of this volume should focus on Synge's plays in production, in

Ireland and beyond, from original productions to more recent ones, including a consideration of his profound impact on contemporary Irish drama.

Given the range of Synge's intellectual, cultural and artistic pursuits and influences, and the variety of academic approaches that his work has inspired, the challenge of introducing him is a formidable one. It is prudent, therefore, in the remainder of this opening essay, to offer an overview of some of the key ideas and debates relevant to readers embarking on an early encounter with Synge, rather than a summary of the contents of this *Companion*. Since the commissioned essays that follow this introduction – written by a diverse team of distinguished international scholars – address specific texts and themes from unique and valued perspectives, the task of this introduction will be to consider some of the important ideas and issues that are relevant across the entire body of Synge's work.

J. M. Synge's life (1871–1909) coincided exactly with one of the most pivotal phases of Irish history which saw the agrarian unrest of Charles Stewart Parnell's era of the late nineteenth century give way to the revolutionary republicanism that led to the 1916 Rising. Born with firm roots in the landed aristocracy of County Wicklow and into a resolutely conservative Anglo-Irish family, Synge not only witnessed the decline of the ascendancy but, in his own maverick way, contributed to the demise of Anglo-Irish privilege. His involvement in the turbulent early years of Ireland's national theatre – the Abbey Theatre – was crucial to its success in securing a foothold at the centre of Irish cultural life and debate. Also, with his unique perspectives on both the decline of the ascendancy and the rising trajectory of nationalist cultural revival, Synge was well placed to diagnose the ills of Irish society and culture. To an almost eerie degree the major events in his life were to mirror those of his fellow Wicklowman, C. S. Parnell. Both were prominently unconventional Anglo-Irish gentlemen who became notorious for courting international controversy over matters of sexual morality – Parnell over the Katharine O'Shea affair, Synge over the *Playboy* riots. Having ignited the passions of national controversy, both men went to early graves shortly afterwards – Parnell at 45 and Synge at 38 years old. Although a generation apart, Parnell and Synge cast long shadows after their deaths and endured as potent spectral presences in Irish cultural memory, most prominently in the work of W. B. Yeats and James Joyce.

Given the highly dramatic nature of the times that he lived through, it is hardly surprising that the narrative of Synge's life is often condensed into a simplified and manageable version of a complicated set of events and contexts. Students of Synge need to be somewhat wary of the standard account which has informed much of the critical response to his work since his death in 1909. The conventional narrative usually follows a familiar pattern: an ascendancy dilettante dabbles in the bohemian fads of *fin-de-siècle* Europe before coming to his senses during his famous sojourns on the Aran Islands, where be becomes a willing convert to Irish Revivalism on discovering the richness of Irish folk culture and the power of the Irish language; having bravely faced down both the inherited prejudices of his Anglo-Irish background and the chauvinistic extremes of Irish nationalism, Synge becomes a martyr to 'art', brought down by the philistinism and intransigence of those consumed by the 'narrow' concerns of Irish politics.

This version of the J. M. Synge story was largely created by W. B. Yeats in the years and decades immediately after the writer's death. Yeats's famous essay, 'J. M. Synge and the Ireland of his Time'[2] (1910) is particularly important for its role in the distillation of Synge's achievements along the lines favoured by the influential poet. In this essay he effectively removes Synge from the material domain of quotidian concerns and elevates him to the status of 'a pure artist' (323) who – in that oft-quoted line – 'seemed by nature unfitted to think a political thought' (319). Despite the fact that critics increasingly have questioned the self-serving distortions of Yeats's assessment, the portrayal of Synge by the elder poet has been stubbornly enduring, not to mention restrictive of the interpretative potentials within Synge's work. Tellingly, in one of his later poems, 'The Municipal Gallery Revisited', Yeats, as he surveys the portraits in what is now the Hugh Lane Gallery, frames Synge as an icon of Irish Revivalism.

Perhaps unfairly, then, Synge became a stable signifier for classic Irish Revivalism early on and did not live long enough to challenge attempts to cast him in that role. His innovative use of dialect informed by the rhythms of Irish language syntax and his vivid renderings of rural customs and landscapes, particularly in the west of Ireland, were easily co-opted to the nation-building agendas of the new Irish State. Because of Synge's willingness to go 'into the cabins of the poor', ardent nationalist critics such as Daniel Corkery could forgive his Anglo-Irish roots and enlist him to the cultural programme of independent Ireland.[3] Meanwhile, almost simultaneously, a younger generation of writers coming of age in the early years of Irish independence were eager to overthrow the certainties of Yeatsian Revivalism. Not surprisingly it was Yeats's great exemplar, Synge, who often bore the brunt of their critique.

In his iconoclastic expressionist play, *The Old Lady Says 'No!'* (1929), playwright Denis Johnston called time on the Irish Revival by mercilessly parodying Synge's 'peasant-speak'.[4] Some years later Patrick Kavanagh, one of Synge's greatest posthumous antagonists chimed in with his rejection of the Revival as 'a thoroughgoing English-bred lie'.[5] The meteoric rise of the reputation of James Joyce in the twentieth century and the gargantuan body of critical commentary that accompanied it, further pigeonholed Synge and routinely placed him at the opposite end of the spectrum from that inhabited by Joyce. Invariably Joyce was cast as an open-minded cosmopolitan, happy to leave the parochialism of his native place behind, while Synge was sequestered to illustrate the kind of narrow-focused nativism that the author of *Ulysses* (1922) was trying to escape.

From this vantage point it is increasingly clear that counter-Revivalist disavowals of Synge as the embodiment of a regressive nativism were strategically motivated by a youthful intolerance of the overbearing dominance of Yeats rather than by any deep engagement with Synge's work. If anything, writers such as Johnston and Kavanagh were more properly the great inheritors of Synge rather than his antagonists. Synge was much more deeply informed by the traditions of European avant-garde theatre than Johnston ever was, notwithstanding the latter's fondness for German expressionism. And the notion, advanced by Kavanagh and others, that Synge was the purveyor of twee Revivalist pastoral was disingenuous indeed.[6] Synge, after all, repeatedly drew attention to the psychic, material and cultural impoverishment of life in remote rural Ireland, not only in essays like 'The Oppression of the Hills' (CW II, 210–12) but also in plays such as *The Shadow of the Glen* and *The Playboy of the Western World*. Ironically, Kavanagh in his epic poem 'The Great Hunger' would himself explore psychic territory similar to that already traversed by Synge decades earlier.

It is not the intention here to downplay Synge's involvement in the Irish Revival – that is an indisputable fact demonstrated by his profound contribution to the early Abbey Theatre. But caution does need to be exercised against simplistic and reductive formulations of that broad movement which all too readily associate it with regressive, reactionary and backward-looking traditionalism. As I have argued elsewhere, the Revival 'was characterised by a rich and complex ferment of political and cultural thinking and no small amount of liberational energy'.[7] There is, however, a clear need to differentiate between the brand of Revivalism espoused by Yeats and that articulated by Synge: all too often they are lumped together as if they pursued the same agendas.[8] In actuality, Synge's work provides a systematic critique of Yeatsian methods: from *The Shadow of the Glen*, which offers a counter-version of female agency to that presented in *Cathleen ni Houlihan* (1902) by Yeats and Lady Gregory, to *Deirdre of the Sorrows*, which attacks Yeats's conservative, antiquarian approach to the past in plays like *On Baile's Strand* (1904). If anyone embodies the spirit of progressive Revivalism, therefore, it is J. M. Synge. In his hands tradition is best deployed as a springboard for innovation, liberation and progress, not as a straitjacket to conserve older ways purely to keep the modern world at bay.

Notwithstanding his deep commitment and personal investment in the Irish language, a preparedness to critique and supersede what he perceived to be a persistent attitude of tokenism in Gaelic League circles earned Synge a good deal of suspicion among Irish-language enthusiasts. Although he had been schooled in the Irish language at Trinity College Dublin and had first-hand knowledge of Gaeltacht life he made a deliberate choice not to write in the ancient tongue but, instead, to infuse English with the idioms, rhythms and syntax of Irish. That strategic decision may have undermined attempts to create a modern literature in the Irish language but it also produced a new literary approach. This tactic allowed Synge to transcend both the uncertainties and squabbling over the standardisation of the Irish language, and the provincialism of Anglo-Irish literary practices. Such a pivotal decision to rest his literary reputation on a risky experiment with dialect was due in no short measure to his belief that 'the linguistic atmosphere of Ireland has become definitely English enough, for the first time, to allow work to be done in English that is perfectly Irish in its essence, yet has sureness and purity of form' (CW II, 384).

His very fashioning of a modern, experimental Irish national theatre out of the fragments of a folk tradition further makes the case for Synge's progressive Revivalism. Although much of his work can be read as an elegy for the disappearance of a distinct Gaelic peasant culture, especially *The Aran Islands*, there are many carefully inserted critiques of the passing of the old order which are far from sentimental. *Riders to the Sea*, for example, can easily be read as an exposé of the cloying and atrophying influence of tradition, where youthful ambition is discouraged out of a pathological need to preserve the old ways. Maurya's refusal to give her blessing to Bartley's enterprising journey over sea to Galway explains why life on the island has sunk below subsistence with 'only a bit of wet flour' and 'maybe a fish that would be stinking' (CW III, 24) to look forward to.

A similar diagnosis combining elegy and critique is levelled against his own class in his essay 'A Landlord's Garden in County Wicklow'. As he surveys a crumbling big house with its 'broken green-houses and mouse-eaten libraries', Synge ponders a cultural fate remarkably similar to that encountered in *Riders*. Here, too, he is struck by the fact that 'one or two delicate girls ... are left so often to represent a dozen hearty men who were alive a generation or two ago' (CW II, 231). In this case it is effete aristocratic decadence rather than Gaelic inability to respond to adverse external conditions which leads to cultural liquidation. Yet Synge is very careful to differentiate between the two scenarios: while the profound tragedy of *Riders* is intended to evoke pathos, he states categorically in 'A Landlord's Garden' that 'These owners of the land are not much pitied at the present day, or much deserving of pity' (231). Significantly though, the need to triumph over the cultural torpidity evident within Gaelic *and* Anglo-Ireland becomes a major feature of Synge's work. This is most obviously manifested in the wild, visceral and subversive acts of defiance perpetrated by so many of his heroes and heroines in response to cultural stagnation and fragmentation. As Synge wrote in the Preface to his collected poems: 'there is no timbre [of poetry] that has not strong roots among the clay and worms ... before verse can be human again it must learn to be brutal' (CW I, xxxvi).

Synge's revolutionary impulses, however, are rarely expressed in conventional political terms. Despite his close proximity to cult personalities such as John O'Leary, Charles Stewart Parnell and Maud Gonne, major political figures are surprisingly, if deliberately, absent from his work. Nor is he concerned with the major events and significant dates in Irish history. 'I do not much believe', he wrote to Frank Fay, 'in trying to entice in people by a sort of political atmosphere that has nothing to do with our real dramatic movement' (CL I, 81–2). The suggestion here is not that Synge is the apolitical writer that Yeats claimed but rather that he is a supremely democratic one. The grand narrative of Irish nationalism in and of itself may be of little interest to him, but the outworking of power relations at individual and local level is what consumes him most. His concern is to break down and devolve abstract ideological issues into micro-contexts where questions of power, personal motivations, psychodynamics, group relations and determinisms of environment and culture can be laid bare. Both in his plays and prose works, Synge rarely engages with macro-political issues like the Land War or the fortunes of Irish nationalism. Instead, his method is to concentrate on the details of the material and cultural impoverishment of life among the most marginalised of people in remote rural Ireland. The politics of agrarian unrest are not the focus – they are a given. It is the exhaustion and trauma left in their wake at an individual level that is of most concern.

The extreme subtlety of political analysis which characterises most of Synge's creative work, however, gives way to a more overt statement of opinion in a series of articles that he wrote for the *Manchester Guardian* in 1905. These compelling essays owe as much to Synge's serious engagement with the left-wing ideas of Karl Marx and Paul Lafargue as they do to his first-hand knowledge of Irish poverty. Readers of these essays are left in no doubt about his contempt for the dubious practices of the publican-grocers or 'gombeen men', who wielded disproportionate power in the poorest regions of the country. Having visited the congested districts of the west of Ireland he was all too aware that the cosy alliance between business, parliamentary politics, religion and the professions was as culpable in visiting unspeakable misery on the most marginalised of the Irish peasantry as was the colonial administration.

In his famous essay on Synge, Yeats astutely observed that 'low vitality helped him to be observant and contemplative' (321). Synge was indeed dogged by ill-health for most of his life and, consequently, was curious about the source of individual and cultural vigour and vitality. As recorded in 'Autobiography', he anxiously internalised Darwinian notions of the survival of the fittest: 'I am unhealthy', he wrote, 'and if I marry I will have unhealthy children. But I will never create beings to suffer as I am suffering' (CW II, 9). This dark realisation may explain his personal preference for the company of tramps, vagrants and wanderers of various kinds. It is no coincidence that the people of the roads populate the entire spectrum of his writing and stand out as the most heroic and admirable characters in his plays. Christy Mahon, Nora Burke, the Douls, Deirdre and Sarah Casey – wanderers all – are presented as welcome antidotes to the small-minded, repressive, dull consensus of sedentary middle-class life.

In the travel essays, too, Synge repeatedly displays an interest in and empathy with tramps and vagrants, beyond a mere nostalgia for their quaintness. Crucially, his admiration is for their vitality, ingenuity, wit and dogged unconformity. Unlike Yeats's tramps, Synge's (particularly those documented in the reportage of his travel essays) are not idealisations of the collective folk imagination which can be invoked to stem the relentless march of modernity, but rather supreme and diverse embodiments of the power of individual fortitude and imagination to resist assimilation and repressive conformity at particularised moments in Irish history. It is unsurprising, therefore, that Samuel Beckett should count Synge's tramps among his most important influences.[9]

Synge's wanderers are alternative *flâneurs* – not jaded and effete like the metropolitan variety that he had encountered in Paris but muscular, autonomous and vital. In Gustave Caillebotte's classic painting 'Paris Street: Rainy Day' (1877) the alienation and ennui of the umbrella-carrying *flâneur* is unmistakable. This contrasts very interestingly with Jack B. Yeats's illustration of 'A Wicklow Vagrant' (CW II, 205) which accompanied an essay by Synge on the travellers of Wicklow.[10] Clearly in dialogue with Caillebotte's painting, Yeats's drawing highlights a congruent dandyism which attaches to the Wicklow tramp but unmistakably contrasts the tramp's robust physicality with the effeteness of the Parisians by emphasising his nonchalant imperviousness to the teeming rain. Synge performs an analogous manoeuvre in the essay itself by offering his literary renderings of the full-blooded tramp life he had encountered, as an alternative to decadent *fin-de-siècle* tastes exemplified by Joris-Karl Huysmans' novel, *Against Nature* (1884). Significantly in that novel, the ailing and reclusive aesthete, Des Esseintes, is the last surviving member of a noble aristocratic family. In his self-indulgent excesses and experiments he embodied all that Synge despised, not only in the European literature of the period but in the habits of his own declining class. Such literature, in his view, pandered to the cynical monotony of privileged modern life instead of challenging it. Books like this, argued Synge, appealed to 'young men without health, and to women without occupation, rather than to those who count, singly or collectively, in contemporary intellectual life' (CW II, 395). By drawing comparisons between the temperament of the vagrant and that of the artist, Synge hammered home the point and offered one of the most revealing insights into his own aesthetic:

> In the middle classes the gifted son of a family is always the poorest – usually a writer or artist with no sense for speculation – and in a family of peasants, where the average comfort is just over penury, the gifted son sinks also, and is soon a tramp on the roadside. (CW II, 203)

In such a formulation Synge opened up the possibility for the discovery of avant-garde potentials within local and traditional culture and for a critique of the settled orthodoxies of Irish middle-class life from a marginal perspective. In Synge's view, this was far more satisfactory than the wholesale importation of undigested and inappropriate conventions from elsewhere. Not surprisingly, his picaresque modernism was deeply sceptical of the arcane experimentalism soon to be in vogue among his modernist contemporaries: Synge's preference instead was for literature that could be 'read by strong men, and thieves, and deacons, not by little cliques only' (CW I, xxxvi).

In all of this it seems increasingly disingenuous to set Synge and Joyce apart as polar opposites. Joyce's tetchy and grudging response to *Riders to the Sea* is often taken as evidence enough that their respective aesthetic projects were antagonistic. Yet Synge, too, was in a similar way falsely dismissive of Ibsen's 'joyless and pallid words' in the Preface to *The Playboy* (CW II, 53) despite their profound influence on him: it would seem that homage paid to literary exemplars must be disguised as churlish carping. The fact that Joyce openly criticised and repeatedly parodied certain aspects of Synge's work is often remarked upon, but what is less readily appreciated is the extent to which Joyce was clearly in sympathy with, and indebted to, Synge's work and influence. Both writers soaked up the avant-garde energies of *fin-de-siècle* Europe – the hand of Ibsen touched both of them and can be detected in striking similarities across texts. *The Shadow of the Glen* and Joyce's 'Eveline', for example, reward careful comparison.[11] Both fashioned different but, in many ways, analogous experimental modernist literatures which are solidly anchored in the Irish locale. *The Aran Islands* can be read as Synge's *A*

Portrait of the Artist as a Young Man with a reverse trajectory from Paris to the west of Ireland; and in the homeless wanderings of Stephen Dedalus in *Ulysses* we can detect another version of the artist-tramp model proposed by Synge. In the end, both writers, informed by sustained engagements with European literatures, were consumed by the issues surrounding Ireland's material advancement and spiritual liberation. It seems reasonable, therefore, that their various points of consensus and not just their obvious divergences should command critical scrutiny. The redress of this imbalance may facilitate the emergence of new perspectives – not just on the work of Synge and Joyce – but also on the trajectories of the Irish Revival and of the progress of Irish modernism.

As this volume attests, Synge's work continues to be of central importance within and beyond the broad field of Irish Studies: theatre historians invest much effort poring over the details of original productions and tracking the later influence of Synge; cultural historians maintain a keen interest in his contribution to the complex dynamics of cultural nationalism in advance of the 1916 Rising; his experiments with the Irish language persistently attract the interest of Irish language scholars and specialists in Hiberno-English; cultural theorists explore Synge's interest in, and relationship to, left-wing thought; his detailed analysis of the actual conditions of rural Ireland at the turn of the twentieth century make him an important source for sociologists and anthropologists; his spirited challenge to Victorian moral propriety in the form of a radical on-stage representation of female desire continues to be of consequence to feminist critics; the nature of his experimentalism commands debate among students of modernism; and his profound awareness of the operations of culture in colonial contexts make him a fitting exemplar for postcolonial writers and critics. This list may provide a useful catalogue of approaches to Synge's work that readers will encounter over the course of the essays collected here. Inevitably, however, it does not exhaust all possibilities. Of necessity in a collection such as this, some themes and ideas that might otherwise have merited a fuller treatment have been dispersed across a number of essays, and difficult editorial choices and selections have had to be made. In the end the final shape of the volume is intended to address, in the first instance, the needs of those whose interest in the work of J. M. Synge is just awakening.

One of the most significant trends to emerge from this collection of essays is the ongoing internationalisation of Synge Studies. Synge's indebtedness to the rich traditions of European literature and drama is receiving renewed attention, and the extent to which he was nourished by some of the most radical nutrients within the intellectual bloodstream of late nineteenth-century Europe is now being fully appreciated. His impact on a whole range of the most influential dramatists of global significance becomes more apparent with the passage of time: of all the modern Irish playwrights to work exclusively in the Irish theatre, Synge is the one whose place among the great figures of world drama is secure. Despite his rejection by the audience of the Abbey Theatre more than a century ago, Synge's appeal to Irish audiences has never been greater than at the present moment. The enduring power of his work to address the Irish context was illustrated by the popular success of Bisi Adigun and Roddy Doyle's version of *The Playboy* produced by the Abbey Theatre in 2007. It is significant in these globalised times, therefore, that Synge's rising international reputation has not been achieved at the expense of local indifference. Indeed there is a compelling symmetry in the fact that – a century after he was vilified for misrepresenting the people of the west of Ireland – Synge's plays should once again triumph on the international stage in a major production mounted by the Druid Theatre Company from County Galway.

NOTES

1. W. J. Mc Cormack, *Fool of the Family: A Life of J. M. Synge* (London: Weidenfeld & Nicolson, 2000).
2. W. B. Yeats, 'J. M. Synge and the Ireland of his Time', *Essays and Introductions* (London: Macmillan, 1961), p. 318.
3. Daniel Corkery, *Synge and Anglo-Irish Literature* (Cork: Mercier Press, 1966), p. 235.
4. Denis Johnston, *Selected Plays of Denis Johnston*, ed. Joseph Ronsley (Gerrards Cross: Colin Smythe, 1983).
5. Patrick Kavanagh, 'Self-Portrait', in Antoinette Quinn (ed.), *Patrick Kavanagh: A Poet's Country, Selected Prose* (Dublin: Lilliput Press, 2003), p. 306.
6. Patrick Kavanagh, 'Paris in Aran', in *Patrick Kavanagh: A Poet's Country*, pp. 189–92.
7. P. J. Mathews, *Revival: The Abbey Theatre, Sinn Féin, the Gaelic League and the Co-operative Movement* (Cork: Field Day / Cork University Press, 2003), p. 148.
8. See, for example, Joe Cleary, *Outrageous Fortune: Capital and Culture in Modern Ireland* (Dublin: Field Day, 2006), pp. 92, 132, 147.
9. See Gregory Dobbins's essay below for further consideration of Synge's influence on Beckett.
10. See Elaine Sisson's essay below for further discussion of Yeats's illustration.
11. See P. J. Mathews, '"A.E.I.O.U"': Joyce and the *Irish Homestead*', in Anne Fogarty and Timothy Martin (eds.), *Joyce on the Threshold* (Gainesville, FL: University of Florida Press, 2005), pp. 151–68.

2

OONA FRAWLEY

The Shadow of the Glen and Riders to the Sea

John Millington Synge's first two performed plays, *The Shadow of the Glen* (1903) and *Riders to the Sea* (1904), marked a significant point of departure for both Synge's own writing and, more broadly, for the Irish theatre. In discovering that he could quite literally grant voice to the people he had long observed, Synge found his forte. With these two strikingly original one-act dramas the budding playwright lent considerable impetus to the early experiments of the Abbey Theatre movement, indicated the directions his future work would take, and created a focus for the divisive nationalisms that would later rile audiences of *The Playboy of the Western World*.

The Irish Literary Theatre, established by Lady Augusta Gregory, W. B. Yeats and George Martyn in 1899, set out a clear statement of intent:

> We will show that Ireland is not the home of buffoonery and easy sentiment, as it has been represented, but the home of an ancient idealism. We are confident of the support of all Irish people, who are weary of misrepresentation, in carrying out a work that is outside all of the political questions that divide us.[1]

Aiming instead to provide a forum for home-grown drama that expressed the subtleties of Irish life, this experimental theatre movement actively contributed to the political dynamics of its moment. Since his work veered away from mawkish sentimentality and offered instead a performance of 'the deeper thoughts and emotions'[2] that the founders of the movement had hoped for, Synge can be credited with providing the embryonic Abbey Theatre with its first robust articulation of an innovative national drama. His brand of realism was a shift away not only from the tomfoolery and false naivety that was the Irish peasant's representation on the English stage, but also from a merely symbolic representation of Irishness that achieved such success in plays like *Cathleen ni Houlihan* (1902) by W. B. Yeats and Lady Gregory. Despite the Irish Literary Theatre's expressed hope of finding a 'tolerant welcome', however, it would discover that some perceived a contradiction between the 'ancient idealism' the movement had hoped to present and the Irish life that Synge represented.[3]

Synge's particular experience enabled his invocation of authentic peasant life: not only had he wandered the Irish countryside among the peasantry, especially in Wicklow, but he had formalised his study through a commitment to Irish language and folklore, underlined by his time on the Aran Islands and in other Irish-speaking areas. Both of his first two plays exhibit the influence of these various experiences: a familiarity with nature and local rural place in Ireland; an interest in experimenting with dialect; and knowledge of Irish folklore alongside an appreciation of its connections with wider European folk traditions. Even before his first two plays were performed, then, Synge was committed to a type of realism uncommon among his Irish literary contemporaries. This led to later discussion about Synge's indebtedness to 'foreign' influence, including, most obviously, that of Ibsen. While his dismissal of Ibsen in the preface to *The Playboy* has rung untrue for many critics, Synge's denial of the impact of a major contemporary playwright whose work was performed in Dublin during the period is significant. An admission of 'foreign' influence might well have lessened the controversy sparked by *Shadow* particularly: Synge, though, repeatedly emphasised that his plays were drawn from observations of a specifically Irish reality. In this sense, he inaugurates an Irish national theatre that not only attempted to diminish the stage Irishman, but also initiated the Irishwoman into the drama in a new and significantly vocal way, in a manner comparable to Ibsen's initiative.

Given that *Riders* and *The Shadow* were Synge's first attempts at drama – beyond the early experiment *When the Moon Has Set* and other fragments of dramatic poetry – their success is all the more remarkable. The compressed form of the one-act play provided for the tight focus of each piece, allowing the action to unfold in real time and heightening the dramatic quality of Synge's language. The two plays had compositional overlap, and in many ways offer sisterly contrasts: while *Riders* hinges on an old woman, *The Shadow* focuses on a young one; *Riders'* atmosphere is determined by the sea, while *The Shadow* draws strange energy from the menace of the hills; *Riders* relies on tragedy and tension, while *The Shadow* allows for some comedy and release. These contrasts, though, are best seen in the context of the plays' similarity in determinedly reflecting an Ireland that had been kept off-stage; in their preoccupation with landscape and Irish literary tradition; and in their representation of women who are subject to tragedies that are the result of presiding social mores.

Riders to the Sea, quietly published in Yeats's *Samhain* (1903) prior to its first performance on 25 February 1904,[4] has been called a 'flawless masterpiece'.[5] The drama takes shape around what an early critic astutely called the 'expectant anxiety and imaginative awe'[6] that builds: we await the inevitable news that Maurya has lost her last son, Bartley, to the sea, on the same day that confirmation comes of the drowning some days before of another son, Michael. Some critics have argued that *Riders* does not follow Aristotelian principles closely enough to be tragic: James Joyce, for instance, who admired the play enough to translate it into Italian, called *Riders* a 'dwarf-drama'.[7] *Riders* does, however, contain a form of tragedy that Ronán McDonald describes as 'a pattern of response, a cultural structure through which profound loss is mediated and represented'.[8] This tragic pattern is related to the peculiar and defining relationship that characters have with nature and landscape, as well as to what an earlier Synge critic, writing of *Deirdre of the Sorrows*, called 'feminine tragedy'.[9] The 'sublime tragedy' of *Riders* and *The Shadow*, I argue, renovated notions of the dramatic in Irish theatre with a social realism that altered the perception and function of the woman on-stage, while highlighting expectations placed on Irish women off-stage; it also granted new dramatic importance to landscape and place by refusing simple idealisations of rural Ireland. In this sense, Synge can be seen to do for rural Ireland what James Joyce was to do for its capital city: diagnose a profound social malaise.[10]

As an island nation, Ireland has an intimate relationship with the sea, and *Riders* draws on practical, mythical and literary aspects of Ireland's seafaring tradition. Aran provided first-hand experience of the sea's ruthlessness and the constant negotiation with weather that curagh-travel demanded. Synge repeatedly notes the threat of drowning in *The Aran Islands*, and variously experiences exhilaration, terror and profound dejection – all aspects of the sublime – in the face of the churning sea. 'Even, I thought, if we were dropped into the blue chasm of the waves, this death, with the fresh sea saltness in one's teeth, would be better than most deaths one is likely to meet' (CW II, 97). This impassioned state of mind is soon eroded, however: 'After a few hours, the mind grows bewildered with the endless change and struggle of the sea, and an utter despondency replaces the first moment of exhilaration' (CW II, 108). This emotional shift, so vividly captured in *The Aran Islands*, is significant for *Riders*, because it is embedded in the keen, which Synge described as a 'profound ecstasy of grief' (CW II, 74). This tradition, he felt, embodied

> no personal complaint … but seems to contain the whole passionate rage that lurks somewhere in every native of the island. In this cry the inner consciousness of the people seems to lay itself bare for an instant, and to reveal the mood of beings who feel their isolation in the face of a universe that wars on them with winds and seas. (CW II, 75)

Considered against the background of the 'easy sentiment' that the Irish Literary Theatre wished to transcend, the passion of grief and resignation Maurya displays when Bartley's death is confirmed is startling, revealing Synge's familiarity with funeral traditions as he witnessed them on Aran, as well as with literary conventions of elegy, which he had been drawn to in his poetry. The *Vita Vecchia*, for instance, a prose piece interspersed with poetry, is elegiac in tone, but where it falls short in attempting to accommodate several literary traditions, *Riders* succeeds. The powerful wail of the keen caps the play's involvement with conventions of elegy: we have seen repetitions and refrains of speech, reiterated questions, and outbreaks of anger – all before the death even occurs. We finally witness a procession of mourners and an attempt by Maurya to move from grief to a type of consolation: 'there isn't any more the sea can do to me' (CW III, 23), she tells herself, concluding that 'No man can be living forever, and we must be satisfied' (CW III, 27). Maurya's performance of grief thus summarises Synge's literary loyalties to both pan-European and specifically Irish traditions.

When Maurya follows Bartley to deliver a blessing she had failed to utter and bread the daughters have forgotten to give him, she experiences a vision which, like other events of the play, derives from Synge's time on Aran. Synge records the tale of a woman who saw her dead son riding a horse with a man who was subsequently to drown. This type of vision has roots in folklore concerned with the return of the dead to escort another to their realm. Also noteworthy, though, are links between Maurya's visionary qualities and those of her medieval Irish counterparts, whom Synge had studied first as an undergraduate at Trinity College, and later on his own initiative as he continued his study of the Irish language. Synge was thus aware of an Irish literary tradition that frequently granted visionary capacities to central figures like Finn. The seer in medieval Irish literature was, like Maurya, frequently connected to nature and possessed an ability to 'read' the natural landscape correctly: as the only one to see the inevitability of Bartley's death should he sail under the prevailing conditions, Maurya has direct links to the medieval Irish visionary. The priest, that central figure in Irish bourgeois culture, is kept off-stage by Synge, and the priest's reassurances, communicated through the daughters, are dismissed by Maurya: 'It's little the like of him knows of the sea', she says (CW III, 21). Instead it is Maurya, with her more traditional, even pre-modern knowledge of the natural world, who foresees what is to come. The seer in medieval literature is also often a liminal figure 'stranded in nature', who 'acquires special knowledge'.[11] This description is apt for Maurya, whom we see marginalised by her son and her daughters when her words and warnings go unheeded. Synge, though, makes her central, thus seeming to comment on the status of 'folk' knowledge as well as on the status and place of such women in the community.

Synge's play also offers the flipside of an often-told Irish narrative, that of the voyage tale, or *immram*. Early Irish voyage literature reveals the importance of the sea to Irish culture. Figures such as the seventh-century Bran or the ninth-century Maelduin set off on adventures, leaving the land (and predictability) behind for the mystery, danger and possibility of the sea. Synge, whom we know read *The Voyage of Bran* at least,[12] and who in *The Aran Islands* repeatedly considered the possibility of death on the water, provides in *Riders* the inversion of this narrative by focusing on those who remain behind while the voyage occurs. This inversion means that the dramatic focus is necessarily shifted: first, to the women frequently absent from or marginal in voyage literature, and second, by offering a critique of male heroics from the perspective of female sacrifice, an enactment of anxiety rather than action.

This second point is crucial to a consideration of the play as sublime feminine tragedy: Maurya's awareness of the threat of the sea, garnered through the loss of her husband and her sons, has granted her a fearful connection with the natural world. Unlike the Aristotelian tragic figure, Maurya's tragedy is precisely about *in*action – about having to remain behind as a woman, about the fallout after loss. The tragedy of *Riders* is not to be associated with Michael or Bartley, but with Maurya. She sees herself as part of a society in which women's roles are strictly defined and in which the loss of the male in a household can seem catastrophic. When Bartley advises his sisters about handling affairs in his absence, Maurya immediately asks how Cathleen would 'get a good price for a pig' (CW III, 9), revealing a sense that her own inability to act or exert agency is tied to her position as a woman. The priest, in contrast, despite having no experiential basis for his judgements, offers false reassurances that Bartley will survive because God would not deprive an old woman of her only son, and receives veneration and attention. Within the culture of the play, men can be said to dismiss or undercut the female voice. These attempts at control ultimately fail, though, since Synge reveals that much of the power of the play resides in nature, which overwhelms the men who would not listen to the words of an old woman in full possession of the knowledge of the sea's sublime power.

Maurya's relative powerlessness and her household's tragic circumstances have been alternatively explained as the result of consistent violations of folk ritual pointed out by many critics.[13] If actions had been carried out according to prescription, Bartley's death might have been averted – had Maurya issued the blessing and the girls remembered Bartley's bread. It is more likely, though, that Synge purposefully positions these folk violations in the play in order to demonstrate the way the culture *suggests* that control and agency lie within the grasp of women (and men), when he himself recognises that they do not. In the end Maurya is granted only the verbal power which Synge himself provides her. This can, though, be read as a breakthrough: after the priest's repeated words have proven empty, and after Bartley, the male head of the household, is silenced by the sea, the last word is Maurya's. The old woman, not the priest, performs and utters what seems like a funeral oration at the close.

Conversely – and herein lies much of the play's genius – we can also see Maurya's triumph of speech at the close of the play in a more sinister light. Maurya's complaint that she goes unheeded can and indeed has been read as indicative of a generational clash;[14] Maurya attempts to impose a rigid world-view and a confining operating procedure on the next generation, resisting change and clinging to traditional modes of thought. Read this way, Maurya's refusal to listen to her children or to risk change means that the triumph of speech at the close is considerably diminished, since her last word comes at the cost of having lost her last son. Maurya's tragedy, then, is compounded not only by her inability to act, but, in this reading, by her unwillingness to act outside of perceived strictures of behaviour. The very predictability of Maurya's tragedy, Synge implies, lies in the stasis she wishes to preserve.

First responses to *Riders* in the national press were marked by objections: it contained 'studies of melancholy',[15] according to the *Independent*, and, despite 'much of the old charm and delicacy', was 'too dreadfully doleful to please the popular taste'.[16] In the *United Irishman* – Arthur Griffith's paper so important in the controversy over *The Shadow* – *Riders*' 'tragic beauty' was noted, but the reviewer found the play wanting: 'we need sunshine badly'.[17] Such reviews make evident that the Irish Literary Theatre was perceived to have responsibilities other than the simple performance of its chosen plays – the plays were held accountable for their entertainment value, but also for their politics and their representation of an Irishness whose definition was still under construction.

While *Riders* was not granted an easy passage by theatre critics, it was *The Shadow of the Glen* – first performed several months earlier on 8 October 1903 – that had assured Synge's position as the most controversial among the new playwrights. On a bill that included *Cathleen ni Houlihan*, *Shadow* was teamed with one of the most successful and iconic plays of the Irish theatre movement. In *Cathleen*, set in 1798, a young man abandons his bride on the eve of marriage for the principles of national freedom and revolution. In *The Shadow*, Nora's husband Dan feigns death to test her fidelity, and orders her out of the house once he discovers what he believes to be her disloyalty.

Nora subsequently departs with a tramp who has chanced on their cottage during a storm that provides the backdrop to a far from idealised rural existence. The public appeal of *Cathleen* is usefully considered against the debate sparked by *The Shadow*, since it reveals considerations of appropriate behaviour for men and women in turn-of-the-nineteenth-century Dublin: while the young man's departure in *Cathleen* (and the less focused-on abandonment of his bride) was considered an heroic and symbolic act of sacrifice for Ireland, Nora's exit into the wild Wicklow darkness with a stranger aroused passionate disclaimers about the character of the women of Ireland.

The charge was led by Arthur Griffith, who mounted hyperbolic retorts to Synge's play, proclaiming Irish women 'the most virtuous in the world',[18] and accusing Synge even a year later of creating a 'foul echo from degenerate Greece' in Nora, who, he claimed, could not be Irish.[19] Yeats countered Griffith's attacks by eloquently defending the play, the theatre's right to produce even nationally unflattering art, and the possibility that what Synge had written reflected Irish experience.[20] Despite Yeats's defence and Synge's own, the controversy raged on. With 'Mother Ireland' and 'Cathleen' dominant metaphors for Ireland during this period, Nora was seen as an abomination. As is often noted,[21] the original 'Cathleen ni Houlihan', Maud Gonne, left a performance of *The Shadow* in protest and wrote against 'the insidious and destructive tyranny of foreign influence'.[22] That Gonne would shortly seek a divorce herself to escape an abusive marriage did not deter her from protesting at the representation of Irish women as possibly disloyal to their husbands.

The emphasis Synge placed on the authenticity of productions was crucial to the controversy. A 1906 brochure for the Theatre's first tour outlined what came to be known as the 'Abbey Method' as it developed out of performances like that of *Riders* and *The Shadow*:

> The Folk Play needs a special kind of acting, and the Company ... are all familiar with the ways of the Irish peasantry, and in their acting take care to keep close to the actual movements and gestures of the people. Their costumes and their properties are ... thoroughly appropriate and accurate, while the scenes in which they play are actual replicas of some carefully chosen original; forasmuch as these plays are portions of Irish life, so are they put upon the stage with a care and accuracy of details that has hardly been attempted before.   (CW III, xix)

The Shadow's 'accuracy' was, though, just what was contested. In the later preface to *The Playboy*, Synge offered as a further defence the fact that his language was 'genuine': 'When I was writing *The Shadow of the Glen* some years ago, I got more aid than any learning could have given me, from a chink in the floor of the old Wicklow house where I was staying, that let me hear what was being said by the servant girls in the kitchen' (CW IV, 53). While the image of the Anglo-Irish Synge listening to servants through floorboards was itself enough to cause offence, Synge was attempting to justify not just what was perceived as the difficult language and rhythm of his speech, but the seemingly impossible realities addressed by his plays.

Despite objections that the play did not reflect Irish life and Griffith's claim that *The Shadow*'s roots were Greek, sources for the play came from Synge's time on Aran, where he was told the story of 'the unfaithful wife'. The tale is close to that of *The Shadow*: while a young woman sits with what she thinks is the body of her husband, a stranger comes to the door; the woman asks the stranger to sit with the body while she alerts a neighbouring man to her husband's death. While the woman is out, the dead man sits up and reveals his plan to the stranger. The wife then returns with the young man, who, at her suggestion, lies down for a rest; the woman soon follows the young man into the bedroom. The version told to Synge on Aran ends thus:

> Then the dead man got up, and he took one stick, and he gave the other to myself. We went in and saw them lying together with her head on his arm. The dead man hit him a blow with the stick so that the blood leapt up and hit the gallery. (CW II, 72)

Narrated in the first person, the folktale gives centrality to the viewpoint of the stranger. Synge's innovation is to shift away from his tramp to highlight the woman who, in the Aran version, remains voiceless and seemingly unimportant except as an object who precipitates a crisis over ownership: in Synge's version, as he wrote to actor Frank Fay, 'the woman should dominate' (CW III, xx). Focusing on Nora provides for a devastating window into the mind of a young woman who would have been considered fortunate in her day for having married, for having a home and land. A final shift that Synge contrives in the tale makes his drama extremely subtle. While uproar about the play depended crucially upon reading Nora as unfaithful, there is, in fact, no concrete evidence presented to this effect. Synge offers nothing so obvious as the version of the tale told on Aran; Nora is not caught red-handed, and this provides the play with much of its power to disturb. Behind the vehement charge against Nora must have hidden a reluctance to face another possibility: if Nora was not unfaithful to Dan, the focus would have to shift to the acceptability of Dan's behaviour in tricking his wife and then asking her to leave.

This leads to a second element crucial to the uproar: the belief that Nora *chooses* to leave. Nora's departure cannot, in fact, be equated with her Ibsenian namesake's decision to leave her husband in *A Doll's House*. What the furore over *The Shadow* ignored – perhaps by necessity in a culture that had felt itself emasculated under colonisation and was in the process of creating new concepts of masculinity – was the critique Synge levelled at the role played by the husband in the 'loveless marriage'[23] described by Yeats's father in his own eloquent defence of the play. Synge critiques the commodification of marriage, comparing the way that woman seemed indispensable as a symbol of nation and country but often lacked value outside of these nationalist constraints.[24] As Robin Skelton perceptively notes, Nora's question about what way she would have lived without marrying Dan is not rhetorical: it is 'one of the real questions asked and answered in the play'.[25] Nora's 'departure' is, in fact, closer in character to eviction, with all of the resonances that that would have had for an Irish audience: it is little wonder that critics focused instead on denying the possibility of the play's realism, for to confront an eviction of a wife by a husband would have been to confront not only the colonial legacy but also the impact it continued to have on male–female relations in Ireland. The large-scale eviction crises of the 1840s and 1850s would have loomed large in the cultural memory of Synge's audience. Synge himself witnessed his own brother evicting tenants on their estate, as well as evictions on Aran. But to recognise Dan in the role of evicting landlord and Nora as tenant demanded a shift in understanding of power and gender relations that Synge's audiences did not seem capable of. Nora, not unlike Kavanagh's Patrick Maguire, is full of a profound spiritual hunger. But as a young, married woman in a seemingly privileged position, her ruminations were hard for critics to bear – hence the long line of critique that focuses on her perceived wrongdoing instead of on the circumscribed society she comes from.

Nora's cottage is modelled on one in Glenmalure, County Wicklow, and the idea of what Synge called in an essay 'The Oppression of the Hills' might well have been inspired by a visit to this remote, dramatic valley. Synge's Wicklow experiences exposed him to a side of nature different from the one that his contemporaries (and he himself as a younger writer) were so eager to idealise in the service of an Irish nationalism. At twilight one evening, regarding the natural world, Synge experiences a 'vague but passionate anguish' (CW II, 196) that he would later assign to Nora:

> Among the cottages that are scattered through the hills of County Wicklow I have met with many people who show in a singular way the influence of a particular locality. These people live for the most part beside old roads and pathways where hardly one man passes in the day, and look out all the year on unbroken heath. (CW II, 209)

The relentlessness of weather in such locations means that it becomes, like the sea in *Riders* and *The Aran Islands*, a character in its own right, with the

ability to influence people: the climate, Synge suggests, 'has caused or
increased a tendency to nervous depression among the people, and every
degree of sadness ... is common among these hills' (CW II, 196). Rather
than presenting his audience, then, with an idyllic representation of a country
cottage scene, Synge challenges closely held ideals with Nora, who is indeed
deeply affected by her environment, but not positively: like Maurya, Nora's
experience of nature is marked by sublime tragedy. While she has an appreciation of some of the beauty of the place, Nora is acutely aware of the
loneliness it induces, and of her lack of power over her circumstances: she
can no more control the outcome of her life than she can the weather.

Synge's language emphasises the impact that life is having on Nora.
Words like 'queer' and 'odd' resonate with the atmospheric tension of
'mists' and the darkness of the hills: 'it's always up on the hills he was,
thinking thoughts in the dark mist', Nora says of Dan (CW III, 35). Dan is
ruminative, suspicious of 'talk' and words, while Nora is desperate for talk,
and speaks to the tramp as if to herself about her isolation and anguish, the
sense of her own dashed hopes, her resignation. In the play's short term we
see her move from a sobriety at her husband's death to an increasing distress
as she talks through her possibilities, and, eventually, towards despair as she
realises that her husband is going to expel her from the house. Alone on the
doorstep in the presence of the three men, she is left to the environment that
has shaped her isolation until the tramp offers his company. Synge uses
landscape as a background on which he can project crucial social problems,
so that the environment itself, in a sense, becomes responsible for this state
of affairs. If Nora is displaced, abandoned or even disloyal, the environment
has shaped her.

The striking overlap in names used in *Riders* and *The Shadow* heightens
Synge's critique of Irish mores. Rather than assigning characters distinct
names, Synge consciously redeploys 'Nora', 'Michael' and 'Patch' across the
two plays. While one could argue that Synge was simply using common
names, others were equally common – and in fact Synge uses them for
peripheral figures, like the 'Colum' and 'Eamon' who help to carry
Michael's body in *Riders* (CW III, 23). The interplay of names implies an
inter-changeability and critiques the impossibility for individuation under
rigid social strictures like those that determine Nora's fate.

One character beyond both the realm of names and the social realm
inhabited by the other characters is, of course, *The Shadow*'s tramp. As an
outsider, he remains nameless, and this seeming lack of identity is, for Synge, a
sign of his realised freedom. Synge had been drawn to the life of the tramp:
'He is not to be pitied', he writes of one tramp that he meets. 'There is
something grandiose in a man who has forced all kingdoms of the earth to

yield the tribute of his bread and who, at a hundred, begs on the wayside with the pride of an emperor' (CW II, 196). Synge imbues the tramp with the royalty that such marginal figures were often assigned in medieval Irish literature: legends of wild men (and, less often, women) situated them in the wilderness 'as the point of departure on the way towards acquisition of sovereignty'.[26] Sweeney, for instance, like Synge's tramp, lives in the natural world, and is a fallen king; Finn, equally a wanderer, retains a regal-like status in the culture. Synge thus adapts for a modern audience the medieval Irish preoccupation with vagrant figures. Not unlike the medieval bard, the tramp is implicitly an artist figure who moves freely. He is also a liminal figure who exists beyond the clutches of a culture's mores, an aspect of tramp life that Synge, a critic of bourgeois Victorian morals, found appealing.

The near-mysticism Synge personally connects to nature and place is also personified in the figure of the tramp, and is apparent in many of Synge's early poems. 'The Fugitive', for instance, enacts a flight 'from all the wilderness of cities' (CW I, 15, 1) and the speaker in 'Prelude' removes himself so thoroughly that he 'did but half remember human words, / In converse with the mountains, moors, and fens' (CW I, 32, 7–8). Synge's early emphasis on the possibilities of a communion with nature were fed by his study of Irish-language material, since the Irish tradition is steeped in variations on pastoral forms. But, as with *Riders*, Synge employs Irish and folklore traditions only to make them his own: by the time he writes *The Shadow*, there is no simple idealisation of Irish country life and landscape, but a complex rendering of the sometimes contradictory realities of rurality that his urban audience found difficult to accept.

In her departure into nature, Nora also retrieves from Irish literary tradition other female figures who live in nature. Nature, for such women, is a space of madness as for the male, but simultaneously a space of control and freedom: and what often retrieves their sanity is sexual intercourse. Synge, unlike many of his contemporaries, does not try to sanitise Irish representations of sexuality, male/female relationships, and power dynamics, and if we extrapolate from the Irish literary traditions on which he draws, we could conclude that Nora might well be embarking on a more satisfying relationship and existence, though beyond the bounds of the only culture she has experienced. The only known reality is that which we are given with the play's ending, however, when Synge ironically suggests that the status quo has been maintained: if Nora's 'departure' has unsettled her husband, he does not show it. Instead, we have the 'comic relief' of witnessing the pseudo-couple of Michael and Dan sitting down at the hearth to share a drink, appropriate for a play that has mimicked and mocked wake traditions, many of which centred around drink, and for a type of tale in which alcohol is central. Synge thus ends the play with a sobering commentary on the centrality of alcohol to male agency and power in Ireland, allowing drunkenness to take central stage only as the curtain falls, just as rampant alcoholism and its inevitable effects on Irish family life during this period were similarly cloaked and hidden.

Both *Riders* and *The Shadow* continue to reward inspection and analysis; the complexity of Synge's constructions has certainly not been fully mined. Synge's skill as a playwright means that dichotomies – nature–culture; woman–man; displacement–belonging – are continuously explored and interrogated, in turn challenging some of the most stalwart ideologies of both colonial and nationalist mindsets of Synge's time. In drawing female characters whose lives are shaped by the tragedy of inaction and the effect of their particular environment, Synge critiqued contemporary Irish culture and exposed the strain that results from insisting that women remain merely symbolic for a nationalist and chauvinist society. Rather than relying on such trite symbolism himself, Synge created a realist drama rooted in medieval Irish tradition and dispensed with romanticisations of landscape that would have softened the blow. The controversy generated by his mode of operation only led him to redouble his efforts, and, in the few years left to him, to produce some of the finest drama of the Irish stage. More than a century after their composition, these two one-act plays continue to unsettle and provoke audience response, and remain significant foundations for Synge's mature drama.

NOTES

1. Lady Augusta Gregory, *Our Irish Theatre* (New York: Capricorn Books, 1965), pp. 8–9.
2. Ibid.
3. Ibid.
4. *Riders*, while thus performed after *Shadow*, was the first published.
5. Maurice Bourgeois, *John Millington Synge and the Irish Theatre* (New York: Benjamin Blom, 1965), p. 171.
6. Ibid., p. 162.
7. In Richard Ellmann, *James Joyce* (Oxford University Press, 1982), p. 129.
8. Ronan McDonald, *Tragedy and Irish Literature* (London: Palgrave, 2002), p. 27.
9. Ellen S. Spangler, 'Synge's *Deirdre of the Sorrows* as Feminine Tragedy', *Éire-Ireland*, 12:4 (1977), p. 98.
10. W. J. Mc Cormack notes that *Riders to the Sea* and *The Shadow of the Glen* anticipate *Dubliners* in 'an unblinking attention to death and deep-rooted unhappiness, a sardonic but generous humour, [and] aesthetic patience in allowing implication to emerge at its own pace'; *Fool of the Family: A Life of J. M. Synge* (London: Weidenfeld & Nicolson, 2000), p. 252.
11. Joseph Falaky Nagy, 'Liminality and Knowledge in Irish Tradition', in *Studia Celtica* 16/17 (1981/2), p. 138.

12. Declan Kiberd, *Synge and the Irish Language* (Dublin: Gill & Macmillan, 1993), p. 167.
13. See Edward A. Kopper, Jr., 'Riders to the Sea', in Kopper, ed., *A J. M. Synge Literary Companion* (Westport CT: Greenwood Press, 1988), pp. 39–49, p. 43; and also Kiberd, *Synge and the Irish Language*, p. 167.
14. See Judith Remy Leder, 'Synge's *Riders to the Sea*: Island as Cultural Battleground', *Twentieth Century Literature*, 36:2 (Summer 1990), pp. 207–25.
15. Cited in Robert Hogan and James Kilroy, *Laying the Foundations 1902–1904* (Dublin: Dolmen Press, 1976), p. 116.
16. Ibid., p. 117.
17. Ibid., p. 117.
18. Ibid., p. 80.
19. 28 January 1905, *United Irishman*, in Robert Hogan and James Kilroy, *The Abbey Theatre: The Years of Synge 1905–1909* (Dublin: Dolmen Press, 1978), p. 12.
20. 'The Irish National Theatre and Three Sorts of Ignorance', in Colton Johnson (ed.), *The Collected Works of W. B. Yeats*, vol. X: *Later Articles and Reviews* (New York: Scribner, 2000), pp. 99–100.
21. See, for instance, Mary Fitzgerald-Hoyt, 'Death and the Colleen: *The Shadow of the Glen*', in Alexander G. Gonzalez (ed.), *Assessing the Achievement of J. M. Synge* (Westport, CT: Greenwood Press, 1996), p. 51.
22. 24 October 1903, *United Irishman*, pp. 2–3.
23. John B. Yeats, 10 October 1903, *United Irishman*, in Hogan and Kilroy, *Laying the Foundations*, p. 76.
24. For a more detailed critique along these lines, see Rob Doggett, '*In the Shadow of the Glen*: Gender, Nationalism, and "A Woman Only"', *English Literary History*, 67:4 (2000), pp. 1011–34.
25. Robin Skelton, *The Writings of J. M. Synge* (London: Thames & Hudson, 1971), p. 60.
26. Pádraig Ó Riain, 'A Study of the Irish Legend of the Wild Man', *Éigse* 14 (1972), p. 194.

3

SHAUN RICHARDS

The Playboy of the Western World

'On Those That Hated *The Playboy Of The Western World*, 1907'

Once, when midnight smote the air,
Eunuchs ran through Hell and met
On every crowded street to stare
Upon great Juan riding by:
Even like these to rail and sweat
Staring upon his sinewy thigh.
W. B. Yeats.[1]

In setting *The Playboy of the Western World* 'near a village, on a wild coast of
Mayo' (CW IV, 55), Synge appeared to conform to the Literary Revival's
preference for an idealised west-of-Ireland location, whose distance from the
anglicised east had preserved Irish authenticity, and so enabled the embryonic
nation-state to 'draw its vitality from that hidden spring'.[2] However, while
many of his contemporaries maintained a 'double focus on past and peasant',[3] Synge's play was resolutely present-orientated. As signalled by the
speculation that Christy had been 'fighting bloody wars for Kruger and the
freedom of the Boers' (71), the world of Mayo might have been geographically distant from Dublin's Abbey Theatre in which the play was first performed on 26 January 1907, but they shared the same fraught historical
moment. The Boer War ended in May 1902, but the well-known exploits of
the Irish Transvaal Brigade raised by Major John MacBride to support the
Boers' fight against the British Empire, and the pro-Boer enthusiasm of the
future-founder of Sinn Féin, Arthur Griffith, and MacBride's wife-to-be,
Maud Gonne, ensured that *The Playboy*'s audiences would grasp that what
was being staged was Ireland's recent and rebellious reality. The set-
directions' observance of dramatic realism's demand for the maximum of
verisimilitude, coupled with a density of place names from County Mayo,
ensured the credibility of the location. But the suggestion that Christy might
have been fighting for the Boers, coupled with the aftermath of that conflict in
'the loosèd khaki cut-throats' (75), projects the play into a conflicted, contemporary reality, where violence and displacement are deemed to be the

norm. This hard-edged intervention into a world often dramatically imaged as anodyne was Synge's objective; it was also the cause of the play's controversy – and its dramatic power and cultural significance.

The phrase which resonates throughout the Preface to the play, which Synge wrote shortly before its premiere, is 'fiery and magnificent and tender' (54), a distillation of his feelings for the Aran Islands, perceived as the last outpost of a pre-Christian, pre-colonial Ireland where the people still had 'the agile walk of the wild animal' (CW II, 66). But if the islands were a primitive Eden, the rest of Ireland was Paradise Lost: 'How much of Ireland was formerly like this and how much of Ireland is today Anglicised and civilised and brutalised?' (CW II, 103). This new world was one where, according to the Preface, 'the springtime of the local life has been forgotten, and the harvest is a memory only, and the straw has been turned into bricks' (54). While the rural and seasonal metaphors mask the brutal reality of irrevocable loss, the observation that the Aran islands will 'gradually yield to the ruthlessness of "progress"' (CW II, 103) makes clear that the 'bricks' referenced in the Preface are those of capitalist modernity. Synge's elegiac sensibility sees the imaginative and linguistic richness of Ireland, which is intimately dependent on that pre-industrial life-style, as existing only 'for a few years more' (54), and *The Playboy* stands as a lament for its demise and a utopian manifesto for its resurrection.

It is important to note that Synge's valorisation of a threatened life-style and language was widely shared at the time. The Gaelic League, established in 1893 to support the speaking of the Irish language, as well as the preservation of Irish dance, music and poetry, was central to the cultural and, increasingly, political life of the period. Synge had a profound knowledge of Irish which deeply informed his work,[4] but progressively he became irremediably hostile to the Gaelic League and many of its self-serving supporters, and it is this which underpins so much of *The Playboy* and the controversy surrounding its first production.

'The Gaelic League,' wrote Synge shortly after *The Playboy*'s premiere, is 'gushing, cowardly and maudlin', producing 'snivelling' booklets which were 'going through Ireland like the scab on sheep', and disseminating a language which, far from the 'old and magnificent language of our manuscripts', was an 'incoherent twaddle' (CW II, 399–400). The echo of 'magnificent' from the Preface to *The Playboy*, and its association with the ancient Ireland of 'manuscripts', correlates with the life of the Aran Islands, 'perhaps the most primitive that is left in Europe' (CW II, 53), in constructing a world-view in which an indigenous Irish vitality was being leached away by a movement which Synge saw as distinguished by a class-based chauvinism and moral timidity. His feelings are expressed in a sketch for a play which he wrote while working on *The Playboy*, *National Drama: A Farce*, where an unnamed cultural nationalist group – as interested in alcohol as art – seeks to define a national Irish drama: 'which contains the manifold and fine qualities of the Irish race, their love for the land of their forefathers, and their poetic familiarity with the glittering and unseen forms of the visionary world' (CW III, 222). But, above all, 'The National Drama of Catholic Ireland must have no sex' (223) and, as Synge observed in a clearly oppositional move, 'I restored the sex element to its rightful place' (CL I, 74).

In *National Drama: A Farce*, the character of Jameson summarises the vapidity of this 'national' theatre, asking, 'In short you think that the Irish drama should hold up a mirror to the Irish Nation and it going to Mass on a fine springdayish Sunday?' (CW III, 222–3). This echoes Synge's own distaste for 'a purely fantastic, unmodern, ideal, spring-dayish, Cuchulainoid National Theatre' (CL I, 74), whose rejection of saga-sentimentality suggests that his work will not only be modern, but unyielding in its search for truth: 'what I write of Irish country life I know to be true and I most emphattically [sic] will not change a syllable of it because A. B. or C. may think they know better than I do,' he declared in 1904 (CL I, 91). And the truth, as he saw it, was that an emerging petit-bourgeoisie was exploiting the peasants it simultaneously idealised as the embodiment of authentic Ireland. Indeed it was the very people nominally dedicated to Irish independence who were 'swindling the people themselves in a dozen ways' (CL I, 116). Synge's complex cultural-political antagonism to this class, which included the owners of village shops where 'the prices charged are often exorbitant' and 'keep the people near to pauperism!' (CW II, 330), is condensed in his vitriolic verdict on what he found during his 1905 visit to Mayo, the setting of *The Playboy*: 'There are sides of all that western life the groggy-patriot-publican-general-shop-man who is married to the priest's half-sister and is second cousin once-removed of the dispensary doctor, that are horrible and awful' (CL I, 116).

Whereas pre-Famine Ireland was distinguished by an economic system based on a powerful aristocracy and 'an impoverished and insecure peasantry', changing economic circumstances 'had begun to transform that proletariat into a bourgeoisie'.[5] The contemporary reality was that this class sought to achieve a political power commensurate with its growing economic strength and cultural self-confidence, and while the Gaelic League was non-sectarian in its origins, indeed Douglas Hyde, its founder, was a Protestant: 'By the middle of the first decade of the twentieth century, an organization which had been started with inter-faith cultural intentions had been transformed into a mass organization dominated by Catholics and increasingly subservient to political forces that were republican, separatist or clericalist.'[6] Synge's perception was that this nexus of interests preferred to idealise, rather than analyse Ireland, and was creating a society which feared 'any gleam of truth' (CW II, 400). But, he asserted in the rhetorically titled 'Can We Go Back into Our Mother's Womb?', 'This delirium will not always last' and, in language which resonates with *The Playboy*, he continued: 'It will not be long – we will make it our first hope – till some young man with blood in his veins, and logic in his wits and courage in his heart, will sweep over the backside of the world to the uttermost limbo this credo of mouthing gibberish.' While Christy Mahon is no language campaigner, his final vivacity, achieved by striking down repressive authority in all its manifestations, marks him as the apogee of 'the nation that has made a place in history by seventeen centuries of manhood' (CW II, 399–400), but whose full glory shone 'Before the merchant and the clerk / Breathed on the world with timid breath'.[7]

However, the Christy who enters in Act I belongs more to the world of clerks than heroes, being described as 'a slight young man … very tired and frightened and dirty', and the stage directions continue this tone, noting him as speaking 'in a small voice' (67) and being 'shocked' by the suggestion that he 'followed after a young woman on a lonesome night' (69). Indeed, in terms of character, the closest parallel to Christy in Act I is Shawn Keogh, around whom the negative associations cluster – and remain throughout the play. In Act I he 'looks round awkwardly' when he sees that Pegeen is alone (57); he is described as being 'scandalised' (59) and 'in horrified confusion' (63) at the suggestion that he should stay with Pegeen while her father, Michael, attends Kate Cassidy's wake. At the end of the play he is still 'in terror' (171), but this time of Christy, who has become 'the champion of the world' (139), and is prepared, 'almost gaily' (171), to face the prospect of going to the gallows for the murder of his father. That transformation is at the dramatic and thematic heart of the play.

The Playboy opens with Pegeen, 'a wild-looking but fine girl of about twenty' (57). And across the multiple rough sketches and drafts of the play the constant note Synge strikes is as to her strength of character. In an early draft, *Murder Will Out*, she is described as a 'bold big girl' (304) and elsewhere as 'masterful and rather impetuous', 'haughty and quick tempered' (56). As she is alone on stage the audience has to focus on the fact that she is writing out the order for her trousseau, but when the fact rapidly emerges that she is destined to marry the 'fat and fair' (57) Shawn Keogh, whom early drafts describe as 'innately slow, awkward and helpless' (56), they have to be struck by the disparity between their physical and psychological characteristics. But this is a world of depletion and poverty in which emigration is the lot of those lacking the material wealth necessary to survive in the face of 'the broken harvests' and in which Michael can readily assume that Christy's crime is larceny, as 'There's many wanting' (69). The only men of the community seen on stage are Philly O'Cullen, 'thin and mistrusting' (in earlier drafts 'elderly, thin and political'), and Jimmy Farrell 'who is fat and amorous, about forty-five' (60–61). In this context it is not only Shawn's youth, but also his wealth, which makes him the obvious husband for Pegeen. However the attitude of the other men towards him is revealing.

Shawn's refusal to stay with Pegeen is met with 'cold contempt' (65), and while Michael celebrates his choice of Shawn as son-in-law since his sexual timidity will ensure there is no infidelity in the marriage, Synge's marginal note to an early draft, 'work through Shawn's righteousness in contrast with Christy' (64), clearly suggests that 'righteousness' is to be seen as negative. Crucially, Shawn's moral principles are derived from the fact that he is 'afeard of Father Reilly'. This, coupled with his preference for his bed rather than the drunken wake for Kate Cassidy, suggests that he is the product of the 'devotional revolution' which, inspired by Cardinal Paul Cullen, sought to replace semi-pagan practices, such as wakes, with standardised, Church-approved alternatives. The emerging bourgeoisie of post-Famine Irish society embraced this morally upright life-style which accorded with their distain for profligacy and preference for the consolidation of wealth. Indeed, as argued by Luke Gibbons, this religious 'revolution' was 'part of an overall modernising thrust', one of several features demonstrating Ireland's 'direct integration into the capitalist world economy'.[8] And in Shawn's case financial power appears to be the corollary of righteousness and the 'weapon' on which he relies in first acquiring and then retaining Pegeen as his intended.

In the cast list for the play, while both Philly and Jimmy are described as 'small farmers', Shawn is given simply as 'farmer'. This demonstrates Synge's awareness of the class divisions operating in rural Ireland in which 'small farmers', who still largely survived on the basis of an economy of potato cultivation, were subordinate to the 'strong farmers', who were progressively consolidating their land holdings and shaping the transition to an agrarian capitalism based on cattle. The fact that Shawn has promised Michael a 'drift of heifers' and a 'blue bull from Sneem' (155) as part of the marriage arrangements demonstrates that he is part of this economic elite – while also showing that this coupling is based more on property than passion, Shaun referring to the match as 'a good bargain' (59). That Michael is a publican who adds to his income by selling illegal poteen, further adds to the grim picture that Synge is painting of rural Ireland in which the 'congested districts', the poverty-stricken regions of the rural west, were becoming the preserves of vested interests who consolidated their power and wealth; much as Michael aims to do by marrying Pegeen off to Shawn, her second cousin. AE (George Russell) shared Synge's distaste for these 'gombeen men' – the word derived from the Irish for usury – and his condemnation of their abuses indicates how powerful an alliance of publican and 'strong farmer' could be in the deprived society of early twentieth-century Ireland:

> In congested Ireland every job which can be filled by the kith and kin of the gombeen kings and queens is filled accordingly, and you get every kind of inefficiency and jobbery. They are all publicans, and their friends are all strong drinkers. They beget people of their own character and appoint them lieutenants and non-commissioned officers in their service ... in fact round the gombeen system reels the whole drunken congested world, and underneath this revelry and jobbery the unfortunate peasant labours and gets no return for his labour.[9]

Michael's drunkenness clearly imperils his dynastic ambitions, but Shawn is single-minded in seeing his wealth as the means by which to gain Pegeen. In seeking to obtain the Widow Quin's support in the venture he offers so much in the way of livestock, property rights and other gifts that she interrupts him with 'That'll do, so' (117). Clearly the amount of disposable property that Shawn can command is considerable in this context of impoverishment, but while it has brought him to the brink of marriage to Pegeen it has not brought him respect: in addition to the 'contempt' for his sexual timidity displayed by the men, it is Pegeen's attitude to him – and then to Christy – which takes us into the heart of the drama.

While the play opens with Pegeen ordering the necessities for her wedding, her first reference to it with Shawn is directed 'with scornful good humour' (59) as she suggests he cannot take their marriage as a certainty. Early stage directions state that she speaks to him 'impatiently' (59) and 'sharply' (60), and in stark opposition to his moral rectitude imitates his voice to demand 'Stop tormenting me with Father Reilly' (59). Although she defends him against her father, Philly and Jimmy, asking what right they have 'to be making game of a poor fellow for minding the priest', the stage directions indicate that she is simply 'taking up the defence of her property' (65). Clearly, while the marriage might be arranged, Pegeen, 'ambitious in all ways' (56), as an early draft describes her, is no passive partner in the relationship. Christy's entry, and the revelation that he has killed his father, immediately throws the marriage into doubt – and this, notably, before Christy's triumphant transformation through the power of his tale and the admiration of the girls of the community. Shawn's attempted interventions in the conversation are now met 'very sharply' (75) by Pegeen, who is 'snapping at him' while she speaks to Christy 'with a honeyed voice' (77) as she persuades him to stay and rest. Shawn is verbally emasculated by Pegeen's 'jeering' suggestion that Father Reilly puts him in 'the holy brotherhoods' (79), while she watches Christy 'with delight' and pronounces him 'a fine, handsome young fellow' (79). 'What would I want wedding so young?' (81), her rhetorical response to Christy's question as to whether she is single, indicates how far, and how rapidly, her clearly passionless partnership with Shawn has deteriorated, and by the close of Act I she announces with finality, 'I wouldn't wed him if a bishop came walking for to join us' (91). Christy is the catalyst in bringing the relationship to an end, but the cause lies in the nature of the society which Synge was at pains to diagnose.

When Pegeen declares 'We're a queer lot these days', she explicitly establishes a contrast between a fallen present of cripples and lunatics and a recent, more 'heroic' past in which 'knock[ing] the eye from a peeler' and 'maiming ewes' (59) can be seen, not as petty offences, but as acts of rebellion against landlords and colonial law. But Pegeen is less concerned with their political implications than with the emotional extremes they suggest; a search for sensation, and above all emotional fulfilment, which, as she acknowledges to Christy in Act III, had her 'tempted often to go sailing the seas' (151). This echoes the Widow Quin's sexual reverie about 'thinking on the gallant hairy fellows are drifting beyond, and myself long years living alone' (127), to suggest that Pegeen's frustration with Shawn, and increasing attachment to Christy, just as the impulse which drives the girls of the village to seek him out in Act II, is born of the emotional barrenness of her life.

In this context the roles of the various 'fathers' are significant. The Church-enforced emotional repression sanctioned by Father Reilly has been noted. At the other extreme is the drunkenness of Michael, whose celebration of the 'five men, aye, and six men, stretched out retching speechless on the holy stones' (151) at Kate Cassidy's wake is only surpassed in debauchery by Old Mahon's recollections of experiencing delirium tremens of such severity that he saw 'rats big as badgers sucking the life blood from the butt of my lug', and only three weeks previously 'drinking [himself] silly and paralytic from dusk to dawn' in the company of 'the Limerick girls' (143). The attempt to force Christy into marriage with the Widow Casey was so that he would 'have her gold to drink' (103), and while Michael's role in arranging the marriage of Pegeen is not so overtly and brutally mercenary it is still a match he has 'chosen' (153). Father Reilly's power over Shawn is no less complete for being driven by devotion, for what all three 'fathers' look to achieve is the removal of autonomous free choice from their various 'off-spring'; the difference between Shawn and Christy and, to a lesser extent, Pegeen, is the extent to which they resist incorporation within the patriarchal power-structure, and it is the basis of that resistance, and its implications for the individual and society, which is Synge's major interest.

Michael's description of Shawn as a 'shy and decent Christian' (153) establishes one end of the spectrum on which he in turn is viewed, by Shawn, as an 'old Pagan' (65). The idea of a pagan substratum to Irish culture was central to Synge's thinking as made clear in a passage from *The Aran Islands* where he recounts how an old man knelt by a funeral graveside and repeated a prayer for the dead. But, for Synge, this expression of Christian faith was a superficial accretion on a bed-rock reality: 'There was an irony in these words of atonement and Catholic belief spoken by voices that were still hoarse with the cries of pagan desperation', which, more truly, expressed 'the inner consciousness of the people' (CW II, 75). While Michael's mix of drunkenness and cupidity is a corruption of any indigenous pagan impulse, enough remains for him – temporarily at least – to prefer Pegeen's marriage to Christy, as 'I liefer face the grave untimely and I seeing a score of grandsons growing up gallant little swearers by the name of God, than go peopling my bedside with puny weeds the like of what you'd breed, I'm thinking, out of Shaneen Keogh' (157). His description of Pegeen as 'a heathen daughter' (153), and her rejection of Shawn as one 'with no savagery' (153), captures the profound level at which the unrestrained expression of passion in the pursuit, or defence, of the fully realised self is a virtue; albeit now but a flickering remnant of a reality driven to the verge of extinction through commerce and conformity. Therefore, while Christy's 'killing' of his father is a lie, and the place where the blow was struck merely a potato field, its gradual transformation by Christy into a battle of epic proportions is both parody of the sagas expressed in the 'old and magnificent language of our manuscripts', and their profound evocation. In displacing Shawn he vanquished an Ireland in thrall to 'squeamishness' and which recoiled from dealing 'with the entire reality of life' (CL I, 74). Moreover he strikes down 'authority' in all its repressive manifestations. This charged agenda places Synge within a European avant-garde whose objectives, while having resonances with the political specificities of Ireland, were even more wide-ranging and provocative.

In this context *The Playboy* can be compared with *Ubu Roi* (1896) by French dramatist Alfred Jarry, in the intensity of its anti-bourgeois stance. Both plays caused riots; nominally because of a word which disturbed the audiences' sensibilities – 'shift' in *The Playboy* and 'shite' (*merdre*) in *Ubu*. However they are worlds apart in terms of style, *The Playboy* observing the major tenets of dramatic realism, while *Ubu*'s flimsy, proto-Dadaist plot was a puppet-style parody of *Macbeth* and *Hamlet*. But in Jarry's description of the 'ignoble' Ubu as 'really rather a spoiled child',[10] who, like the bourgeoisie, demands that his every appetite is granted immediate satisfaction, one starts to see a unanimity in their attitudes to their audiences, and the society from which they were drawn.

Synge was a frequent visitor to Paris between 1895 and 1903, which 'gave him a back-seat row at some of the rowdier sideshows of European civilisation entering crisis – the Dreyfus affair, the Arms Race, Alfred Jarry's *Ubu Roi*.[11] However, and unlike Yeats who recorded his experience of witnessing the first production, there is no evidence of him attending the play, despite being in Paris at the time. But the final version of *Ubu* had been published five months before the premiere, and the political and artistic turbulence of the period permeated publications and conversations to which Synge's command of French would have given him unmediated access. Jarry was part of the *zeitgeist* of late nineteenth-century Europe in which Synge was immersed, and in which Jarry's writings on the theatre provided a provocation to action to which Synge was to become increasingly sensitised. It was clearly *Ubu* which staged the Europe-wide reality of bourgeois brutality, but Synge was equally committed to the attack, and for reasons which, like Jarry's, can be seen to have affinities with anarchism and the concept of '*l'acte gratuit*', the explosive act of violence directed against the bourgeoisie.

Declan Kiberd astutely recognises that *The Aran Islands* might be read as a document in the history of 1890s anarchism, with the community on Inis Meáin presented as 'a version of the commune, a utopian zone where most of the discontents of civilisation seem to be annulled'.[12] However, the anarchism which infuses the work is that of the commune that lives outside, or in Synge's terms, 'before', convention; and it is pacific not combative. But while *The Aran Islands* was not published until 1907, it was completed in 1901, and so before Synge's exposure to the full wrath of bourgeois hostility experienced around *Shadow of the Glen* in 1903. In the increasingly confrontational relationship which followed, the idea of an Irish '*acte gratuit*' clearly gained in attraction until it found expression in the loy raised by Christy Mahon against a whole society of repressive fathers, both on stage and in the auditorium.

While Synge's private correspondence was full of disgust at the class of 'fat-faced, sweaty headed swine' (CW II, 283) which he saw swamping Ireland, in 1905 he felt he was held back from dramatising this world: 'All that side of the matter of course I left untouched in my stuff. I sometimes wish to God I hadn't a soul and then I could give myself up to putting those lads on the stage. God, wouldn't they hop!' (CL I, 116–17). Two years later, *The Playboy* realised his repressed desire to flay the mean-spirited materialism of an Irish bourgeoisie, for the strong farmer Shawn Keogh and drunken publican Michael James are members of the very class idealising itself as the upholders of Ireland's ancient idealism. In the play Synge was presenting his audience with a world which, in Jarry's phrase, 'should confront the public like [an] exaggerating mirror ... in which the depraved saw themselves'.[13] This was striking at the bourgeoisie with a vengeance, and the presence in the audience of many Gaelic Leaguers and nationalists added to the play's impact – and their fury at a 'misrepresentation' which the Abbey had supposedly been founded to eradicate. In the words of *The Freeman's Journal*: 'A strong protest must, however, be entered against this unmitigated, protracted libel upon Irish peasant men and, worse still, upon Irish peasant girlhood. The blood boils with indignation as one recalls the incidents, expressions, ideas of this squalid offensive production.'[14] The full extent of Synge's violent inversion of the norms of bourgeois, nationalist drama can be seen by comparing *The Playboy* to two contemporaneous works; Padraic Colum's *The Land* (1905) and Douglas Hyde's *Casadh an tSúgáin* (*The Twisting of the Rope*; 1901).

Synge had attended the premiere of Hyde's piece and commented sarcastically on the young Gaelic League girls talking, 'in very bad Irish', to their male companions who were 'pale with enthusiasm' (CW II, 381). He was clearly aware of the import of the evening as Hyde's was the first play written in Irish, but although he described it as 'a charming little piece' (381), whereas Hyde's play sees the community cunningly exclude the intruder, Hanrahan, who has threatened the marriage of Oona and Sheamus, leaving Sheamus triumphant and Hanrahan cursing and powerless beyond the locked door, *The Playboy* sees Christy's triumphant exit and Shawn rejected.[15] The time of *The Land*, like *The Playboy*, is 'contemporary with the stage-presentation'[16] and Colum's description of its concern with 'the revolt of the young against parental possessiveness' (7) over the issue of marriage and inheritance of land, suggests a significant parallel with Synge's work. However, while acknowledging Ellen's desire to 'have a chance of knowing what is in me' (32) rather than observe the dictates of her father, the play's conservatism resides in the community's ability to retain stability in the face of this revolt. Colum gives the last words to Cornelius who, while he may be 'struggling with words' (47) and so parallels Shawn Keogh's ineffectuality, gives a celebratory speech which projects a vision of the redemption of self and society following on from the departure of those in revolt against its norms: 'Stay on the land, and you'll be saved body and soul; you'll be saved in the man and in the nation' (47). The difference from Michael's slothful 'we'll have peace now for our drinks' and Shawn's soon-dashed hopes that 'Father Reilly can wed us in the end of all' (173) could not be more striking, especially as *The Playboy*'s final triumphalism is individual, rather than communal, and conducted by Christy, who poetically renders, and realises, the desire articulated by Ellen in Colum's play: 'it's my freedom I want' (44).

But while Christy's initial act of transformative violence lies at the heart of the play, and the sheer brutality of its on-stage repetition accounted for much of the audience's disquiet, the force which attracts Pegeen is the fusion of 'savagery [and] fine words' (153). And, further to the argument concerning her desire for sensation, she provides the template for the resurrection of Christy as Playboy in her early speculation that, were he not so tired, he could equal the Gaelic poets for 'talk and streeleen [gossip]', matching creativity with the capacity for violence in declaring 'it's the poets are your like, fine fiery fellows with great rages when their temper's roused' (81). Indeed, as drama-tised in the courtship scene in Act III, the poetic impulse is realised in both Christy and Pegeen as they imagine, 'with rapture' and 'real tenderness,' a life of wandering abroad at night, 'coaxing bailiffs' (149) in a continued flouting of authority. Christy's reference to them 'making mighty kisses with our wetted mouths, or gaming in a gap of sunshine with yourself stretched back into your necklace in the flowers of the earth' (149) makes explicit the sexual charge which informs their exchange, and Pegeen's response, 'I'd be nice so, is it?' (149), signals her acquiescence. Yet within minutes of swearing that 'I'll wed him and I'll not renege' (157) she rejects him as 'an ugly liar' (163) and leads the crowd in attempting to capture him for the gallows. Christy's rejection by Pegeen, and the community which had idealised him, expresses Synge's darkest and most despondent judgement on the fallen state of Irish society.

While Pegeen's transformation through the relationship is captured in her amazed 'And to think it's me is talking sweetly' (151), she is still sufficiently uncertain about a future with Christy as to greet it 'with a qualm of dread' (149). And when, with the revelation that he has not killed his father, the potent mixture of violence and poetry is diluted, and she appears to have exchanged Shawn for one who was 'only playing the hero' (165), her anger and anguish drive her back into conformity with the community and its obeisance to Father Riley and fear of (English) law. The play opened with her preparation for a wedding; it closes on her 'keening' 'wild lamentations' (173) over the death, with Christy's departure, of all the poetry and passion he promised. However, while her racking realisation of absolute loss is in sharp contrast to Christy's exultant liberation from restraint, the nature of his triumphant exit requires more than unexamined celebration.

While Christy's future is projected 'from this hour to the dawning of the judgment day' (173), his transformation, and the community's response to him, is based on the heroic past. Christy's Act II rendition of the 'killing' evokes the epic battles of the sagas, but it is the poetry, as much as the violence, which has its origins in the 'ancient manuscripts'. Declan Kiberd has shown the extent to which the love-exchange between Christy and Pegeen is derived from Synge's reading of Douglas Hyde's translations of ancient Irish poetry, *The Love Songs of Connaught* (1893), and his knowledge of these and other originals. As Kiberd observed: 'In [Synge's] hands, the mean-ing of Gaelic tradition changed from something museumised to something modifiable, endlessly open.'[17] In striking down his father Christy frees himself from the past and starts out on his journey of liberation, but through his final reconciliation with Old Mahon Synge demonstrates that the corollary of the overthrow of the past is its necessary reintegration into the future. The process by which the community, and especially Pegeen, enabled Christy to become the Playboy is one of complementary wish-fulfilment and self-realisation; he is the heroic past made flesh. But when it faces them in all its bloody reality they make the choice of mediocrity over magnificence. In this particular 'battle of two civilisations' the victor is bourgeois conformity and its associated allegiance with the law. But alongside their failure is the apparently available alternative of a cultural revivalism which provides a genuine, rather than ersatz, redemption of self and society. However, as noted by Una Chauduri in her comparison of the conclusion of *The Playboy* with the exit of Nora from Ibsen's *A Doll's House* (1879), this 'heroism of departure' is actually 'an impossible ideal'. Christy's departure is 'radically transgressive'[18] in terms of the norms of nationalist expectations and celebrates the potency of the heroic past at the same time as dramatising its practical impossibility in a world now given over to the 'gombeen men'.

As Synge acknowledged, his values were dependent on a social stasis in which modernity was held at bay, and he had 'a dread of any reform that would tend to lessen their [the peasants'] individuality' (CW II, 286). While he dramatises a process by which Christy and, by implication, Ireland, can be transformed through drawing on its heroic and poetic past there is no suggestion of any systematic socio-political programme by which this could be effected. Rather Christy's celebratory exit is more expressive of a romantic anarchism in which the community's failures are dramatised, but the radical alternative occupies an ungraspable off-stage infinity. Only by projecting Christy beyond economic imperatives could Synge make him the embodiment of a liberation whose precise lineaments are finally more easily suggested than defined.

NOTES

1. W. B. Yeats, *The Variorum Edition of the Poems of W. B. Yeats*, eds. Peter Allt and Russell K. Alspach (London: Macmillan, 1973), p. 294.
2. Maude Gonne MacBride, 'A National Theatre', *United Irishman*, No. 243, 24 October 1903, p. 2.
3. Joep Leerssen, *Remembrance and Imagination* (Cork: Field Day / Cork University Press, 1996), p. 221.
4. Declan Kiberd, *Synge and the Irish Language*, Dublin: Gill & Macmillan, 1993.
5. F. S. L. Lyons, *Ireland Since the Famine* (London: Fontana, 1973), p. 50.
6. Tom Garvin, *Nationalist Revolutionaries in Ireland, 1858–1928* (Oxford: Clarendon Press, 1987), p. 85.

4

MARY BURKE

The Well of the Saints and *The Tinker's Wedding*

In John Millington Synge's dramas *The Well of the Saints* (1905) and *The Tinker's Wedding* (published 1907), peripatetic characters unconscious of ageing, sinfulness or ugliness live in a pre-lapsarian state that is disrupted by contact with the fallen realms of the Church and proprietorship. At the close of both, the by now tainted nomads reject any further dealings with the corrupting and implicitly entwined ideologies of capitalism and established religion and attempt to return to their original condition. The plays both centre on the loss of innocence of the wanderer foolish enough to initiate dealings with God's representative and the earthly values that he is ultimately seen to uphold. In a reversal of the folkloric associations of the rambler from which the plot of *The Tinker's Wedding* derives,[1] worldliness is represented by the dogmatic churchmen and their nominally pious congregations, naivety and a genuine closeness to real divinity and pre-capitalist artlessness by the animistic peoples of the road. In short, despite their mythic echoes, both of these plays are deeply engaged with Revival-era debates on religious practices, economic transformation, and cultural difference, and constitute significant responses by Synge to the wider cultural shifts of late nineteenth-century Ireland.

At the outset of *The Well of the Saints*, Mary and Martin Doul share an unselfconscious contentment, dwelling in what they alone perceive to be an Arcadian idyll. However, their fall to knowledge on being cured of blindness by the saint reveals their own moral corrosion as well as that of the wider community, and they come to understand that the capitalist misfortunes of ill-paid labour and hunger will supplant their former pre-modern ease. In like manner, the tinkers who had functioned predominantly within the pre-capitalist barter system are drawn more deeply into the modern financial nexus by the priest's demand for cash payment for the wedding vows he will perform in *The Tinker's Wedding*. The dramas' shared theme of the clash of an upwardly mobile, propertied and increasingly standardised contemporary Ireland with an earlier and more individualistic cultural and economic order is exemplified by the difference between the wandering Michael Byrne in *The Tinker's Wedding* and the ambitious and sedentary Timmy in *The Well of the Saints*: both are smiths, but the former operates in a haphazard exchange economy while the latter can boast of business premises and a paid employee.

The Well of the Saints has been unduly disregarded, though it should rank as a primary Synge text in light of its likely influence on Samuel Beckett's absurd tramp characters and its unrecognised engagement with the overt themes of Synge's more canonised drama. Beyond the obvious thematic pairing with *The Tinker's Wedding*, the play also echoes the unambiguous depiction of the unhappiness caused in the marriage relationship by the entwined strictures of property and propriety of *The Shadow of the Glen* and, to a lesser extent, *The Playboy of the Western World*. However, *The Well of the Saints* does so in a manner that is too subtle for critics to have recognised that it is of a continuum with Synge's overall concern with the challenge to individualism presented by cultural homogenisation. The consistent inattention to *The Well of the Saints* may be ultimately traced to its inauspicious first production in February 1905, when attendances were poor and reviews were negative,[2] though the drama never gained the ultimately beneficial notoriety of *The Playboy of the Western World* and *The Shadow of the Glen*. In addition, *The Well of the Saints* has also suffered from the weight of critical consideration given to W. B. Yeats's famous preface and to the play's sources, at the expense of detailed engagement with both the text itself and its creative dialogue with *The Tinker's Wedding*. Nevertheless, *The Well of the Saints* has not suffered the degree of neglect of its sister drama: the response to Synge's most difficult play has been either crude or non-existent, and it has commonly been regarded as his least significant work – when considered at all. Daniel Corkery's damning summation, that 'the play is scarcely worth considering either as a piece of stagecraft or as a piece of literature', is characteristic of most twentieth-century deliberations on *The Tinker's Wedding*.[3] The fact that Corkery even bothered to refer to the play is in itself unusual: a glance at the index of the standard essay collection concerning Synge's drama often yields no reference to the play whatsoever.

The Tinker's Wedding was published in 1907 and premiered in London two years later (and after Synge's death) at the Afternoon Theatre Company at His Majesty's Theatre. Poignantly, Synge's only two-act play finally made its Abbey debut in April 1971 on the centenary of his birth, and even then it was paired with *Riders to the Sea* rather than with its obvious companion piece. Although it was the perceived anti-clericalism of *The Tinker's Wedding* which led to initial fears regarding its potential offensiveness, uneasiness about the play's seemingly crude and farcical action and incendiary title likely mitigated against its being staged in the wake of the political mobilisation of

Irish Travellers during the 1960s; prior to this period, the term 'tinker' was uncontroversially deployed in dominant culture to refer to the population currently known as Travellers, though it has since been considered pejorative.[4] However, a work such as Marina Carr's *By the Bog of Cats* suggests that dramatic treatments of Traveller culture utilising the term 'tinker' or its cognates do not inevitably offend actual members of that community, as critics and theatre directors fearful of the implications of Synge's play may assume. Indeed, Synge's depictions of tramps and tinkers is clearly admiring of peripatetic culture in a manner that foreshadows the more nuanced literary depictions of Travellers that begin to emerge after that community's radicalisation. The erroneous nature of the assumption that *The Tinker's Wedding* is inevitably offensive to the minority portrayed is underlined by the ironic fact that the drama has been staged by Traveller amateur acting troupes on a number of occasions since the 1970s.[5] In addition, the lack of critical consideration of the subtly subversive nature of Synge's sympathetic representation of peoples of the road in *The Tinker's Wedding* has further contributed to its being disregarded. This neglect is not a reliable indication of the play's innate insignificance, since it has yet to be fully appreciated as a work that both queries the prejudice of the settled against the unsettled, and presciently celebrates minority identity.

The acclaim that greeted the coupled productions of *The Well of the Saints* and *The Tinker's Wedding* by DruidSynge (the Druid theatre company's 2005 marathon of all of the dramatist's work), intimates that their humour and skilful construction is more apparent on the stage than on the page; implicitly, the very dearth of productions of *The Well of the Saints* and *The Tinker's Wedding* throughout much of the twentieth century has successively reinforced the hasty early consensus that the works concerned were Synge's least successful dramas. Most importantly, DruidSynge's double bill allowed the hitherto unacknowledged conversation that exists between *The Well of the Saints* and *The Tinker's Wedding* to finally find its voice. This all suggests that the time is ripe for a reassessment of the plays' centrality to Synge's oeuvre, to recent Irish drama that depicts marginalised Irish identities, and to the active engagement of Irish minorities themselves with their representation by canonical writers.

This examination of *The Tinker's Wedding* and *The Well of the Saints* as companion pieces is ultimately predicated upon earlier beliefs regarding the shared culture of diverse peripatetic populations such as tinkers and tramps. Travellers are members of a historically nomadic indigenous community that has provided seasonal labour, trading, entertainment, and smithing services to the settled population for generations. At present, the culture is regarded as being ethnically and culturally distinct both from majority society and from other historically nomadic groupings. However, *The Tinker's Wedding* and *The Well of the Saints* have arguably suffered from a critical misunderstanding of both the perception of itinerant subcultures in the period in which Synge was writing and the profound transformation such communities have undergone in the era after the dramatist's lifetime. This lack of knowledge of both the literary construct and historical reality of peripatetism in twentieth-century Ireland has shaped ahistorical and apolitical critical responses to *The Tinker's Wedding* that present it as a naturalistic portrayal of an *actual* and unchanging Traveller temperament. Aoife Bhreathnach's groundbreaking study of twentieth-century government policy and the Travellers posits that a complex set of post-partition welfare, school attendance and zoning policies gradually led to the disappearance of all historically unsettled populations other than Travellers, thereby rendering them the only visible antithesis of settled *mores* in the public sphere.[6] Additionally, a sense of when this population became culturally distinct to begin with is difficult to pluck out from Irish written sources in many instances, since, for the most part, tinkers tend not to be evenly differentiated from similarly nomadic and occupationally overlapping groupings prior to the Revival. Furthermore, Traveller culture is historically non-literate, so the community itself does not possess a written archive. A nascent sense of the Traveller ethnicity enshrined in British law since the close of the twentieth century is doubtlessly iterated in Revival writings about tinkers and arguably contributed to this later official recognition of difference. Nevertheless, until the early twentieth century, a variety of itinerant subcultures were often enfolded within a broadly allied peripatetic class that included tinkers.

Despite the fact that in Synge's period tinkers were still often collated with what were then other equally visible peripatetic groupings under a broad umbrella of the 'unsettled', it should be stressed that members of that community were often considered to be a particularly distinctive population segment. Folkloric beliefs such as those detailed by Lady Gregory[7] suggest that the early twentieth-century farming class believed tinkers to be a largely untrustworthy population descended from those forced onto the roads by the famines and political upheavals of earlier eras. These narratives veered from intimating that tinkers possessed supernatural powers to dismissing them as unproductive, promiscuous and heathenish rogues. In short, they and other peripatetic groupings were always outsiders to the dominant culture's overlapping values of sexual continence, frugality and religiosity. In defiant contrast to this popular discourse, Revival-era scholars such as Kuno Meyer and Eóin MacNeill theorised that tinkers were a throwback to the archaic Irish, which rendered the minority an alluring literary theme at a time when attempts were continually being made to recover traces of a lost aboriginal culture.[8] The chasm between the beliefs regarding tinker origins and status in agrarian society and their elevation as the remnants of an idealised pre-colonial order by elite Revivalists informs the depiction of nomads in *The Well of the Saints* and *The Tinker's Wedding*: Synge's tinkers and tramps partake of the folkloric tradition of the roguish wanderer even as his sympathy for such communities places him squarely in the camp of educated peers who considered tinkers to be the living vestiges of an ancestral dreamtime.

The scholarly theory that tinkers embodied an archaic or essential Irishness underlines Synge's attempts to uncover the unacknowledged ties that bind peoples of the road to the settled majority in *The Tinker's Wedding* and *The Well of the Saints*. If *The Aran Islands* gradually yields to a profound despair regarding the encroachments modernity has made into island society, then the unregimented and non-literate nature of peripatetic communities allows Synge to celebrate them as the last living relics of a once-widespread culture of rural non-conformity in the plays concerned (and in short prose pieces such as 'People and Places' (CW II, 193–201) and 'The Vagrants of Wicklow' (CW II, 202–8)). Nevertheless, *The Tinker's Wedding* and *The Well of the Saints* ostensibly pit settled culture and broadly allied and implicitly admirable 'unsettled' subcultures in opposition, since both culminate in shockingly irreverent clashes of wanderer and Church representative: the nomads attack a priest in the former and violently strike a can of holy water from a saint's hand in the latter. Of course, even the motif of a tin can upon which much physical action centres is repeated from one play to the other. Significantly, however, both plays ultimately illustrate that the contending settled and 'unsettled' populations have more in common than either realise: Synge destabilises sedentary stereotypes of the nomad and reveals that the perceived moral chasm between the minority and majority communities is largely constructed. Indeed, well-intentioned liberal humanist readings that have praised the wanderers' lack of piety and civility as proof of the yawning gap between an unadventurous sedentary order and an inherently colourful peri-patetic culture have tended to reinforce a breach that Synge attempts to seal. The folkloric belief of his era which suggested that peoples of the road were the descendants of those who had been expelled from orderly society implied that contemporaneous tinkers had no connection whatsoever to majority culture. However, for Synge, tinkers and tramps are the custodians of local and autonomous values within a broader rural order that is acquiescing in the conformity and homogeneity required by modernity, prosperity and the Catholic Church's imposition of standardised devotional practice after the mid-nineteenth century.

Synge's critique of settled aspirations in *The Well of the Saints* and *The Tinker's Wedding* challenges the sense of sedentary superiority that underlines the dominant culture binary of immoral wanderer and upstanding member of rooted society. In order to highlight the sublimated bond between spaces usually understood to symbolise the antithetical values of sacred and profane, the opening stage directions of both plays place the wanderers' temporary resting place in close proximity to a church, and this juxtaposition serves to deconstruct the link between church membership and rootedness implied by the very word 'parishioner'. Although prospective groom Michael Byrne speaks of the clergyman as 'playing cards, or drinking a sup, or singing songs, until the dawn of day' (CW IV, 13), critical readings of *The Tinker's Wedding* that interpret the man of God as the antithesis of the tinkers have downplayed the irregularity of the priest's conduct. For instance, seemingly unconcerned about the spiritual consequences for the sinfully cohabiting Michael Byrne and Sarah Casey should they not be able to afford the fee, the clergyman initially demands the substantial sum of one pound for performing what is his priestly duty. He also voices his suspicion that Sarah was never christened, but does not suggest rectifying a situation that would, according to Church teaching, endanger the young woman's soul. Moreover, the initial teasing banter between God's representative and the raucous Mary Byrne suggests that he has finally met his match in capacity for alcohol and seditious-ness. The tinker matriarch urges drink upon the priest with the playful suggestion that he is as much of a sinner as she is, revealing that she is aware of his secret taste for the substance. His tongue loosened by the alcohol, the clergyman subsequently reveals his envy of Mary's autonomous existence and his impatience with the demands of his pious parishioners. Even more audaciously, Synge intimates that this intrinsic like-mindedness makes the older man and woman sexually compatible: Mary flirtatiously places her hand upon the priest's knee during this exchange, and implies that her drinking companion is romantically available by referring to him as a 'single man' (CW IV, 19). In both *The Well of the Saints* and *The Tinker's Wedding*, men of God are drawn into a bodily realm traditionally associated with the wanderer: the tinkers' adversary is described by Sarah as being 'near burst with the fat', while the saint has a 'big head' and 'welted knees' (CW IV, 43; CW II, 149). The binary opposition of holy priest and unholy itinerants is further challenged when the dramas concerned are read side by side: the 'villain[y]' of Martin and the 'villainies' of the tinkers are referred to by others, but the latter have the final word when they brand the priest 'an old villain' (CW III, 147; CW IV, 45–9) at the close of the action in *The Tinker's Wedding*. Finally, and in contrast to the commonplace Irish folk-loric trope of the woman or man of the road's capacity for casting curses, it is God's representative who threatens maledictions upon the wanderers in both plays.

46

The tinkers and tramps of *The Tinker's Wedding* and *The Well of the Saints* have not internalised the negative beliefs concerning their peripatetic subculture that circulate in the dominant society, and their pronouncements suggest that they even consider their own lifestyle to be superior to that of the economically productive house-dwellers: Martin derides Timmy's abode as a 'shanty' (CW III, 111), and when forced to work for wages rather than rely on begging, the Douls scorn the restrictions placed upon the individual by capitalism. The symbiotic relationship of such Church-endorsed virtue with the capitalist work ethic is suggested in the opening scene of *The Tinker's Wedding*, when Sarah urges Michael to solder her wedding ring in the priest's presence, 'for it's great love the like of him [the priest] have to talk of work' (CW IV, 13). Moreover, the Christian metaphors of 'light' and 'dark' are invoked in a subversive manner in *The Well of the Saints*. Once Martin has been led 'into the light' – which involves being cured of blindness *and* forced to take a stake in the religio-capitalist order – he labels the world of work, property and propriety as 'dark'. Similarly, the Douls only begin again to notice the sunlight and the joys of nature with which they were first associated once they are about to be expelled from the community. Given the use of the plural noun in the title of a play concerned with an individual Church representative and with the muddying of moral hierarchies, the 'saints' referred to can only be the Douls.

In 'People and Places', Synge explicitly links Irish beggars' physical and mental robustness to their nationality:

> These vagrants have no resemblance with the mendicants who show their sores near the churches of Italy, for ... the greater number that one sees are vigorous women and men of fine physique ... [The] freshness of wit which is equally sure in the women and the men ... is a peculiarity of Irish tramps and distinguishes them, I think, from the rural beggars of other countries of Europe.
>
> (CW II, 196–7)

Here, and in *The Well of the Saints* and *The Tinker's Wedding*, Synge elevates the wanderer as the noble remnant of a threatened native culture that had valued expression and freedom over social climbing, avariciousness and close-mouthed conformity. The writer's ability to envision the world through the eyes of the outsider suggests a personal identification with a grouping that, like his own class, could not be contained within the narrowest contemporary definitions of Irishness, which excluded both 'heathenish' tinker and Protestant Anglo-Irishman alike. This empathy with the nomad in a writer whose background was continually invoked in critiques of his 'unpatriotic' plays draws attention to Ireland's cultural and religious diversity in an era in which elements within nationalism were attempting to claim the term

'Catholic' as an equivalent of 'Irish'. In a further sense of his personal identification with the marginalised, the display of individual conscience of peoples of the road in *The Well of the Saints* takes on overtones of the evangelical Protestant tradition within which the young Synge had been raised; despite his predilection for cures, the austere wandering saint who does not intend to charge a fee to wed Molly and Timmy is a sympathetic figure drawn both from traditions of the 'uncorrupted' Celtic Church from which Irish Protestantism claims lineal descent and from Biblical narratives of desert-dwelling ascetics. Though he was predictably hostile, Arthur Griffith incisively deployed the term 'Calvinistic' in his review of the play, and Synge's 'Protestantisation' of the saint was foregrounded in the DruidSynge production.[9] Thus, the 'Protestant' saint is implicitly contrasted with the house-dwelling and rapacious Catholic priest, even if equally implicated in the religious establishment's enforcement of sedentary norms in the end.

As represented in the numerous Revival writings in which the values of propertied middle-class and farming existence are rejected, free-spirited tinkers and tramps embodied the bohemian values with which the more liberal writers of the period identified. Synge's plays and prose works centred on itinerant groupings exist within a huge constellation of comparable pieces concerned with wandering musicians, tramps, beggars and tinkers by diverse contemporaneous writers.[10] Even as Synge utilises the purported paganism and anti-materialism of peoples of the road as a stick with which to beat the religiosity and acquisitiveness of the upwardly mobile petit bourgeois class, his depictions are more humanising, personally resonant and explicitly seditious than those of his peers, however, who often deploy wanderers as undifferentiated and romanticised symbols of a free-floating non-conformity. For instance, the commonplace trope of tinker heathenism that goes unquestioned in most other depictions is revealed by Synge in *The Well of the Saints* and *The Tinker's Wedding* to be more admirable than the self-serving professions of piety of a corrupt settled culture. This message is consistent with Synge's critique of the Church for bolstering the sectional interests of nationalist middle Ireland: in this respect both plays are deeply political, despite Yeats's claim that the playwright was incapable of thinking a political thought.[11] Synge was commissioned in 1905 by the *Manchester Guardian* to write on the distressed state of the Congested Districts of the west, and he subsequently excoriated the stifling social cohesion that emanated from the relationship between the Catholic Church, the professions, and commercial interests in that region, a consensus that excluded those who had no wish to partake of rooted capitalist society. 'There are sides of all that western life … that are horrible,' he wrote, 'in one place the people are starving but wonderfully attractive and charming and in another place where things are going well one has a rampant double-chinned vulgarity I haven't seen the like of' (CL I, 116–17). In Synge's reading of post-Famine culture, the more affluent or aspirational the smallholder or businessperson, the more likely he or she is to conform to an orthodox Catholic doctrine and practice that overlaps with economic self-interest.

In *The Tinker's Wedding*, the young cohabiting couple who have had children together obviously subvert the institution of marriage, attitudes towards which had become intrinsically entwined with the acquisition and passing on of assets by the Revival period. It seems plausible, too, that Mary and Martin Doul of *The Well of the Saints* are also possibly a common-law rather than a legally married couple if the name Doul (from the Irish *dall*, 'blind') is understood as a nickname rather than a shared surname. However, even if Mary and Martin have cemented their union in the eyes of the Church, the couple's casual partings, reconciliations and their insistence on the necessity of the sexual partner's youthful appearance still undermine an institution that relied on strict sexual chastity and the pairing of elderly grooms with fertile brides in order to ensure patrilineal inheritance; in the turn-of-the-twentieth-century Irish context, the Catholic rhetoric of the necessity of chastity both within and without marriage conveniently reinforced the economic advantageousness of that decree to agrarian culture, which often relied on the delayed marriage of the inheriting son and the celibacy of stay-at-home siblings to maintain the economic viability of smallholdings. In particular, women whose primary role was to provide the heir bore the brunt of the pressure to maintain sexual continence at all costs, a fact illuminated by the outrage that greeted Nora Burke's decision to abandon her elderly but financially secure farmer husband for a penniless tramp in *The Shadow of the Glen*. Moreover, even if the Douls really are married, then this merely serves to underline further the rejection of settled rural values inherent in Mary's refusal to provide her husband with offspring, a subversiveness echoed by the landless Sarah Casey's *choosing* to have children outside of wedlock.

Nevertheless, the hasty manner in which the never-seen children of Sarah and Michael are referred to in passing by their father in the opening scene of *The Tinker's Wedding* and the fact that two child characters included in an early draft were cut in the final version suggests that a playwright who had been subject to excoriation in relation to *The Shadow of the Glen* had come to understand that nationalist audiences had little tolerance for the overt undermining of normative sexual mores. The implicit nature of Synge's critique of the marriage institution's absolute subservience to economic concerns in *The Well of the Saints* and *The Tinker's Wedding* contrasts with the explicit critique of a social configuration that commonly trapped young women in loveless marriages with older smallholders in *The Shadow of the Glen*. Synge's necessary caginess regarding the Byrne–Casey children and the precise legal status of the Douls' relationship may be yet another reason why the thematic connections of the works concerned to Synge's more highly regarded plays are not fully appreciated.

The youthful Molly may briefly dally with the silver-tongued Martin, but acts in her own best interests by choosing the equally aged but financially stable Timmy the smith in the end. The recurrent condemnation of rural marriage custom in Synge's dramas both illuminates the stress that is placed throughout *The Well of the Saints* on the vivacious Molly's choice of the ugly but solvent Timmy as her groom and elucidates the ironic tone of its ending. The drama closes with the expulsion of the Douls as preparations for the wedding of Timmy and Molly are being made, and it becomes apparent that the tramps' banishment from the community is necessary for the restoration of the sedentary values called into question by their refusal to conform to normative work and matrimonial practices. This further explicates Timmy's seemingly odd complaint that Martin's harping upon the weathered nature of Mary's visage has made the whole community begin to self-consciously examine their faces: the Douls' insistence on the necessity of the attractiveness of the sexual partner (echoed by Sarah Casey's repeated avowal of the value of her beauty) draws attention to the elision of such human concerns within a discourse of marriage compatibility that insisted upon economic security and the protection of patrilineal inheritance above all other considerations. Thus, Synge's celebration of the unorthodox alliances of both *The Well of the Saints* and *The Tinker's Wedding* is not so much to reinforce the stereotype of itinerant promiscuity that has become a critical given, as to highlight the profound link between marriage and economics in the rural Ireland of his time. It is striking that despite flirtations with others, the wandering couples in both plays make the conscious decision to stay together in the end, which contrasts with the obligatory nature of the partnership in which property is at stake in *The Playboy of the Western World* and *The Shadow of the Glen*.

In response to Martin's insinuation that Molly is far too attractive for the ageing Timmy, the smith responds that she has 'no call' (CW III, 111) to mind his looks, given that he will provide his bride with a freshly built four-roomed house upon their marriage: part of an emerging Catholic propertied class, Timmy fully expects this real estate to ensure his chances in the matrimonial market. The theme of the clash of a newly upwardly mobile Ireland and those whom the changed economic order excludes that is shared across *The Well of the Saints* and *The Tinker's Wedding* makes these companion plays strikingly relevant to a globalised Ireland of recent years in which the demands of the Celtic Tiger work ethic created social, cultural and economic homogenisation akin to the conformity enforced by the nineteenth-century standardisation of religious practice. From the early 1990s onwards, property speculation became a prime source of new Irish wealth, and those with no access to the capital required to enter the fray emerged as the latest disenfranchised class. Had *The Well of the Saints* and *The Tinker's Wedding* received their due critical attention, the contemporary resonance of dramas in which the danger of the unthinking acquiescence required by economic prosperity is explored might have been foregrounded in the landmark DruidSynge production.

NOTES

1. A priest agrees to marry a tinker couple for a low fee on condition they provide him with a tin can, but when they subsequently forget the offering the enraged clergyman refuses to perform the vows and calls them 'a pair of rogues'. See 'At a Wicklow Fair' (CW II, 228–9). The tale is predicated upon Irish folkloric traditions of the tinker's dishonesty and lack of piety.

2. The *Freeman's Journal* review of 6 February 1905 complained that Synge knew 'nothing of Irish peasant religion' (5), while the *Evening Herald* of the same date suggested that no 'such types of the Irish peasant' as the Douls could be found in 'any part of Ireland' (3).

3. Daniel Corkery, *Synge and Anglo-Irish Literature* (Dublin: Educational Company of Ireland, 1931), p. 149.

4. My utilisation of the term 'tinker' in this analysis is not intended to be derogatory, but is deployed to differentiate between the literary representation and pre-1960s concept of the Traveller and the *actual* Traveller.

5. My thanks to Pat Burke of St Patrick's College, Drumcondra, for this information.

6. Aoife Bhreathnach, *Becoming Conspicuous: Irish Travellers, Society and the State 1922–70* (Dublin: University College Dublin Press, 2006).

7. Lady Gregory, 'The Wandering Tribe', *Poets and Dreamers* (New York: Oxford University Press, 1974) pp. 94–7.

8. Kuno Meyer, 'On the Irish Origin and the Age of Shelta', *Journal of the Gypsy Lore Society*, 2.5 (1891), p. 260; Eóin MacNeill, *Phases of Irish History* (Dublin: Gill, 1919), respectively.

9. Arthur Griffith, 'All Ireland', *United Irishman*, 11 February 1905, p. 1.

10. See, for instance, W. B. Yeats's *Where There is Nothing* (1902), Douglas Hyde's *An Tincéar agus an tSídheóg* (1902), and Lady Gregory's *The Travelling Man* (1910).

11. W. B. Yeats, 'J. M. Synge and the Ireland of his Time', *Essays and Introductions* (London: Macmillan, 1961), p. 319.

5

ELAINE SISSON

The Aran Islands and the travel essays

One wonders in these places why anybody is left in Dublin, or London, or Paris,
when it would be better, one would think, to live in a tent or hut with this
magnificent air, which is like wine in one's teeth.
J. M. Synge, 'In West Kerry', *The Shanachie*, 1907

In a letter to Lady Gregory dated August 1905 Synge revealed that the Blasket
Islands off the Dingle Peninsula in West Kerry were the most interesting place
he had ever been. The close association of Synge with the Aran Islands in
Galway, through his plays and prose writings, has meant that his emotional
and spiritual connection to the Blaskets is often overlooked. Part of his
fascination with the Kerry islands was the almost complete absence of
English as a spoken language and, as he writes to Lady Gregory, the necessity
of being 'thrown back on my Irish entirely' in order to communicate (CL I,
122). The Irish language is woven into the topography of the landscape with
the name of every hillock, inlet and outcrop carrying a local history of
meaning. Synge's travel essays are acutely attuned to the landscape: from
the Blaskets to Mayo, from Wicklow to Connemara, he documents the
geography of the land as keenly as he records his conversations with local
people.

Synge's travel essays, collected under the title *In Wicklow, West Kerry and
Connemara* (1910) and his long prose piece on his Aran sojourns, *The Aran
Islands* (1907), illustrate how he can be understood as an early modernist.
The concept of modernity is sometimes misunderstood as a descriptor of
what is current and contemporary but often, paradoxically, modernity is
concerned as much with the past as with the present. Modernity has a Janus
face: one side turned towards progress and the other towards tradition.
Modernism (one of the aesthetic discourses of modernity) may display a
seemingly primitivist interest in folk culture as well as a desire for the new.
This tension between the authentic and the progressive is at the heart of much
of Irish Revivalist writing and culture. While many Revivalists' work displays
a sentimentalised yearning for more 'authentic' times, the very act of photographing, documenting, recording and describing rapidly disappearing peasant ways of life (as seen in the works of Synge, Douglas Hyde, Patrick Pearse

and Lady Gregory, for example) is in itself part of the technocratic apparatus of modernity.

This essay situates Synge's travel essays and his work on the Aran Islands within some of the emergent discourses of modernity such as photography, ethnography, anthropology and documentary realism. Synge's work avoids the sentimentality found in much Revivalist writing on the west of Ireland in particular and he eschews an easy nostalgia for the past. As a realist he recognises that the social conditions of poverty may be alleviated through economic innovation and agricultural technology. Yet what prevents Synge's travel essays from being solely journalistic comment is his humane, poetic and lyrical eye. These shorter pieces are abundant with images of the landscape and topography of Ireland and of people's lives which are shared, rather than observed. *The Aran Islands* also records Synge's growing sensibility as an artist; the writing's discursive mode is both documentary and autobiography, describing events and places but also recording an inner consciousness which is poetic, reflective and, at times, elegiac.

Born into late nineteenth-century urban privilege, Synge belongs to that class of European gentlemen for whom culture and learning was accumulated in the great cities of the world. He started his education in Dublin, and travelled to London and Paris as men of his class tended to do. In Paris Synge studied at the Sorbonne and read extensively in European literature. Records show he was reading Wagner, Pater, Wilde, Wordsworth, as well as contemporary French literature: Baudelaire, Verlaine, Maupassant and Flaubert.[1] The Synge whom W. B. Yeats met in Paris in 1896 was struggling to articulate himself in the language of the material he was reading: that of the aesthete and the urbane scholar-poet. When he revealed to Yeats that he had some knowledge of the Irish language from his time studying at Trinity College Dublin, Yeats urged Synge to go to the Aran Islands. 'Perhaps I would have given the same advice to any young Irish writer who knew Irish,' recollected Yeats, 'for I had been that summer upon Inishmaan [Inis Meáin] and Inishmore [Inis Mór] and was full of the subject.' Yeats's exhortation to Synge to find a life that had not yet been expressed in literature rang true to the young man who was writing second-hand pastiches of a kind of life already well documented within contemporary literature. As Yeats so astutely observed, the work Synge had written in Paris was 'as of a man trying to look out of a window and blurring all that he sees by breathing upon the window'.[2]

Released from his unfulfilled literary life in Paris, Synge returned to Ireland, yet when he first went to Aran in 1898 his European sensibility accompanied him. In his baggage was a copy of Flaubert's *Madame Bovary*, an edition of Gabriel Rossetti's poems, and works by Swedenborg and the Breton ethnographer Pierre Loti.[3] Synge had experienced the life of the urban *flâneur*: the cultured existence of the financially independent gentleman scholar. Yet his life was discontented and he was unable to capture its joys, decadence and ennui in writing as effectively as had Baudelaire and Rimbaud. Synge travelled to Aran five times between 1898 and 1901. He first journeyed to Inis Mór in May 1898 and after two weeks there, took a boat to Inis Meáin staying with Patrick McDonagh, whose son Máirtín became his tutor. By late 1898 he had returned to Paris and stayed in Europe until May of the next year. That autumn, in September 1899, he revisited Aran, staying for a month. He did not return for a full year, owing in part to the first appearance of the symptoms of Hodgkin's Disease, when he then spent another month in the autumn of 1900, mostly on Inis Oirr. On his fourth trip in 1901 he spent almost three weeks, dividing his time between Inis Meáin and Inis Oirr, and returned a few weeks later for his fifth and last trip in late October 1901, staying for the entire time on Inis Oirr. By late 1901 Synge had finished writing *The Aran Islands* although it remained unpublished until 1907.

Synge's many trips to Aran had been in a private capacity: he was enthralled by the landscape, the language and the people. However, his essays on other parts of Ireland published collectively as *In Wicklow, West Kerry and Connemara* served a more public, even at times political, agenda. Although for the most part Synge travelled alone, writing and publishing his thoughts in Dublin literary magazines, in 1905 he was commissioned by the *Manchester Guardian* newspaper to write on aspects of Irish rural life. C. P. Scott, the editor, asked Synge and Jack B. Yeats, the illustrator, to travel to the Congested Districts of Connemara and North Mayo to record the devastation of the region which had suffered a famine for the fourth time in fifteen years.[4] In 1897 the newspaper had been involved in previous relief efforts, initiating the highly successful Manchester Relief Fund, a private charitable drive, to help the Congested Districts Board eliminate starvation. Yeats's and Synge's commission was, in part, to update the *Manchester Guardian* readers on the effects, if any, of the earlier relief works. They also travelled to Spiddal, Co. Galway, and Swinford, Co. Mayo, recording for the newspaper their impressions of prevailing social and economic conditions. In all, Synge and Yeats had twelve illustrated articles published in the *Manchester Guardian*.

The travel essays reveal different aspects of Synge the writer; he is poet, journalist, social commentator, naturalist, lyricist and traveller. They are divided into three sections: the writings on Wicklow are the most lyrical and least journalistic; the West Kerry essays are vivid and expressive, evoking the type of expansive language and wildness to be found in Synge's dramatic writings, and the Connemara pieces, written while travelling with Jack Yeats, are social comment and reportage commissioned by the *Manchester Guardian*.

On his solitary trips through Wicklow and Kerry, Synge does not so much travel through Ireland as within it; he sleeps in ditches, rests lying by the side of the road, hiking through bogs and up heather-sided mountains. Along his journey he meets fellow-companions of the road, often walking aimlessly, engaged by the conversation and with ear tuned to local turns of phrase. Synge writes that 'tramp life' invites a particular way of thinking about the world that is akin to the artist's. 'In all the circumstances of this tramp life,' he writes in 'The Vagrants of Wicklow', 'there is a certain wildness that gives it romance and a peculiar value for those who look at life in Ireland with an eye that is aware of the arts also' (CW II, 208). As Alan Price noted, Synge saw similarities between the position of the artist in society and the nomadic life of the vagrant – both symbolising marginality yet freedom.[5] Closer in spirit to Walt Whitman than to Baudelaire, Synge as tramp is the antithesis of the sophisticated urban gentleman and he anticipates Charlie Chaplin's and Samuel Beckett's use of the tramp as a paradoxical figure within modernity. Working from Synge's text and photographs, Jack Yeats provided a pen and ink illustration for the publication of Synge's 'The Vagrants of Wicklow' (CW II, 205), visually drawing attention to the tramp as anti-*flâneur*. Yeats's vagrant has all the ease and stature of the cultured man of leisure. His clothes are threadbare although his stance is elegant and debonair with cocked hat and a blackthorn stick in the place of a dandy's cane.

The *Manchester Guardian* articles are first-hand journalistic observations drawn with a poet's eye. Synge chronicles the lives he sees without sentiment or sanctification in essays such as 'From Galway to Gorumna'. In Spiddal, for example, he notices tidy groups of girls 'sitting out by the hour, near enough to the road to see everything that was passing, yet far enough away to keep their shyness undisturbed'. Their clothes with their red petticoats are 'peculiarly beautiful' against the green grass with the splendour behind them of the 'strip of sea' and in the distance 'the grey cliffs of Clare' (CW II, 288). Yet earlier in the journey he had observed wretched, emaciated people, 'pinched with hunger and the fear of it' (CW II, 287). All through the Congested Districts he remarks on the bureaucratic meddling which impacts on local peoples' ability to make a sustainable living. The *Manchester Guardian* articles show Synge to be a compassionate and realistic social investigator mindful of the responsibility of representing people with honesty yet respect. For example he exposes the myth that local people are lazy by illustrating that what may seem to be unwillingness to participate in agricultural schemes is often prudence based on a local experience of the inhospitable landscape. 'The Inner Lands of Mayo' cites the failed forestation of Carna in Connemara as a good example of experts dictating schemes for areas without adequate knowledge of local land conditions (CW II, 332). Instead Synge suggests practical remedies that might be undertaken, such as the supplying of good-quality manure and new seed potatoes, the extension of land purchases and the improvement of rail and sea links (CW II, 339–43).

Adele Dalsimer has noted that although Synge's writings on Connemara and Mayo reprise the 'exhilarating strangeness' he had already encountered among the people of Wicklow and West Kerry his investigative writing in the *Manchester Guardian* is more restrained.[6] Perhaps mindful of his liberal English readership he refrains from recounting the types of wilder episodes which he witnesses in West Kerry and in Wicklow. In 'The Vagrants of Wicklow' Synge recounts an altercation between local people and the police in which a drunken flower-woman rips her clothes from her back in fury at her ill-treatment (CW II, 207). At a circus in Dingle, he records how a group of 'wild hillside people, fishwomen and drunken sailors' surged into the circus tent until 'three or four of the women performers ran out from behind the scenes and threw themselves into the crowd', forcing back the intruders and demonstrating 'in an extraordinary tumult of swearing, wrestling and laughter' (CW II, 242).

These keenly observed sketches of the energies, passions and chaos of Irish life are entirely missing from the domesticated, sanitised descriptions of rural life found in much Revivalist writing. Although at times Synge can be idealistic he is rarely sentimental and, more importantly, he does not shy away from dealing with the underbelly of impoverishment. He chronicles dirt, violence, alcohol abuse, neglect, hunger and brutality with a candour that is missing from the writings of his contemporaries. Synge's immersion in rural life as a traveller rather than as a Revivalist tourist means that his travel writing largely escapes the romanticism often found in contemporary narratives on rural Ireland. The tendency within Revivalism to privilege the rural over the urban created discourses of romantic nationalism which located rural life as a repository of spiritual authenticity. The investment in the authenticity of the rural within Revivalism was in keeping with a larger European-wide interest in folk-culture as an aspect of the modernist concern with primitivism. The nationalist demand for the authentic as expressed through a search for the 'true', the 'real' or the 'original' Ireland was firmly focused on the west of Ireland as the locale of the 'true' nationalist self, which also had the effect of throwing an essentialising eye over the people who lived there. A commonly held Revivalist conception was that the west of Ireland had a mystical quality lacking in other parts of the country where English prevailed. Consequently an interest in the Irish language and literature, rural regeneration and the folk primitivism of peasant life meant that the privileging of the west of Ireland over the urban centres of Anglicisation was central to cultural nationalist discourse.

The appellation 'Irish Ireland'– first coined by the journalist and writer D. P. Moran – made a distinction between 'real' Ireland (and by definition Irishness) as being rural and Irish-speaking, and a domesticated Ireland which was urbanised and anglicised. Moran's book, *The Philosophy of Irish Ireland* (1905), in which he outlined these differences, is a polemical manifesto for the future of a Gaelicised Ireland. The Gaelic League had already been in existence for more than ten years, ever since Douglas Hyde's plea for the revival of Irish had sown the seeds for its establishment in 1893.[7] However, Moran felt that the Gaelic League's efforts in revitalising Irish had neglected to address the underlying social and economic realities which linked poverty to the decline of the Irish language.[8] His understanding that rural Ireland's cultural disenfranchisement from its past had contributed to its state of social and economic impotence was a radically articulated insight into the decline of the Irish language. In his vehement distaste for what he disparaged as the drawing-room literary Revivalism of the Celtic Twilight, he argued that urban-based and Anglophone appraisals of Ireland's culture were embedded within establishment discourse and prejudices. Unfairly for Synge, Moran initially included him as part of this urban literary coterie, which neglected to take into account two important factors in Synge's favour. The first was Synge's knowledge of the Irish language – which was far superior to Moran's – and the second, his articles for the *Manchester Guardian* which diagnosed many of the same ills as Moran. In fact Moran and Synge shared points in common as both men recognised the need to address questions of cultural and economic poverty as a crucial factor in regenerating rural Ireland.

Despite Moran's polemical attacks on bourgeois Revivalism the Aran Islands continued to attract interest from enthusiastic nationalists in search of 'Irish Ireland'. Synge's appetite for journalism and his capacity for incisive social comment are not as much in evidence in *The Aran Islands*, which was of course written prior to his visit to the Congested Districts for the *Manchester Guardian*. Consequently, *The Aran Islands* sits more easily as a Revivalist text evoking the islands as a place of spiritual purity and artistic inspiration, of topographic 'otherness' and wild beauty, and as an outpost of Gaelic oral civilisation. There was a long-established expeditionary traffic to Aran well before Synge first made his way there in 1898. The Aran Islands had been the subject of archaeological and ethnographic academic inquiries as far back as the eighteenth century. The islands had long exerted a fascination to antiquarians, but in the 1890s the new science of anthropology also expressed an interest in investigating ethnic strains in the Irish population to identify an 'original' or 'authentic' Irish type. However, the earliest studies of the Aran Islands were concerned with antiquities and archaeology rather than with an investigation of ethnicity. Studies of life-style, folklore and local culture as part of anthropological inquiry did not emerge until the late 1880s. The earliest recorded academic field trips to the islands are T. J. Westropp's *Notes on Connaught and Clare, especially the Aran Islands and Sligo* in the late eighteenth century (1770). Later visitors to the islands include George Petrie and John O'Flaherty in the 1820s, which resulted in O'Flaherty's publication of 'A Sketch of the History and Antiquities of the Southern Isles of Aran' in 1824.[9] In the 1830s the antiquarian John O'Donovan arrived on behalf of the Ordnance Survey of Ireland. Cultural interest aroused by the Young Irelanders in the 1840s (consider Thomas Davis's rousing lines 'The West's Awake, the West's Awake') inspired an increased curiosity in archaeological sites around Ireland generally, but in particular on Aran. After the 1850s trips began with increasingly regularity as local fishermen rowed boatloads of historians, archaeologists, philologists and antiquarians to and from the islands. Sir Samuel Ferguson, Whitley Stokes, Eugene O'Curry, John Windele and Charles Hartshorne all conducted expeditions to the islands during the 1850s.

The most extensive historical, architectural and archaeological study of the islands during that period was Martin Haverty's study for the British Association. Haverty's report *The Aran Islands* was first published in 1857 and later reprinted, due to its popularity, in 1859.[10] Nicola Gordon Bowe has suggested that Haverty's study 'provided the sort of structured search for the vernacular which artists, archaeologists and historians would increasingly favour'.[11] The Royal Irish Academy commissioned a report on Aran antiquities in the 1860s, but by the 1870s the focus on the islands had shifted from the interests of antiquarians to those of folklorists.[12] Both Sir William Wilde, father of Oscar, and Jeremiah Curtin were producing works in the 1870s which examined issues of ethnicity and folkloric culture rather than sites of archaeological significance.[13] These works anticipated the mythic significance the islands would hold for the Revivalist movements of the next few decades. The modernist and nationalist agendas within discourses on primitivism collide in the belief that the roots or 'truth' of a civilisation are accessible through excavation, although sometimes to uphold very different agendas. The contradictory nature of discourses of modernity and national identity have been examined by Clifford Geertz, who suggests that emergent discourses on nationalism and modernity contain a tension between the authentic (the past) and the progressive (the future) which he has referred to as an internal conflict between 'essentialism' and 'epochalism'. Epochalism can be read as a desire for progress, while essentialism has a primitivist impulse which seeks to preserve an intangible essence of a race or people and therefore is driven to enshrine 'authentic' language or culture.[14]

The significance of Aran to cultural nationalists was not only in its association with early Christian monastic settlements like those of St Enda but with an older pre-Christian civilisation. The remains of the Christian settlements on Aran coupled with the island's mystical pagan history fed the imaginations of literary Revivalists. Cultural nationalism dictated that the Aran Islands take on the properties of the imaginary islands of mythology as well as 'the transcendently imaged islands of medieval Christianity'.[15] From the late nineteenth century there had been a steady stream of nationalists seeking cultural absolution in the islands' holy wells, peasant cabins and monastic sites. William Butler Yeats and Arthur Symons were among the first of these to go in 1896. Visits were localised and cultural tourists tended to go to the same places as each other. The fact that Synge and Pearse shared the same language teacher, Máirtín McDonagh, albeit on different trips, suggests just how localised trips were. Lady Gregory recounts her territorial indignation at finding a 'stranger' on her beloved Inis Mór. She recorded in the *English Review* that she was staying on Aran

> gathering folk-lore, talking to the people, and felt quite angry when I passed another outsider walking here and there, talking also to the people. I was jealous of not being alone on the island among the fishers and seaweed gatherers. I did not speak to the stranger, nor was he inclined to speak to me; he also looked on me as an intruder. I only heard his name.[16]

It was Synge.

Nationalist pilgrimages seeking 'primitive' cultural purity coincided with expeditions of a 'modern' scientific nature. A. C. Haddon's expeditions between 1891 and 1893 marked the first modern anthropological trip which used anthropometric instruments and photographs to catalogue physical types. Haddon's 'Studies in Irish Craniology: The Aran Islands, Co. Galway', and Haddon's and C. R. Browne's 'The Ethnography of the Aran Islands, Co. Galway' include head, face and body measurements, detailed lists of hair and eye colour, the documentation of local folk culture (songs, stories, superstitions), as well as the health status and psychology of the islanders.[17] Synge too had an ethnographic interest in the folkways and mores of the islanders. He noted carefully local customs and rituals and took a number of photographs which were later published in conjunction with *The Aran Islands*. Declan Kiberd has noted the influence on Synge of the work of the Breton ethnographer and folklorist Anatole le Braz, observing how customs which were common in Brittany such as the lighting of bonfires on St John's Eve (23 June) were also practised on Aran. As Kiberd notes, Synge 'detected a fiercely defiant paganism underneath a thin film of Christian belief'.[18]

Synge's writings demonstrate quite beautifully what James Clifford has coined 'the ethnographic allegory'. Clifford suggests that ethnographic writing about people and cultures has an allegorical function which transcends mere observation or documentary and which is capable of making 'moral, ideological and even cosmological statements'.[19] Synge's description of a funeral on Inis Meáin captures in material detail the habits and rituals of the islanders' customs and infers larger existential questions from what he sees. He observes how the coffin is 'carried out sewn loosely in sailcloth, and held near the ground by three cross-poles lashed upon the top'. The older women, wearing their petticoats pulled up tight around their heads, join the family procession as they weave their way down to the graveyard. Gathered around the coffin the old women begin to keen and Synge intuits how the keening articulates 'the whole passionate rage that lurks somewhere in every native of the island'. In this instant he sees how the crying lays bare the 'inner consciousness of the people' and 'reveal[s] the mood of beings who feel their isolation in the face of a universe that wars on them with wind and seas'. Between the simplicity of the grave and the mumbled Catholic prayers, Synge deliberates on 'the cries of pagan desperation' and 'the pitiable despair before the horror of fate' that the presence of death reveals (CW II, 74–5). Robin Skelton noted that Synge was a 'time-haunted man' with an acute sense of his mortality because of his chronic poor health.[20] His familiarity with illness gave him a discriminating awareness of the physical hardships of the lives of the rural poor, recognising that if he had not been born into the comforts of his social class he might never have survived infancy. As Clifford argues, and Synge demonstrates, the transcendent meanings are not just reflective interpretations added on to the writing or reading of the initial 'simple' event; they are intrinsic to the meaning of the event itself. In *The Aran Islands* the islanders become a human ideal existing outside of history, transformed from the local into the universal.

Synge was sufficiently aware to realise that his presence on the islands brought the threat of change and hastened the progress of modernisation. Yet, as Kiberd notes, it did not prevent him from bringing different kinds of technology to the Aran Islands, including an alarm clock for a people who measured their day's routines by movements of sun and shadow.[21] Synge's interest in the relatively new technology of photography was, on the one hand, a method of capturing a disappearing culture and yet, on the other, it illustrated to local people their own geographic isolation and lack of sophistication. The photograph, as an apparatus of modernity, captures the tension between the desire for preservation of the 'authentic' and the impulse towards progress. At one stage, when Synge wishes to photograph a local island boy, they argue when he tries to change into his Sunday clothes instead of remaining, as Synge desires, in his native homespuns. Synge is critical of the boy's apparent shame of his 'primitive' clothes and his wish to appear modern for the camera, and yet is guilty, through photographing him in the first place, of introducing the conflict (CW II, 134). Synge is aware of the power of the photograph. On a quayside in Aran he takes out his wallet of photographs in order to quieten a crowd; in Kerry he shows a picture of himself among marble statues in the Luxembourg Gardens in Paris and is beguiled to hear a man muse that 'in those countries they do have naked people standing around in their skins' (CW II, 252).

On his first visit to Aran in 1898 Synge bought a Lancaster hand camera from a fellow-visitor to the island. It was a heavy box camera holding twelve quarter plates which were later developed by his nephew, Francis Edmund Stephens. Later, Synge owned a Kilto box camera which he used to take fifty-three photographs of Aran, the Blaskets and Galway city, later published by Lilo Stephens.[22] It was mostly from Synge's photographs that Jack Yeats based his pen and ink illustrations which accompanied both the travel essays and *The Aran Islands*. While Yeats's strong linear style complements Synge's written descriptions of the stark, yet robust, lives of the rural poor, Yeats's artwork in turn was influenced by Synge's photographs. The images, like Yeats's drawings, are neither sentimental nor condescending to the life of the peasant; instead they both offer realistic and humane portraits of their subjects.

Yet it would be a mistake to consider *The Aran Islands* primarily as an ethnographic text, a guidebook or even a travel essay. Unlike the travel essays it contains a more sustained interior narrative and records the growing consciousness of a writer and a poet. While Synge has a photographer's eye for light and shade, composition and colour, he has a poet's eye for description and an ability to translate the inner life into lyrical language. *The Aran Islands* is also the autobiography of an artist. As Synge steps on to the currach that brings him from Inis Mór to Inis Meáin for the first time, he experiences 'a moment of exquisite satisfaction' to find himself 'moving away from civilisation' (CW II, 57). In any real sense Synge is not moving very far as he travels from one island to the next but he is, in effect, sailing into a different landscape: the landscape of the artistic imagination. He found on Aran not merely an unfamiliar rhythm of speech which he was to utilise in his plays and poetry, but something greater: a connection beyond language to a greater consciousness; an awareness of the abandonment, terror, lamentation, joy, agony, despair and exultation of being alive. One dark night in Aran he listens to the 'low rustling' of the waves and the 'whistling and shrieking' of wild birds and is released into such an immense solitude that 'I could not see or realise my own body, and I seemed to exist merely in my perception of the waves and of the crying birds, and of the smell of seaweed' (CW II, 129–30). The annihilation of the body and the merging of the individual into a universal consciousness is an intensely felt emotional and spiritual experience, and what Aran, in particular, offered was a rich imaginative seam of life out of which Synge produced a carefully sustained meditation. Within the bardic tradition of Irish-language literature lies the concept of *dinnseanchas*: a recognition of the importance of place. Sometimes literally translated as topography, *dinnseanchas* is more than the knowledge of local geography but is learning invested with the meaning and significance of nature, genealogy and memory. What the travel essays and *The Aran Islands* illustrate is not only Synge's ability to read the Irish landscape, captured in language, but his acceptance of mortality, beauty, fragility, death and the cyclical nature of life.

NOTES

1. Ann Saddlemyer, 'Synge and the Doors of Perception', in Andrew Carpenter (ed.), *Place, Personality and the Irish Writer* (Gerrards Cross: Colin Smythe, 1977), p. 103.
2. W. B. Yeats, 'My First Meeting with Synge', in E. H. Mikhail (ed.), *J. M. Synge: Interviews and Recollections* (London: Macmillan, 1977), p. 5.
3. Richard Fallis, 'Art as Collaboration: Literary Influences on J. M. Synge', in Edward A. Kopper (ed.), *A J. M. Synge Literary Companion* (New York: Greenwood Press, 1988), p. 151. See also a discussion of the influence of the Breton ethnographers on the work of Synge and Gauguin in James F. Knapp, 'Primitivism and Empire: John Synge and Paul Gauguin', *Comparative Literature*, 41.1 (Winter 1989), pp. 53–68.
4. The Congested Districts were poor areas mostly in the west of Ireland where the quality of the land was unable to sustain local populations. The Congested Districts Board was established by the Land Purchase Act of 1891 to support local communities by dividing large land estates into smaller, more workable holdings. It also devised a number of schemes with the aim of improving rural infrastructure and alleviating poverty.
5. Alan Price, *Synge and Anglo-Irish Drama* (London: Methuen, 1961), p. 122.
6. Adele Dalsimer, *Visualising Ireland: National Identity and the Pictorial Tradition* (London: Faber & Faber, 1993), p. 208.
7. Douglas Hyde, 'The Necessity for De-Anglicising Ireland', in Breandán Ó Conaire (ed.), *Language, Lore and Lyrics* (Dublin: Irish Academic Press, 1986), pp. 153–70.
8. D. P. Moran, 'The Gaelic Revival', *The Philosophy of Irish Ireland* (Dublin: James Duffy, 1905), p. 83.
9. Royal Irish Academy Transcripts XIV *Antiquities*, pp. 79–140.
10. Martin Haverty, *The Aran Isles: or a Report of the Excursion of the British Association from Dublin to the Western Isles of Aran*, (London, 1857).
11. Nicola Gordon Bowe, *Art and the National Dream: The Search for Vernacular Expression in Turn of the Century Design* (Dublin: Irish Academic Press, 1993), p. 197.

12. Henry Kinahan, 'Notes on Some of the Ancient Villages in the Aran County of Galway', *Proceedings of the Royal Irish Academy*, 10 (1866), pp. 25–30.

13. See Diarmuid Ó Giolláin, 'Irish Pioneers', *Locating Irish Folklore: Tradition, Modernity, Identity* (Cork: Cork University Press, 2000), pp. 94–113.

14. Clifford Geertz, 'Thick Description: Toward an Interpretive Theory of Culture', *The Interpretation of Cultures* (London: Hutchinson, 1975), pp. 3–32.

15. John Wilson Foster, 'Certain Set Apart: The Western Isle in the Irish Renaissance', *Studies* (Winter, 1977), p. 265.

16. Lady Gregory, 'Memories of Synge', *English Review* (London), XII (March 1913), pp. 556–66.

17. A.C. Haddon and C.R. Browne, 'The Ethnography of the Aran Islands', *Proceedings of the Royal Irish Academy*, 2nd, 3rd Series, 1891–1893, pp. 452–505. Also see A.C. Haddon, 'Photography and Folklore', *Folklore*, 6 (1895), pp. 222–4.

18. Declan Kiberd, *Synge and the Irish Language* (London: Macmillan, 1979), p. 156.

19. James Clifford, 'On Ethnographic Allegory', in James Clifford and George Marcus (eds.), *Writing Culture: The Poetics and Politics of Ethnography* (Berkeley: University of California Press, 1986), p. 98.

20. Robin Skelton, *The Writings of John Millington Synge* (London: Thames & Hudson, 1971), p. 62.

21. Kiberd, *Synge and the Irish Language*, p. xiv.

22. J.M. Synge, *My Wallet of Photographs* (Dublin: Dolmen Editions, 1971).

6

DECLAN KIBERD

Deirdre of the Sorrows

The legend of Deirdre and the Sons of Uisneach has been arguably the most popular of all Irish tales with artists and with audiences. It became famous as one of *'trí truaighe na scéalaíochta'* ('the three sorrows of storytelling'). In the twelfth-century Book of Leinster it is referred to as a *'longas'*, a narrative of exile. That version centralises the three doomed brothers in a harsh account of warrior life. Deirdre's role is only briefly described – she is wild and rude, compelling Naoise to undertake with her the elopement to Alban. In one memorable scene, she grabs him by the ears to make him do her will, but she is not otherwise pivotal. After the brothers die, she is forced to live for a year of humiliation with an enemy of her lover, Naoise, after which she dashes her brains out upon a rock in a terrible image of female derangement and suffering.

It is only in much later medieval versions that Deirdre's emotional graph is made a crucial element all through the narrative. Now, she moans with pain and in the end commits suicide on her lover's grave. In the words of Celtic scholar Eleanor Hull, the wild woman of the Book of Leinster has been 'transformed into the Lydia Languish of a later age'.[1] Those changes reflect the growing importance of women as an audience for the heroic tales, with a consequent increase in the profile of female protagonists. After this reconfiguration the tale is seen as a love story rather than simply one of warrior honour: and indeed the clash between love and honour allows for a developing subtlety in the psychological portrayal of a tragic heroine.

Even after the collapse of the Gaelic aristocracy in the early 1600s, the legend retained its fascination for poor peasants and fisherfolk, who listened spellbound to it around cottage fires. It had all the interest of the eternal triangle – a young man and an older one vying for the love of a beautiful aristocratic girl – but its appeal may also have been due to its treatment of the theme of emigration, whose pleasures and pains would have been well known in most rural communities. Many men in the west of Ireland had, after all, migrated to Scotland (Alban), either on a seasonal or a semi-permanent basis:

and those who returned thereafter discovered what James Joyce would articulate in his great play *Exiles* (1918): that a nation exacts from every emigrant a moral and emotional price, payable most often upon return. If leaving proved almost always a heart-rending thing, coming home could often be even worse. A people whose community was ravaged by emigration of the young (often seeking to escape the prohibitive codes of the elderly) might also be fascinated by the abusive treatment offered to returnees. Those who came back often did so in the naive belief that they could take up things where they had left off.

J. M. Synge was a shrewd observer of migrations from the western sea-board, noting that the tradition had become self-sustaining – not always a matter of economic necessity but simply the bright thing for young people to do, with a consequent impoverishment of social life for all who remained. In an essay he wrote of the complex, even contradictory, impulses behind emigration:

> In the poorest districts of all they go reluctantly, because they are unable to keep themselves at home; but in places where there has been much improvement the younger and brighter men and girls get ambitions which they cannot satisfy in this country, and so they go also. Again, where there is no local life or amusements they go because they are dull, and when amusements and races are introduced they get the taste for amusements and go because they cannot get enough of them. They go as much from districts where the political life has been allowed to stagnate as from districts where there has been an excess of agitation that has ended only in disappointment. (CW II, 341)

His conviction was that the only real remedy for emigration was the 'restoration of some national life to the people' (341). He believed that the Gaelic League was doing more than any other movement to check the demoralisation, but noticed with dismay in *The Aran Islands* that a young woman who had returned from exile seemed disoriented and listless, at once sophisticated and disillusioned:

> She has passed part of her life on the mainland, and the disillusion she found in Galway has coloured her imagination. As we sit on the stools on either side of the fire, I hear her voice going backwards and forwards in the same sentence from the gaiety of a child to the plaintive intonation of an old race that is worn with sorrow. At one moment she is a simple peasant, at another she seems to be looking out at the world with a sense of prehistoric disillusion and to sum up in the expression of her grey-blue eyes the whole external despondency of the clouds and sea. (CW II, 114)

As he translated *Oidhe Chloinne Uisnigh* (*The Tragic Fate of the Children of Usna*) into Hiberno-English during a sojourn on the Aran islands from

21 September to 9 October 1901,[2] Synge would have noted the painful realities of these themes all around him. Just a couple of months earlier, the first act of George Russell's mystical play titled *Deirdre* had been published in the *All Ireland Review*.[3] It lacked psychological or sociological realism, being a reverie on the fated doom of Deirdre (whose name means 'troubler', because of the prophecy of a druid at her birth that she would bring ruin to the men of Ulster). In Russell's version Deirdre, though weak and passive, is seen as the destroyer of the Red Branch Knights. Five years later, W. B. Yeats would produce his own *Deirdre*, which did centralise the heroine as a tragedy queen, but his play treated the characters more as symbols than as persons of flesh and blood.

Synge's own take on the legend, when his turn came to dramatise it, was different – rooted not just in the realities of rural Irish life but also in a modern psychology of love and of its frustration. Its theme anticipates that of Freud in *Civilization and Its Discontents*: that a massive price must be paid in terms of self-repression if one is to enter and partake in a given culture.[4] Synge began his work on 5 September 1907, a year after the performance of Yeats's version in the Abbey Theatre and some months after the *Playboy* controversies. 'I am half inclined to try a play on "Deirdre" – it would be amusing to compare it with Yeats' and Russells' [*sic*],' he wrote to Frederick Gregg, an American journalist on 12 September, 'but I am a little afraid that the "Saga" people might loosen my grip on reality' (CL II, 56). He needn't have worried, but he continued to fret, writing on 4 January 1908 to John Quinn: 'These saga people when one comes to deal with them, seem very remote; – one does not know what they thought or what they ate or where they went to sleep, so one is apt to fall into rhetoric' (CL II, 122).

Such reservations, far from being realistic scruples attendant on the enterprise, are built into the very structure and style of *Deirdre of the Sorrows*. Before writing it, Synge in his performed plays had written solely of the peasantry: and there is a very deep sense in which this play is itself a critical exploration of the relationship between the rather remote, aristocratic characters of the old tale and the warmly human peasant world in which alone it now lingered. The underlying project is democratic: to present the characters in all their humanity not as regal personages so much as terrified persons caught up in an insoluble crisis of human relations. Synge achieves this effect by resort to a technique which might be called anti-pastoral: whereas in traditional pastoral, kings and queens dressed for a day as shepherds and shepherdesses, Synge puts his well-honed peasant dialect of Hiberno-English on to the lips of royalty. Traditional pastoral tended to be conservative, even reactionary, in the way it wished away an all-too-palpable division of social classes:[5] but Synge exacerbates our sense of these tensions by the deliberate incongruity with which he has a character say that the king will be 'in a blue stew' (CW IV, 185), if he discovers what is afoot. When peasants play at royalty, as the storytellers did every night on which they retold the legend, all social hierarchies are reversed.

This is why, for all his scruples, Synge confidently told his nephew, Edward Stephens, that his play would never be open to the danger of being branded a mere imitation of Russell's or Yeats's: 'People are entitled to use these old stories in any way they wish. My treatment of the story of Deirdre wouldn't be like either of theirs.'[6] Many caustic critics had felt frustrated by the unreal characters in Russell's version. 'Who are his people?' George Moore inquired testily after a viewing: 'Ours were cattle-merchants.'[7]

Synge had always been somewhat sceptical of the rather ethereal values subscribed to by such Revivalists as Russell. In a poem, 'The Passing of the Shee', he seemed to link Russell and Yeats:

> 'The Passing of the Shee'
> *After looking at one of A. E.'s pictures.*
>
> Adieu, sweet Angus, Maeve and Fand,
> Ye plumed yet skinny Shee,
> That poets played with hand in hand
> To learn their ecstasy.

The phrase 'hand in hand' is a reference to Yeats's 'The Stolen Child', in which an infant is 'taken' by fairies. Against this other-worldly view of the Celtic Twilight, Synge posited a warmly humane and very specific reality couched in clear images of monosyllabic urgency:

> We'll search in Red Dan Sally's ditch,
> And drink in Tubber fair,
> Or poach with Red Dan Philly's bitch
> The badger and the hare.   (CW I, 38)

Likewise, when it came to renditions of the ancient queens of Irish and other sagas, Synge invoked them in a poem, only to demonstrate the stronger claims of living men and women:

> 'Queens'
>
> Seven dog-days we let pass
> Naming Queens in Glenmacnass,
> All the rare and royal names
> Wormy sheepskin yet retains,
> Etain, Helen, Maeve, and Fand,
> Golden Deirdre's tender hand,
> Bert, the big-foot, sung by Villon,

Cassandra, Ronsard found in Lyon.
Queens of Sheba, Meath and Connaught,
Coifed with crown, or gaudy bonnet,
Queens whose fingers once did stir men,
Queens were eaten of fleas and vermin,
Queens men drew like Mona Lisa,
Or slew with drugs in Rome and Pisa,
We named Lucrezia Crivelli,
And Titian's lady with amber belly,
Queens acquainted in learned sin,
Jane of Jewry's slender shin:
Queens who wasted the East by proxy,
Or drove the ass-cart, a tinker's doxy.
Yet these are rotten – I ask their pardon –
And we've the sun on rock and garden,
These are rotten, so you're the Queen
Of all are living, or have been.   (CW I, 34)

This technique of listing the names of ancient exemplars only to press the superior claims of contemporary life would be emulated by Yeats, who clearly got the underlying point, in such poems as 'Easter 1916'. In Synge's lyric the majestic queens of the past are all rotten in the earth. Even the vellum of the bards, who thought that they had salvaged the royal names from oblivion, is now but a wormy sheepskin. As heir to those bards, Synge in his title seems to promise an encomium in celebration of ancient ladies but instead produces a lyric to his own girlfriend, Molly Allgood, the Abbey actress. He registers the decline of that tradition from Etain and Helen to a latter-day tinker's doxy – but he doesn't appear to be too worried. Faced with the pressure of actual experience now, he must excuse himself his bardic duty: 'I ask their pardon.'

It is much the same in Synge's dramatisation of the Deirdre legend. He arouses the expectations of his audience with an unashamedly Revivalist title, only to deliver something quite anti-Revivalist in methodology. Many Revivalists subscribed to a cult of aristocracy – that very thing which England had now, a noble upper class, must have been something which the Irish once enjoyed in the days of their past glory. If every thinker claimed lineage from some old king or prince, the very phrase of greeting in modern Irish, 'a dhuine uasail' (O noble person) expressed a kind of aristocratic fetishism which informed many texts of the national *risorgimento*. Synge, a genuine aristocrat himself but one intent on embracing a more democratic politics, was impatient with those who seemed intent on reversing his chosen trajectory. In a letter to Stephen MacKenna he complained of the 'purely fantastic, unmodern, ideal, spring-dayish Cuchulainoid' (CL I, 74) nature of

Revivalist texts in a world whose realities were neither fantastic nor Cuchulanoid.

So Synge mocks his own chosen title by having Deirdre say, with self-dramatising narcissism: 'Do not leave me, Naisi. I am Deirdre of the Sorrows' (CW II, 207). The story was so well known and so often repeated that all the characters can give the impression that they are posing for posterity, a sentiment difficult to avoid given the prophecy of the druid Cathbhad at Deirdre's birth. The technical challenge faced by Synge was how to infuse tension into such a fated, over-determined tale. This he did by making Deirdre, in other moments, a more sympathetic and less iconic figure. The sighting of Naisi partakes of both worlds, the spiritual-ideal and the real, for a man with hair like the raven, skin as snow, and lips as if blood had been spilt on that snow, may be either a heraldic figure from the tapestry of fate which she has woven *or* a merely accurate description of an actual youth whom she has already spotted passing her home. Her imposition of her will on the rather unsure young swain is in keeping not just with the self-actualising warrior-women of the Celts (Maeve and Aoife), but also reflective of a contemporary rural Ireland in which women, as often noted, had to take the initiative in wooing, so exhausted were their men from the struggle with stony soil.

That mixture of the aristocratic-heraldic and the natural was also remarked on by Synge in the walk of the fisherfolk of Aran, whose lithe movements recalled the thoroughbred rather than the cart-horse (to that degree only did he endorse the aristocratic rhetoric of Revivalism – if it were linked with the poorest of the poor peasantry) (CW II, 66). The young women of Aran seemed at once country girls and primal forces looking out upon the world with a sense of prehistoric doom, exactly like Deirdre in the grip of the prophecy. King Conchubor has isolated and sequestered Deirdre in the countryside until she is mature and sophisticated enough to make a wife for him: but in exposing her to the forces of storm and skyscape he has unleashed in her those vary natural instincts which he intended to curb. Foolishly, he believes that he alone as High King can negate the prophecy and 'stand between you and the great troubles are foretold' (CW IV, 193).

The women in all of Synge's plays are anxious to live in the present moment, but fated instead to take longer and longer views. They are forever looking backward to a lost past or forward to a possibly happier time, which in their bones they know will be no different from what's gone before. In Act One, Deirdre and Naisi anticipate the joy of a life under nature in Alban, but once they are depicted as living that life in Act Two, they are already considering the world which they have lost. Never are they depicted by Synge in scenes of pleasure or of unalloyed fulfilment. The wedding of Deirdre and Naisi has been placed under the sign of nature by his brother, 'by the sun and moon and the whole earth' (CW IV, 215); but nature proves a weathering and exhausting experience for young aristocrats, bred not for hunting game but for killing men. In Alban Deirdre overhears Naisi confiding in the king's emissary Fergus that he fears that some day he might weary of such open-air love. Evil seems, in all the works of Synge, to inhere even in the seemingly golden romantic moment.

This is the psychological dimension – a truly tragic one – which Synge added to all previous versions. In the original story the lovers perform all deeds under *geasa* (obligation), a kind of '*noblesse oblige*' whose bond carries no strong element of personal motivation: but here the couple flees Ulster in order to protect the integrity of their love. In a somewhat similar style, they decide to accept Fergus's offer of a safe passage back to Emain, in hopes of avoiding the decay of their love in the outdoor life of Alban – but then they resort on the edge of the grave, so dishonestly prepared by the false king, to that very bickering which their removal from Alban was designed to avoid. Confronted with a choice, they would prefer death to lost love, but in the end have to endure both.

Fergus had accused Naisi's brothers, Ainnle and Ardan, of being 'hunters only', that is, not true warriors: but when they place their trust in the warrior-bond of the king, it is badly betrayed. The response of the outraged Fergus is to throw his own sword into the lovers' grave. This is Synge's repudiation not only of Yeats's 'drama of swords' (CW IV, 394) as epitomised by that writer's Cuchulain Cycle, but also of the *claidheamh soluis*, the symbolic sword of light which was the emblem of the Gaelic League. In this, as in its 'Cuchulanoid' obsession, the Irish Revivalist elite imitated the heroic values of the English Arthuriad with its validation of knightly honour by symbolic swords – giving rise to the suspicion among radicals that the warrior heroes of the Irish Heroic Cycle were in some treatments little more than English public-schoolboys in Celtic drag. Synge disliked the Gaelic League's saga-cult and its aristocratic self-image, finding in it only the bankrupt values of an outmoded and parasitic upper class. Swords on the stage he considered 'babyish' (394); and for similar reasons he preferred to make his regal persons speak in homely prose rather than in exalted, Yeatsian poetry.

Such poetry as Synge permitted came from Deirdre, in reprises of her beautiful lines of farewell to the woods of Cuan or in her slightly precious but moving claim that the little moon of Alban would be lonely after the lovers' departure. The man who wrote in the Preface to his own poems that poetry must become brutal if it was again to be fully human (CW I, xxxvi) was deeply suspicious of such appeals to pathetic fallacy, such attempts to make the forces of nature into projected symbols of the human mood. Again and again in his plays and poems, Synge is modernist rather than romantic in his view of nature: nature is weathering, mysterious, inexplicably there, but never reducible to the designs which mere humans have for it. To his own fiancée, Molly Allgood, for whom he created the part of Deirdre, he marvelled in letters at the thought that the rivers will run on long after those who have made love by their banks are dead – a sobering fact.[8]

This is the wisdom epitomised in the play by the old soothsayer Lavarcham, whose role is akin to that of the female chorus in Yeats's version. As a choric figure she has, just like Yeats's musicians, a vested interest in advancing the action foretold by the prophecy, so that she will have a rich tale to tell: but that role has already been assumed by Deirdre, leaving Lavarcham free to espouse a more tough-minded approach. Again and again she tries to abort that very plot which it is in her professional interest to propel. Whenever the young people invoke the prophecy and the need to conform to the supplied script, she demurs. When they warn against the humiliation of growing old, she insists that the only bad thing about being old is having to watch young people whom you love making themselves miserable with such folly. There could hardly be a more blatant manifesto against Revivalism in a play from the period of Irish Revival – a play which warns that the only folly is to make oneself a martyr to a text.

At the very end, when all her warnings have gone unheeded, Lavarcham resigns herself sadly to her narrative role, bringing to a conclusion the very plot which she did her utmost to abort: 'Deirdre is dead, and Naisi is dead, and if the oaks and stars could die for sorrow it's a dark sky and a hard and naked earth we'd have this night in Emain' (CW IV, 269). But her key word is *if*: in truth, there is no pathetic fallacy, because the trees and stars don't obligingly die with self-dramatising humans, but live on mysteriously impervious to all that momentous pain. There is nothing left for Lavarcham to do but to protect what life remains, as she assists her broken king from the stage. Unlike Yeats's Cuchulain, he finds no comfort in his monarchic status, being but a spent old man, who now can see that 'one sorrow has no end surely', that of being 'old and lonesome' (CW IV, 259). His reduced state seems a sudden indication of Deirdre's warning that 'there's no safe place … on the ridge of the world … isn't it a better thing to be following on to a near death, than to be bending the head down' (Plays IV, 231).

The Synge who wrote those lines was a man dying in his thirties. He created the somewhat ambivalent but central role of Deirdre for the woman who was, to him at all events, a rather flighty and teasing lover. Like the male poetic heroes of Synge's plays, Deirdre believes that the only way of challenging time is to create a good story; but, like Molly Allgood, she is also whimsical and self-indulgent. As her nurse Lavarcham asks, 'who'd check her like was made to have her pleasure only?' (CW IV, 183). That Synge was himself ambivalent about his fiancée is clear from the undercurrent of hostility towards her to be found in his strange poem titled 'A Wish':

> May seven tears in every week
> Touch the hollow of your cheek,
> That I – signed with such a dew –
> For a lion's share may sue
> Of the roses ever curled
> Round the May-pole of the world
> Heavy riddles lie in this,
> Sorrow's sauce for every kiss.   (CW I, 51)

Perhaps he kept postponing the marriage because he was unsure – from accounts of her flirtations with handsome actors in the Abbey cast – whether he would have even the 'lion's share' of her love.

Synge was sufficiently older than Molly to be able to identify part of himself with the self-deceived and doting old king: 'Young girls are slow always; it is their lovers that must say the word' (CW IV, 195). But, of course, he also saw himself in the hurt young lover: 'It's women that have loved are cruel only' (CW IV, 257). Deirdre in his version does not so much endure Naisi's death as actively send him out to it, with a harsh and challenging word on her lips. Synge's own feelings for Molly were always tortured and ambiguous – they never did marry – and he knew that in writing Deirdre's lament over the grave of Naisi, he was writing in effect an obituary on himself and on their love, to be spoken before the Abbey audience by Molly after his passing. His seizure of the tale as a warning against Revivalism and false heroics – Naisi calls it 'a tale of blood and broken bodies and the filth of the grave' (CW IV, 211) – would, if he had lived, have generated a controversy to match that which attended *The Playboy of the Western World* with its very different unmasking of hero-making; but, in the event, due deference for a dead author overrode whatever reservations people felt, and the play was received in respectful silence.

It is not a fully finished work. Its peasant dialect sounds oddly at times on the lips of aristocrats: and the clown-figure Owen is not really integrated into the action. He appears to be a male choric counterpart to Lavarcham, a sort of Shakespearean Fool who works as a spy for the king but is secretly in love with the heroine. A reminder of mortality, he says his own father never decayed into angry old age because Naisi killed him. He warns Deirdre that Lavarcham is a dire and wrinkled example of what, if she lives, she will one day become. But his disappearance from the action is as arbitrary and as sudden as his introduction to it. All this may call into question whether Synge really considered this a completed artwork. W. B. Yeats and Molly Allgood oversaw it into its first production, out of respect for a great writer and dear colleague, but it has proven singularly hard to produce in a compelling version.

For all that, the underlying techniques have been hugely influential. The example of Synge here helped to pave the way for James Joyce's *Ulysses* (1922), another democratisation of an epic tale. By juxtaposing the mythical and the matter-of-fact, and by submitting a story of ancient warriors to the deliberately banal language of contemporary life, Synge created a model which, however shakily, provided the basis for later work of more lasting achievement. Joyce, ever since he had read *Riders to the Sea* as a young man in Paris, felt that Synge was the man to beat:[9] and he remained fascinated by his work and by its effects on audiences. An acerbic critic of Yeatsian Revivalism himself, he must have been interested to find so many of his reservations coded into Synge's final play.

Synge's influence has never been fully appreciated. It is obvious in the work of subsequent Irish playwrights. Brian Friel's *Faith Healer*, for instance, reworks the Deirdre legend, by its focus on the penalties imposed on an emigrant who dares to return. That very description, however, might lead many to suspect that Joyce's own *Exiles* would hardly have taken the form it did without Synge's example. If the 'stranger in the house' of *The Shadow of the Glen* was Synge's realist variation upon a Yeatsian theme adumbrated in *Cathleen ni Houlihan*, then the further variation on the idea played by Blazes Boylan in *Ulysses* may have been a complication made possible for Joyce by Synge's existential drama set in a Wicklow landscape. Synge's essays on migration and social decay in the west of Ireland are not just an essential backdrop to an understanding of his last play, but also may have provided both a method and tone for George Orwell's reports from England's own congested districts in *The Road to Wigan Pier*, another exercise in left-wing pastoral.

If Yeats tried to imagine his own generation in the minds and bodies of the ancients, then Synge and Joyce did something even more radical. They asked: what if ancient heroes and heroines were to walk again in the fields and cities of Ireland? This was indeed a case of past narratives flashing forth in the present, not in any attempt to rewind the clock, but rather in order to reveal a socialist, anti-mythological truth at the core of ancient legend. If the legend of Deirdre revealed an aristocratic code in all its moral and emotional bankruptcy, Synge had no compunction in concurring with those latter-day tellers who found such a meaning in the tale.

NOTES

1. Eleanor Hull, 'The Story of Deirdre and the Lay of the Children of Uisne', *Celtic Review* (11, 15 January 1906), p. 288.
2. Synge Manuscripts, Trinity College Dublin, MS 4341.

PART II

Theorising Synge

7

BEN LEVITAS

J. M. Synge: European encounters

Of all the dramatists of the Irish Revival, John Millington Synge is the most intimately connected to the development of modern drama in Europe. His image of Irishness was focused through a European lens. As Daniel Corkery put it: 'It was Synge's European learning enabled him to look at Irish life without the prejudices of the Ascendency class coming in the way ... Europe cleared his eyes ... not entirely of course.'[1] That last cautious caveat goes some way to explain Synge's appeal to modern sensibilities beyond the Ireland he depicted. His later work has an awareness of his problematic complicity in a status quo he wanted to challenge – and one benefit of Synge's continental schooling was a consequently reflexive critique of his own cultural and social predispositions. As a result, his plays' careful calibrations of self and society would in turn become influential interventions in twentieth-century European drama.

Not that this process made his work any less Irish. Synge considered that if any purposeful rebellion were to take place in Ireland it required just such a European dimension. Smarting from the vocal nationalist rejection of *The Playboy of the Western World* in 1907, Synge, adopting the persona of 'a Hedge Schoolmaster', complained:

> Was there ever a sight so piteous as an old and respectable people setting up the ideals of Fee-Gee because, with their eyes glued to John Bull's navel, they dare not be European for fear the huckster across the street might call them English ... some young man with blood in his veins, logic in his wits and courage in his heart will ... teach Ireland again that she is part of Europe, and teach Irishmen again that they have wits to think, imaginations to work miracles, and souls to possess with sanity.
>
> (CW II, 400)

To find Irishness, Synge suggested, it was necessary to look past the coloniser to the continent: to be 'part of Europe' was an alternative to being part of the Empire, crucial if Ireland was to negotiate modernity on its own terms. In taking stock of the shock of the new, Ireland need not renounce its sense of cultural difference, if it could see that was precisely what cultural maturity entailed.

This denial of a notional opposition between Ireland and Europe was far from out of step with its time. It was common for cultural and political nationalists to take comfort and instruction from Europe: particularly the established club of Catholic states (France, Belgium, Italy) to which many thought Ireland should belong; and any small nations (Hungary, Norway, Denmark) which gave clues about how that club might be joined.[2] What set Synge apart were his reference points: less those dimensions of European experience that offered the consolidation of stable national identity, founded on shared religion, language and values; more the culture of contestation that everywhere seemed to be challenging such norms.

The possibility that Ireland might be part of this emerging Europe of uncertain dynamics remains a relatively neglected aspect of his work. This is partly because of a construction of Synge's career popularised by his greatest champion W. B. Yeats; and partly because his subsequent importance as a European (as opposed to simply an Irish) dramatist has seldom been fully considered. Yeats presented Synge's continental explorations as a mere cul-de-sac, and his early development is still sometimes seen in three simple stages: his strict Protestant upbringing and turgid Trinity degree; a dead-end attempt at literary journalism in *fin-de-siècle* Paris; finally, his return to locate his genius in the Aran Islands. But Synge's progress is not so easy to segment. Although he moved beyond the formative evangelism his family practised, he retained close links with them, habitually spending his summers in their company, with his mother, in Wicklow. Such summers continued throughout his travels: his first trip to Germany in 1893 at the age of 22, his three-month trip to Italy in 1895, and his intermittent residency in Paris from 1894 until May 1902. From 1898 to 1901, Synge's trips to the Aran Islands overlaid these spheres of experience with an additional process of discovery. Rather than simple points of departure, where each new location connotes a turning away from the past, there emerges a repeated pattern of movement between locations – at least until the weight of theatre business, for the last five years of his life, limited his travels.

The interplay between Synge's European and Irish modes began when Synge read Darwin as a teenage boy, his existing religious beliefs convulsed into 'an agony of doubt' (CW II, 11). This was one of the great shared shocks of nineteenth-century culture; and as such it opened the door to the wider world. Further doors opened at Trinity College, presenting two options that demanded internationalist sensibilities: music and languages. While his other studies suffered, Synge devoted himself to the violin and classical training in composition (his advanced study in counterpoint would reappear in his structural conception of playwriting). Music offered a model of a pan-European, shared culture: certainly, in Dublin, there existed a shared appreciation among Unionists and Nationalists for recital and opera which naturally looked to the continent for its staples. For shy Synge it was also a social opportunity – his skill with a fiddle would bring him attention in salons and shebeens alike. If musicality suggested a *lingua franca*, languages on the other hand complemented such universalism with a comparative frame of study. Beyond the Trinity prizes for Irish and Hebrew, Synge became adept at German, Italian and French.

It was a combination of these interests that took Synge abroad for the first time, and, as first trips abroad tend to be, it was a profoundly formative experience. Synge left with his cousin Mary Synge (a professional pianist then in middle age) to seek further musical training in Germany. He stayed in Oberworth, near Koblenz, from late July 1893 until January 1894; then in Würzberg, not returning to Dublin until 14 June. The lessons learned that year were more than musical: by Christmas Synge's mother had confided to her diary that Johnnie was 'attributing his unsociableness to his narrow upbringing and warning me!' (CL I, 5). The young writer had discovered that relocation could produce reassessment: as Christy Mahon would say, it was 'the divil's own mirror we had beyond' (CW IV, 95). Arriving in a hostel housing eighteen women, including the hosts – the six von Eicken sisters – could alter a young man's view of himself. It was here that Synge began his habit of striking up close female friendships; Valeska von Eicken, seven years his senior, remained a confidante until his death.

Apart from locating Beethoven and a new 'sociableness', this was a journey of intellectual discovery: language for Synge was a literary and cultural exploration rather than a pursuit of technical facility. In Germany Synge discovered theatre – an introduction that began with Goethe and Schiller.[3] Most significantly, these visits to the theatre came in conjunction with a first exposure to Henrik Ibsen. There must have been a stark disparity between the liveness of Synge's first theatrical experiences (his family remained adamantly opposed) and the German translations of the Norwegian's work – and perhaps this in part explains the ostensible rejection of Ibsen's 'joyless pallid words' (CW IV, 53) in the Preface to *The Playboy of the Western World*. But Synge could also appreciate his debt. During the troubled reception of *The Shadow of the Glen* in 1903, Synge had received a cautious rebuke from his friend Stephen MacKenna. Synge replied:

> You seem to feel that we should not deal with modern matters on the stage in Ireland, because Ireland is 'blessedly unripe' for them. – Do you think that the country people of Norway are much less blessedly unripe than the Irish? If they

are not should Ibsen never have been played in Norway, and therefore never have become an efficient dramatist? Do you think that because the people I have met in the valleys of Würzburg and the Rhein, are quite as unripe as those of Wicklow or Kerry, that Sudermann and Hauptman [sic] should be driven from the boards of Berlin?   (CL I, 74)

The Ibsenism of this outburst is evident in its stress on drama which could test conventional opinion with 'modern matters'; but it can also be detected in the insistence that while the study of social division was international, and was shared practice in cosmopolitan centres, it could still treat and respond to national cultures. Synge positioned his work with European controversialists in the manner of Shaw's *The Quintessence of Ibsenism* – with the theatrical 'pioneer' who could break taboos and lead the charge for change, 'a tiny minority of the force he heads'.[4] At the same time, he could still knock back the Yeats proposal (in 1906) that the Abbey perform foreign masterpieces: the national theatre would be most European when ploughing its own furrow.[5]

Ibsen is ever present in Synge's work: the possibility of folk drama (*Peer Gynt*); the thematic combination of sex and social trespass (*Rosmersholm*, *Ghosts*); the relationship of the artist/individual to social systems (*Brand*, *An Enemy of the People*); strong women (*A Doll's House*, *Hedda Gabler*), and later the possibility of qualifying realism with symbolistic experiment (*When We Dead Awaken*) can all be felt.[6] The thread went all the way back to the German trip, and Synge's first sketched scenario ('Plan for a Play', CW III, 181–2), which featured a cross-class marriage between a young Irish Protestant landowner and a servant. The same theme would be given fuller treatment in *When the Moon has Set* (atheist landowner and nun); by the time of *The Shadow of the Glen* the unconventionality was amplified by adulterous possibilities (peasant woman and tramp). Synge's grudging respect for Ibsen's attitude and 'efficiency' shows his awareness that to effectively tackle difficult issues required both courage and close attention to formal structure. His criticism of his 'joyless' language should be taken in the same light – a specific criticism rather than a general disavowal.

To locate this 'joy' Synge had to look elsewhere. He had concluded his 1903 letter to MacKenna with a much-quoted defence of his work: he had, he said, intended to restore 'the sex element to its natural place, and the people were so surprised they saw the sex only' (CL I, 74). As such it was not simply the play's social problem – unhappy marriage – that upset the audience: it was the sensuality of the solution. It was this sensual 'joy' that, expressed both verbally and physically, brought a new spectrum to Synge's palette. He arrived at this combination of efficiency, controversiality and joy during the next stage of his European adventure, which was to continue, as was *de rigueur*, in Paris.

Synge did not, like many, go to Paris in 1895 to be an artist: he went to learn. His approach was less that of the drifting tramp or poet, but of the diligent, financially independent (if somewhat down-at-heel) student. His £40 per year was enough to support a scholar's life if, like Synge, you rolled your own cigarettes, dressed plainly, wore heavy boots – and had the wherewithal to cook your own breakfast: 'two eggs' reported Maurice Bourgeois, 'which he boiled in a paper-bag long before paper-bag cookery had any official existence'.[7] The first set of courses Synge signed up to at the Sorbonne and the École Pratique des Hautes-Études were of enduring influence. With Paul Passy, he studied comparable phonetics – taking on board his tutor's idea that *patois* could have a literary dynamism, providing the intellectual grounding for his later stylisations of Hiberno-English speech. Auguste Émile Faguet drew Synge into contemporary French literature, schooling him in the moderns: Mallarmé, Baudelaire and Maupassant. These were writers Synge would criticise for their fascination with moral turpitude and morbidity, not least because he feared these proclivities in himself. As with his rejections of Ibsen, such accusations were as much disguised tributes to mesmeric force, as attempts to distance himself from a bohemian licence which he felt both desirable and dangerous. As he later put it (surely with *Les Fleurs du mal* in mind): 'It is absurd to say a flower is not beautiful nor admire its beauty because it is deadly, but it is absurd also to deny its deadliness' (CW II, 349).

Synge offset the apparent decadence of the moderns with a third strand of study: medieval literature with Petit de Julleville. Chaucer, Ronsard and François Rabelais offered the possibility of a literature whose frank ribaldry seemed part of a splendid range of sensual possibility, something that took 'joy' in life without denying its earthiness. Such writers presented a means by which Synge could accept the new artistic licence won by Mallarmé and Baudelaire, while declining a nihilism against which he needed a positive counterweight. The immediacy they offered his poetry and his dialogue is apparent from any comparison of that writing with his direct Hiberno-English translations. The model seemed ideal for Ireland, if only people could see it:

> Am I alone in Leinster, Meath and Connaught
> In Ulster and the South,
> To trace your spirit, Ronsard, in each song and sonnet
> Shining with wine or drouth?   ('To Ronsard', CW I, 30)

The tension between the modern and the medieval was apparent to Synge not only in literary terms. The visual arts remained an important dimension of this dynamic: particularly after his trip to Italy in the first half of 1895, which acquainted him with the glories of the renaissance. Rome and Florence put the inherited chorus of anti-Catholic prejudices firmly in perspective.

Synge also returned to Darwin, who remained a touchstone.[8] Once a naturalist, always a naturalist: the imperatives of natural selection were not to be escaped, however potent imagination appeared. Animal aspects of man are never far away in Synge's plays; nor the skull beneath the skin. The interpretive prism through which his Darwin was refracted was not simple, however: influences included Herbert Spencer, whose profound individualism and defence of laissez-faire economics resonated with Synge's reading in Nietzsche. Then again, it was offset by the criticism of Hippolyte Taine, whose *La Philosophe de l'Art* set out a view of culture paradoxically both determined by race and conditioned by fluctuating social and historical processes.[9]

The individualist impetus of Spencer was also qualified by dynamics of spiritual physicality Synge found in European medieval literature – and in the connected release of music and dance. *Étude Morbide*, a fictionalised self-portrait written in 1899, shows its violin-playing protagonist agonising over women and philosophy. First comes a resigned Spencerian phase: 'For those who fail, there is no hope' (CW II, 29), soon to be replaced by a religious mania, seeking 'saintly exaltation'. That too fails, during an epiphany in which the violinist finds a less rarefied redemption: 'my skin shivers while I play to see that in spite of the agony of the world there are still men and women joyous enough to leap and skip with exultation' (CW II, 33). A sketch for a dialogue between Thomas à Kempis and Rabelais offers a similar model of the carnivalesque: 'At a fair also with ale and the sound of fiddles and dancers and the laughter of fat women the soul is moved to an ecstasy which is perfection and not partial' (CW III, 185). However, when a similar dynamic is generated in *The Well of the Saints*, there is a more evolved, reflexive dimension: one which may explain why Synge also moved beyond this naive sensibility.

This process involved political realignment. Synge shocked his family in the summer of 1896 by reading Karl Marx's *Das Kapital*[10] and he returned to Paris that autumn to study socialist thought. Besides tackling Marx and William Morris, Synge delved into the works of Russian socialist-anarchist Peter Kropotkin, John Hobson's sociological studies of poverty, the reformist socialism of Victor Considerant, and the writings of the then leader of French Marxism, Paul Lafargue. He found his study of that evolving subject complicated by his discovery of a new kind of Ireland: one that, like nascent modernism, inhabited Paris's *rive gauche*. A contingent of Irish nationalists gathered in and around the Hotel Corneille: there he met W. B. Yeats and Maud Gonne for the first time. But also, no less importantly, Synge met

Stephen MacKenna, who would become his closest friend and sounding
post; and Arthur Lynch, who was soon to go off to fight for the Boers.
Synge became attached to Maud Gonne's group *L'Association Irlandaise*
for several months, before resigning in April 1897: he explained to Gonne
that 'my theory of regeneration for Ireland differs from yours ... I wish to
work in my own way for the cause of Ireland and I shall never be able to
do so if I get mixed up with a revolutionary and semi-military movement'
(CL I, 47). This was not merely a case of Synge shying away from physical-
force republicanism: his attempt to distance himself from Gonne should
be seen in the context of her close association with French militarism and
anti-Dreyfusard opinion via her lover Lucien Millevoye. Having read Paul
Lafargue's *Le communisme et l'évolution économique* that April,[11] Synge
likely felt some vindication when Zola re-ignited the Dreyfus debate later the
same year and Lafargue called for socialists to denounce anti-semitism as a
tactic of reactionary clerical and militarist agencies.[12] Later, in 1903, Synge
tied in the socialist influence with that joyousness he found in the medieval
texts, via a comic tradition that ran from Rabelais to Molière and Voltaire,
before concluding with Anatole France:

> No-one, it is possible, will consider ... humorous optimism, even when completed,
> as Anatole France completes it, by socialistic ideals, as a high form of practical
> philosophy, but some may ask where at the present time we can find a better
> one ... In his best work, while remaining true to the distinctive tradition of French
> writing – the tradition which had given us Frère Jean, Tartuffe and Pangloss – he
> has contrived to express with curious exactness the irony and fatalistic gaiety
> which now form the essential mood of the French people ... Those who heard him
> speak in public at the time of the Affaire Dreyfus, and who remember the grave
> power of his words, will not be likely to find him – as some critics have found – a
> shallow sophist without sincerity or depth. (CW II, 395–6)

The combinations that Synge linked via France suggest that the 'joy' missing
in Ibsen could be garnered in a comic tradition, without jettisoning either the
fatalism of post-Darwinian modernism or a practical sense of social critique.
It was an expansive compound, open to elaboration: important, since Synge
was an intellectual omnivore and his reading voracious. To pick a month at
random: in January 1897 alone he tackled Henry Fielding, Dante, Spinoza,
Thomas à Kempis, Leopardi, Hegel, Petrarch, Verlaine, Marcus Aurelius, San
Francesco, Auguste Comte, Wordsworth, Maeterlinck, Villiers de L'Isle Adam,
Shakespeare, Wagner, Keats and Shelley.[13] This critical mass of erudition
brought a certain philosophical reflexivity. Socialist and materialist thought
might act as a mediator between self-denying sainthood and the revelry of
natural physicality; but in the context of Synge's later plays, the relationship is

complicated by a darker examination both of self and the stage. The root of this transition is to be found in Synge's trips to the Aran Islands, which added a new layer of perceptions during the period 1898–1901.

Synge's tendency to exoticise aspects of Island life is evident from the first section of *The Aran Islands*. But this initial naive excitement evolves into a much more complex portrait. Prior to his first visit, Synge had begun studying under Henri d'Arbois de Jubainville, and having already encountered French Celticism through Renan, his studies shifted towards the more anthropological realm of Celtology, encouraged by Kuno Meyer's stringent studies of early Irish epic, and investigations into Breton life made by Le Braz and Pierre Loti. Such thinkers shifted away from idealised 'primitivism' to a less sanitised conception of the cultures they studied.[14] *The Aran Islands* moves with a similar trajectory; Synge's description darkens to the grimmer aspects of Island life. His final, bleak trip to Inis Meáin occurred in the wake of a typhus outbreak, with a backdrop of violent storms. The objective confidence of the narrative voice becomes replaced by reported story, and an internalised recognition of his own alienated position:[15] 'I sat for nearly an hour beside the fire with a curious feeling that I should be quite alone in this little cottage … I became indescribably mournful, for I felt that this little corner on the face of the world, and the people who live in it, have a peace and dignity from which we are shut for ever' (CW II, 162).

One particular writer provided a means of incorporating such reflexive concern into the complex range of influences Synge brought to his stagecraft. As one notebook entry read: 'A wet day with a close circumference of wet stones and fog showing only at my window and inside whitewash, red petticoats, turf smoke, my long pipe and Maeterlinck.'[16] It is an apt conjunction: Maurice Maeterlinck drew down the high-flown mysticism of symbolic art to the 'mere act of living', his treatise *The Treasure of the Humble* arguing that the tragic was a common, not an aristocratic or mythic condition.[17] The influential Belgian's assertion of interior drama – outwardly static, but inwardly and ominously turbulent – was crucial to Synge's oeuvre.[18]

Such sensibilities are central to *Riders to the Sea* and *Well* in their emphasis on drama of the withheld. In *Riders* the delayed confirmation of drowned sons has echoes of Maeterlinck's *Interior* (1894), where a family at home is watched from outside by an old man carrying as yet unknown news of a drowned daughter. A tragic incompleteness of human contact persists in both playwrights' work; and an imaginative potency that may extend beyond the confinements of the real. The addition of this symbolist interiority to Synge's formal range was also crucial in adding metatheatre as an aspect of dramatic performance. Maeterlinck's adrift figures not only evoked the situation of mortality as a universally felt tragic condition – they reflexively commented upon the false presumptions of meaning, fixed upon by naive realists. In *The Sightless* (1891) a group of blind beggars grope for direction and meaning in an unspecific location, waiting for their guide's return: but he is, as the audience can see, already dead. In Synge's elaboration of the metaphor of blindness, the newly sighted Martin Doul mistakes the fair Molly Byrne for his wife, having previously only imagined her beauty. Synge twinned Maeterlinck's symbolism with medieval farce (André de la Vigne's *Moralité de l'aveugle et du boiteaux*)[19] to make Doul's question, 'Which of you all is herself?'(CW III, 95) both existential and comedic. The audience is asked to scrutinise the assumptions of what they can 'see' on stage, what they presume to be real, but also to delight in the artifice.

The particular brand of metatheatrics Synge evolved was a product of his compound influences: if impressed by Maeterlinckian metaphysics, he also felt the need for Ibsenite efficiency and the power of poetic language both medieval and modern; while convinced of the implacable process of Darwinian selection he remained persuaded of the need for joyousness and a socially fair 'practical philosophy'. Fascination with the facts of violence and death came with a need to celebrate sensual tenderness, vitality and sex; tragedy blurred into comedy. There is a noticeable development in the organisation of these influences in Synge's work, a pattern of authoritative command mitigated by observation of lived social relations. The comedic negotiation of lyrical romanticism and darker social realism would shift again once Synge stopped his continental wanderings to unload his heavily laden bags on the Irish stage.

Irish nationalist critics who labelled Synge's work as carrying the whiff of Parisian boulevards produced in their author an irritation that such critics could not discern where he had cherry-picked his influences. Thus, the apostasy of his *Playboy* preface, denying Ibsen and Mallarmé: clearly attempts to point up divergence in the face of whose who would insist his work was simply derivative. Similarly, although Synge famously declared during the *Playboy* week, that he didn't 'give a rap'[20] what people thought of his work, its trajectory would suggest otherwise. The confidence of the cosmopolitian progressive is very much in evidence in Synge's first theatrical forays – the comedic Ibsenism of *The Shadow*, with its emancipatory panache; the materialist symbolism of *Riders*, with its combination of submerged portent and unsparing naturalist detail. In subsequent plays, however, that confidence is opened to doubt. The emancipatory poet outsider (an authority external to *Riders*, but brought within the drama in *The Shadow*, in the form of the tramp) is repeatedly questioned and scrutinised from *The Tinker's Wedding* on. The creative, progressive assertion of individual judgement is increasingly ironic and paradoxical: Synge's tinkers are most outrageous when seeking to be most conventional; Martin Doul's blind choice for the joys of imaginative projection is also a failure to negotiate the real and an inability to cope with any opposing view; Christy Mahon sets off on a romping lifetime when he has already recognised the 'drift of chosen females' (CW IV, 167) as a poor substitute for settled intimacy. By the time we get to *Deirdre of the Sorrows*, Deirdre's attempt to escape from realpolitik has been forced from exile to a complete divorce from reality, a mythic condition of legend – a joyless, pallid compensation for lovers wishing for live warmth. Synge's scrutiny of social conventionality, of collective hostility to imaginative dissidence, operates therefore alongside a scrutiny of presumption, of self-aggrandisement and cocksure individualism.[21]

Participation in the Irish Revival likewise persuaded Synge that it would be political advance by nationalism that was most likely to secure future gains – economic and cultural – in a subdued Ireland (CW II, 343). Thus, his sense of guilt as both a product and a critic of his class helped him acknowledge that the outsider's romanticised view of poverty was implicated in the fact of suffering: 'all the characteristics which give colour and attractiveness to Irish life,' he wrote, 'are bound up with a social condition that is near to penury' (CW II, 286). At the same time, Synge saw there was a danger in trying to impose change – a patronising outsider could also fail to recognise the value of conserving traditional cultures: 'one does not always pardon a sort of contempt for the local views of the people which seems rooted in nearly all the official workers' (CW II, 341).

His theatre would not dictate. The didacticism of provocative realism is tempered by the reflexive questioning of Mahons *père* and *fils*: 'Is it me?' (CW IV, 79, 121). A knowing interrogation of perception demands of its audience a critical evaluation of whether this theatre is itself 'a gallous story' or in fact 'a dirty deed'. The apogee of this crisis of authority was the reception of *The Playboy* itself, which to all appearances was a violent response orchestrated by Synge to resonate with the onstage action.[22] The tripling up of a drama that tests conventionality in terms of subject matter, form and reflexive self-censure is predictably one that is not only influenced by European drama, but also one which, in the course of the twentieth century, would find its way into the heart of European theatrical modernism.

Early 1906 saw two seminal productions – Max Meyerfeld's *The Well of the Saints* at the Deutsches Theater, Berlin; and Karel Mušek's *The Shadow of the Glen* at the Inchover Theatre in Prague. His early appeal to continental theatre was soon confirmed. Soon after Synge's death, his first biographer, the French scholar Maurice Bourgeois, perceptively placed his subject in a contemporary European context, despite public nay-saying from Yeats.[23] Bourgeois's translation of *The Playboy* was produced by a long champion of theatrical provocation, Aurélien Lugné-Poe, at the Théâtre de l'Oeuvre, Paris, in December 1913. It may have gratified Synge that, just as in Ireland, his work was considered too rough and rich by French main-stream opinion, while those closer to the avant-garde took a different view. As Guillaume Apollinaire, writing in his seminal newspaper, *Les Soirées de Paris*, commented on the 1913 production: 'Poets have always tried to murder their fathers, but it is not an easy thing and looking at the house on the first night I thought: too many fathers, too few sons.'[24] That such an *enfant terrible* would identify with Synge is not surprising: Synge's work would always interest an avant-garde *mentalité* once *The Playboy* had taken its place in the series of shocked receptions that chart the impact of modern performance on its audiences.[25]

The tendency for *Le baladin du monde occidental* (as the French transla-tion of *The Playboy* was known) to appeal to the French fringe was also indicated by one of the '*cartel des quatre*', the four directors moulding Parisian opinion between the wars. George Pitoëff, who with his wife Ludmilla moved from Russia to Geneva to form the Companie Pitoëff in late 1918, included the play in that company's first season. *The Tinker's Wedding* followed in 1920, by which time the Pitoëffs had set up at the Théâtre des Arts de Jean Rouché in Paris.[26] In retrospect, Synge's momentum in Europe was, like much that was modernist, given new force by the world war and its devastations. His questioned, questionable heroes were again of their time. Bertolt Brecht and Federico García Lorca both first read Synge in 1920; Lugné-Poe reprised his *Playboy* at the Théâtre de l'Oeuvre in December 1921; and it is likely that (via Lugné-Poe and Pitoëff) Marcel Herrand and Antonin Artaud also caught their first glimpse of Synge around this time.

Significantly, one of the Pitoëffs' other theatrical touchstones was Luigi Pirandello, whom they brought from Italy to a wider European audience. Such points of contact put Synge on a literary line that stretches from Maeterlinck through a Pirandellian exploration of theatrical existentialism and finds later expression in Samuel Beckett. It is easy to see Synge's exploration of imaginative autonomy in *The Well of the Saints* and the contingent realism of *The Playboy* as reopened by Pirandello's *So It is, If It Seems so to You*,[27] especially if one takes the early experiments in 'grotesque theatre' by Luigi Chiarelli as providing a bridge between the two authors.[28] Equally, the collaborative provocations of *The Playboy*'s chal-lenge to the audience can be seen as revisited by Pirandello's *Six Characters in Search of an Author* and the subsequent echo of that play's stormy Rome reception in *Each in His Own Way* ('INTELLIGENT SPECTATOR: They saw a mirror image of themselves and they rebelled against it ... They were particularly horrified at that final clinch! PRODUCER: But then they went and did exactly the same thing themselves!').[29]

The reflexively fictional world that Synge creates is only one side of his coin, however, and on the other is the reflexively real. Interplay between stories and deeds, gallous and dirty, brings Synge into more than one European tradition. A different genealogy could situate him between the influence of Ibsen and the departures of Brecht. By the age of 22, the young German was, by his own account, already benefiting hugely from the study of Synge's use of verbs.[30] This emphasis is significant, for Synge's stylised Hiberno-English emphasised the process of action, rather than the fact of it. The verb is typically a mobile fulcrum between the imaginative, interior world and the real, exterior world of objects and others: 'I'm above many's the day,' suggests the Widow Quin in *The Playboy*, 'darning a stocking or stitching a shift, and odd times again looking out at the schooners, hookers, trawlers is sailing the sea, and I thinking on the gallant hairy fellows are drifting beyond' (CW IV, 127). Rendering action in the present participle invites the actor to re-inhabit the action as it is relived, and in so 'doing', makes action both more immediate and more plastic: open to intervention. More than one aspect of 'Epic Theatre' is anticipated here. That Brecht's and Margarete Steffin's[31] adaptation of *Riders to the Sea*, *Señora Carrar's Rifles* (1937), should prove to be one of the most important of his pre-war works, should therefore not surprise. The obvious difference between the plays is that Brecht has made the issue one of overt political action: the function being to recruit International Brigade volunteers to fight in the Spanish Civil War for the elected republican government against General Franco's Fascist insurgents. Brecht's play does not so much replace Synge's philosophy with his own, as amplify that element of the play which carries their shared debt to Marx, and update the tension to a topical crisis in which passivity itself has become the destructive element.

The shifting perspectives of *The Playboy* also drew Brecht's interest; he selected the play to enhance the Berliner Ensemble's small repertoire of European classics. Brecht's protégé translator Peter Hacks rendered the work a critique of Christy's sudden heroism, his individualism a symptom of the desperate demoralisation that surrounds him. The August 1956 production, directed by Peter Palitzsch and Manfred Wekwerth, has been seen as a crude cold war work: but it does not get it 'all wrong' (as Eric Bentley felt he should tell the ailing Brecht)[32] – it returns to test the logic of contingent authority by which all Synge's 'heroes' are problematised. The political dimensions of Synge's sensibility had understandably been picked up and expanded by Brecht and his followers.[33]

Brecht set *Carrar* on a remote Andalusian coast, to emphasise the inescapable modernity of the new conflict. Meanwhile, a very different play, also inspired by *Riders*, had already been set in southern rural Spain:

Federico García Lorca's *Blood Wedding* (1933).[34] What Lorca found resonant was the generation of heightened poetic language, capable of carrying a local and specific folk tradition.[35] And like Synge, Lorca's poetry operates in tandem with physicality: each seeks to project sexual energy not just by rote, but by example. If Beckett is heir to Synge's metaphysical mode, and Brecht to his social, this third 'embodied' mode is one which carries Synge's sense of the fiddle and the dance: the emphasis on emotional resonance, driven by poetic tonality, structural (dis)harmony, and answered with movement. Lorca was not alone in this Syngian tendency to seek out the audience's inner primitive. Antonin Artaud wrote to the Irish Legation, prior to his visit to the Aran Islands in 1937: 'This isn't a literary project, nor that of an academic or museum curator ... It is vital that I reach the land where *John Millington Synge* lived. That I be received by those people, the people from over there, as one of them.'[36] By travelling in Synge's wake he hoped to fuel what he described as the 'Theatre of Cruelty': a theatre of unifying passion. His ambition was neither dialectics *qua* Brecht, nor style à la Lorca, but the riot itself. Artaud's personalised version of this process led to violent scuffles in Dublin and six days in Mountjoy Prison. He was finally deported, in a state of mental collapse. 'De Valera's Government ... found me too revolutionary, that is to say, too specifically Irish,' he later complained.[37]

Just as in the wake of World War I, the Second World War saw revived interest. Marcel Herrand staged Synge's work repeatedly in occupied Paris: *The Playboy* to acclaim at the Théâtre des Mathurins in 1941; an equally influential *Deirdre* in 1942; and *The Tinker's Wedding* in 1944. One of Jean Vilar's first excursions as director was his 1943 *Well of the Saints*.[38] *The Playboy* in particular enjoyed post-war proliferation: in France, there were five productions between 1950 and 1962,[39] in Germany, eight during a similar period.[40] Synge's continued impact beyond the post-war ruins was always likely, given the range of European playwrights he affected: Brecht, Lorca, Artaud and Beckett obviously offer a wide scope of possibility. Yet it was also directors and performers who carried the flame. Beckett famously could think of Synge's name alone, when asked who had most influenced him: but in the end, *Waiting for Godot* was performed only when he struck a rapport with French director Roger Blin over a common enthusiasm for his Irish precursor.[41] Blin's love of Synge might have originated with Pitoëff, Artaud or Vilar – but in fact came from an earlier French connection: Maurice Bourgeois,[42] who was always happy to tell fellow continentals what he had realised in 1912: '[Synge] was one of the few Irish writers who Europeanised Ireland without degaelicising it – who allied the depth of an intense national spirit to the width of a broad minded international culture.'[43]

NOTES

1. Daniel, Corkery, *Synge and Anglo-Irish Literature* (Cork: Mercier Press, 1931), p. 38.
2. For example, Arthur Griffith's *The Resurrection of Hungary* (Dublin: James Duffy, 1904).
3. W. J. Mc Cormack, *Fool of the Family: A Life of J. M. Synge* (London: Weidenfeld & Nicolson, 2000), p. 114.
4. G. B. Shaw, *The Quintessence of Ibsenism* (London: Walter Scott, 1891), p. 94.
5. Adrian Frazier, *Behind the Scenes: Yeats, Horniman and the Struggle for the Abbey Theatre* (Los Angeles: University of California Press), pp. 186–90.
6. Mc Cormack, *Fool of the Family*, pp. 163, 171.
7. Maurice Bourgeois, *John Millington Synge and the Irish Theatre* (London: Constable, 1913), p. 33.
8. Mc Cormack, *Fool of the Family*, pp. 41–3.
9. Hilary Nias, *The Artificial Self: The Psychology of Hippolyte Taine* (Oxford: Legenda, 1999), p. 150.
10. Edward Stephens, *My Uncle John* (London: Oxford University Press, 1974), p. 104.
11. Diary, 1897, Trinity College Dublin, MS 4341.
12. Leslie Derfler, *Paul Lafargue and the Flowering of French Socialism 1892–1911* (Cambridge, MA: Harvard University Press, 1998) pp. 206–8.
13. Diary, Jan. 1897, Trinity College Dublin, MS 4418.
14. Sinéad Garrigan Mattar, *Primitivism, Science and the Irish Revival* (Oxford University Press, 2004), p. 246.
15. Declan Kiberd, *Irish Classics* (London: Granta, 2000), p. 434.
16. David H. Grene and Edward M. Stephens, *J. M. Synge 1871–1909* (New York: Macmillan, 1959), pp. 89, 95.
17. *The Treasure of the Humble* (London: George Allen, 1897).
18. Katherine Worth, *The Irish Drama of Europe from Yeats to Beckett* (London: Athlone, 1978), pp. 120–39.
19. See Gertrude Schepperle, 'John Synge and His "Old French Farce"', *North American Review*, 214 (1921), pp. 504–13.
20. *Dublin Evening Mail*, 29 Jan. 1907; E. H. Mikhail (ed.), *J. M. Synge: Interviews and Recollections* (London: Macmillan, 1977), p. 37.
21. Ben Levitas, 'Censorship and Self-Censure in the Plays of J. M. Synge', *Princeton University Library Chronicle*, 68.1–2 (2006–7), pp. 271–94.
22. Ben Levitas, *Theatre of Nation: Irish Theatre and Cultural Nationalism 1890–1916* (Oxford: Clarendon, 2002), p. 124.
23. *Freeman's Journal*, 22 January 1912.
24. *Soirées de Paris*, 15 January 1914. Quoted Gerard Leblanc, 'Synge in France', in S. B. Bushrui (ed.), *A Centenary Tribute to J. M. Synge: 'Sunshine and the Moon's Delight'* (Gerrards Cross: Colin Smythe, 1972), 267.
25. See Neil Blackadder, *Performing Opposition: Modern Theatre and the Scandalized Performance* (Westport, CT: Praeger, 2003).
26. Jacqueline Jomaron, *George Pitoeff: metteur en scène* (Lausanne: l'Age d'Homme, 1979), pp. 47–8.
27. F. L. Lucas, *The Drama of Chekhov, Synge, Yeats and Pirandello* (London: Cassell, 1963), p. 81.

28. Principally, via Chiarelli's *The Mask and the Face* (1914). See Walter Starkie, *Luigi Pirandello 1867–1936* (Berkeley: University of California Press, 1967), pp. 12–13.
29. Pirandello, *Collected Plays*, vol. 3 (London: Calder, 1992), p. 133.
30. Anthony Roche, 'Synge, Brecht, and the Hiberno-German Connection, *Hungarian Journal of English and American Studies*, 10.1–2 (2004), pp. 9–32.
31. John Fuegi, *Brecht and Company: Sex, Politics and the Making of the Modern Drama* (New York: Grove Press, 1994) pp. 351–2.
32. Eric Bentley, *The Brecht Memoir* (London: Carcanet, 1989), p. 79.
33. This politicised Synge survived in East Germany. See Klaus Völker, *Irisches Theater I: Yeats and Synge* (Hanover: Friedrich, 1967); Johannes Kleinstück, 'Synge in Germany', in Bushrui (ed.), *A Centenary Tribute*, p. 275.
34. Ian Gibson, *Federico García Lorca: A Life* (London: Faber & Faber, 1989), p. 340.
35. Ramón Sainero Sanchez, *Lorca y Synge: ¿un mundo maldito?* (Madrid: Editorial de la Universidad Complutense, 1983).
36. Letter to the Irish Legation, 6 Aug. 1937, cited in Jonathan Pollock, 'The Aran Islands, One by One: John Millington Synge and Antonin Artaud', in Pascale Amiot-Jouenne (ed.), *Irlande: Insularité, Singularité?: Actes du Colloque de la Société Française d'Études Irlandaises* (Presses Universitaires de Perpignan, 2001), p. 119. Translation by Pollock.
37. Stephen Barber, *Antonin Artaud: Blows and Bombs* (London: Faber, 1993), p. 96.
38. Oscar G. Brockett and Robert R. Findlay, *Century of Innovation: A History of European and American Theater and Drama Since the Late Nineteenth Century* (Englewood Cliffs, NJ: Prentice-Hall, 1973), p. 564.
39. Gerard Leblanc, 'Synge in France', in Bushrui (ed.), *A Centenary Tribute*, pp. 268–9.
40. Kleinstück, 'Synge in Germany', in Bushrui (ed.), *A Centenary Tribute*, p. 272.
41. James Knowlson, *Damned to Fame: The Life of Samuel Beckett* (London: Bloomsbury, 1996) pp. 57, 385.
42. Odette Aslan, *Roger Blin and Twentieth-Century Playwrights* (Cambridge University Press, 1988), pp. 18–19.
43. Bourgeois, *John Millington Synge*, p. 63.

8

ALAN TITLEY

Synge and the Irish language

Experiencing a Synge play for the first time is not just watching any story unfold. Something is happening on the stage that you have never quite felt before. People are speaking in a language which appears to be English, but it is an English once or twice removed. What precisely it is removed from is not that clear either. But the sets and the setting tell you that this is Ireland, and these are people who would be speaking Irish if the audience could only understand them. But most of the people of Ireland could not understand a play in Irish in the early years of the twentieth century and, more assuredly, the greater part of the world could not either.

It is obvious, therefore, that Synge is doing something with his Irish peasantry, and is attempting to mimic some kind of Irish. When characters in a Synge play speak, the air hums with something that does not quite belong. Their relationship with reality is oblique and romantic. Their tongue is a twisted idiom, at times crude, at times poetic. The serious academic question is, what part of his language belongs to him, and what part of it belongs to the Irish language? There is no doubt whatsoever that Synge had a fine command of Irish. Declan Kiberd's book *Synge and the Irish Language* is the most authoritative study of Synge's relationship with the language, and most anything else is likely to be no more than a footnote to that study.[1]

We know that Synge studied Irish at Trinity College Dublin as an under-graduate student. For somebody from his fallen-ascendancy background – at least in the class sense – this was quite a revolutionary choice. Furthermore, his immediate hinterland of south Dublin, which traditionally was a vassal area of Wicklow under the thumb of the wild O'Byrnes from the mountains and even wilder O'Tooles from the vales in the sixteenth and seventeenth centuries, had become the most Anglicised of a rabidly and rapidly Anglicising society. The Irish language vanished from the hills and coasts of Wicklow before any other rural area of the country. Although some vestiges of the language may have been spoken in the wildernesses of Wicklow, and vagrant words and aberrant pronunciations may have survived in the crevices of the mountains above Dublin in his youth, we can be certain that he never heard a living word of Irish in his youth or early childhood. Allied to that, his studies at Trinity College would have been necessarily philological in character, as the living word as text was anathema to the Irish scholars of the late nineteenth century. The Chair of Irish was originally instituted in order to train proselytising clergy to spread the word of the Protestant God among the heretical Irish. Not surprisingly, then, the study of the Bible and other religious texts was central to the academic study of Irish. It appears that he was a good student with a serious academic knowledge of his course, but that he did not evince any real interest in the living language as it was spoken throughout various parts of Ireland at that time. Despite the dullness of his course in the university, some seed had been sown. Synge was a constant diarist, and in 1893 he began to provide entries in Irish for the first time. Although this may have been simply a device to prevent prying eyes from seeking his innermost thoughts, it does appear more likely that he had established some kind of spiritual communion with the language, as artists do.

The classic account of the reawakening of Synge's interest in Irish is Yeats's claim that he should go to the Aran Islands and express a life that had never been expressed before: 'Go to the Aran Islands. Live there as if you were one of the people themselves; express a life that has never found expression.'[2] Yeats's 'life that has never found expression' might have come as a surprise to the islanders themselves, as it is unlikely that they thought they were entirely dumb for thousands of years. Synge's own description of folk tales, legends and poetry in *The Aran Islands* is enough to reinforce our knowledge of Yeats's ignorance of genuine folk tradition. But for all that, it had been an artistic directive, and Yeats always knew more in his heart than his head could ever comprehend. It is unlikely, however, that this was the single and only spur that brought Synge to one of the founts of his imagination. Eighteen months passed between Yeats's diktat delivered in Paris in 1896 and Synge's first trip to Aran. His uncle, the Reverend Alexander Synge, had been a minister on Inis Mór, the biggest of the three Aran Islands, in the 1850s; and it must have been that a family tradition had existed which made him aware of the Ireland of the west. Moreover, there is a palpable sense in all of his writings that he was searching for a form, or for an idiom, that would be commensurable with his imagination.

Before Synge went on the first of his four trips to Aran in May 1898 we can be certain that he had a good knowledge of written literary Irish. He did not however have any conversational ease, and was obviously floundering in his initial halting conversations on Inis Mór. It appears that he quickly acquired sufficient understanding to be able to share passively in the lives of the people, and quite soon to be able to converse with competence. He had an Irish teacher who was his companion and who helped to initiate him into island life. The fact that he was a competent fiddler and played with the local musicians must have made him feel more at home than we would normally suppose. But he was always on a literary errand; his purpose was artistic; and he must have known what he was doing, at least in that part of him in which the imagination glows.

Declan Kiberd's conclusions as to his competence in Irish are apt and authoritative. He could speak the language well and with confidence and was conversant with two of the main dialects. His written Irish was only moderate, enough for him to write letters and entries in his diaries, but not sufficient to write a play in the language, which he may have contemplated. He had a high standard of academic Irish with a corresponding knowledge of its history and literature.[3]

In this regard *The Aran Islands* is a kind of a treasure trove. At a basic level it is a travelogue describing a life that was 'the most primitive that is left in Europe' (CW II, 53) to more sophisticated people in the industrial cities of Britain. That kind of travelogue is now not much more than a curiosity, a paper version of Robert Flaherty's film *Man of Aran*, only more authentic. What remains with us, however, is the sense of an artist coming to self-knowledge, and that self-knowledge growing as his familiarity with Irish, and with Irish folk-culture, became more intimate. He is stirred by the beauty of the language and of the singing when he hears a man 'recite old Irish poetry with an exquisite purity of intonation that brought tears to my eyes though I understood but little of the meaning' (CW II, 56). He hears stories 'so full of European associations' (CW II, 65) that you might wonder if these people were so isolated after all. He is present at the wild keening of a wake, but does not realise yet that this is also a species of poetry. But he remains critical when his own artistic sense is pricked as on 'the south island', where the 'mode of reciting ballads ... is singularly harsh', and when he finds the 'harsh nasal tone' almost intolerable (CW II, 140–1). Everyone seems to want to tell him stories of the fairies, as the islanders most likely supposed that it was this kind of romantic tosh that visitors wanted to hear. Synge's ear, however, is for the local stories, those shards of realistic lore that spark his own imagination. It was one of those stories that gave him the germ of his master-piece *The Playboy of the Western World*.

At the end of Part 3 of *The Aran Islands* he recalls a discussion about the Irish language with an islander who had travelled the world. Interestingly, they discuss Archbishop McHale's translations of the *Iliad* and Thomas Moore's *Irish Melodies*. The islander found them 'most miserable' produc-tions, which might be seen to be a charitable assessment. They then fall to discussing the future of the language, as Irish speakers inevitably do. The man argues that it 'can never die out ... because there's no family in the place can live without a bit of a field for potatoes, and they have only the Irish words for all that they do in the fields' (CW II, 149). This is an interesting argument in favour of the permanence of Irish, but hardly one that sociolinguists would easily accede to. Synge merely reports what he hears – he is a passive observer, noting, watching, listening.

But he did have his own ideas, passionately held and delivered. The great debates of the nineteenth and early twentieth centuries ring through his thoughts. Ever since Stopford A. Brooke's inaugural lecture to the Irish Literary Society in London in March 1893 with the ringing title, 'On the Need and Use of Getting Irish Literature into the English Tongue',[4] the issue of what was going to be done to maintain a 'national' literature, if at all, was a central theme of the culture wars. On the one hand, there were those who were endeavouring to use the Irish language and its resources to create a new literature in English; and, on the other, there were the followers of the Gaelic League who sought the preservation and spread of the Irish language for and in and by itself, and the cultivation of a new literature in Irish.

Although Synge had no problem whatsoever with the preservation of Irish in the Gaeltacht (or Irish-speaking areas), he was a heretic within Gaelic League circles with regard to attempts at a more widespread revival of the language. He denounced the imposition of the English language in the Gaeltacht, a fact which was palpable to him when he encountered islanders who were literate in the government tongue but were forbidden literacy in their own language in the schools. He believed that 'an Irish-speaking Ireland [was] tantamount to a vow of silence for all its people', and therefore that the great silence that came about because of the retreat of the language would be an obvious outcome of an over-zealous programme to reverse the decline.[5] While there may also have been issues of class, background and fear in his beliefs, there must also have been a revulsion against the pretence that Irish was a more spiritual and more holy language than the greasy words of journalistic and commercial English. Although this belief among Irish-speakers was not by any means universal, there was enough of it around to invite opposition. Father Patrick Dineen, by no means a prissy puritan, given some of the quirky entries in his great dictionary, posed a challenge to the Keating Branch of the Gaelic League in 1904:

> This country is, to a large extent, still untainted by the teaching of the positivist, the materialist, the hedonist, which pervades English literature whether serious or trivial ... It will be difficult to prevent that literature from planting the seeds of social disorder and moral degeneracy against even our still untainted population.[6]

The response, of course, was to propose the Irish language – 'a language unpolluted with the very names of monstrosities of sin which are among the commonplaces of life in English-speaking countries', as Fr John M. O'Reilly so plangently put it[7] – as a bulwark against the threats of anglicisation. Even Yeats could indulge himself in this kind of fancy when, in an address to the Gaelic League's Central Branch, he argued (or rather asseverated) that: 'The civilisation which existed in the Irish language ... was an old and better civilisation which had been reeling under the shocks given it by modern vulgarity everywhere, an old and better civilisation which it was their duty to preserve until the deluge had gone by.'[8]

Synge knew better. He had seen the peasant close up, had looked into his smoky eyes, heard his lurid tales, and saw the same cruelty and tragedy in the heart as in the heart of any other man. And there was an attraction in this, albeit an artistic one. Yeats wrote of Synge shortly after his death that he had 'a hunger for harsh facts, for ugly surprising things' (CW I, xxxiv). He had long since bid farewell to 'Sweet Angus, Maeve and Fand', those 'plumed yet skinny Shee' ('The Passing of the Shee', CW I, 38), because his was a world of reality tempered only by the music of language. He was viciously scathing about the Gaelic League in a letter entitled, 'Can we Go Back into our Mother's Womb?' Here, in the persona of 'A Hedge Schoolmaster' he argued that its doctrine was 'founded on ignorance, fraud and hypocrisy', that 'Irish as a living language [was] dying out year by year' and would most likely be dead in a short number of years (CW II, 399). Although this prophecy has been made continuously with confidence since the seventeenth century it has not yet been fulfilled. Synge also mocked the bad Irish of the young Gaelic Leaguers and contrasted this with the natural tongue of the native speaker (400). Significantly, though, as Stephen McKenna recorded, it was the disingenuous hype of Gaelic League rhetoric that Synge loathed the most:

> on the score of one pamphlet in which someone, speaking a half-truth, had urged the youth of Ireland to learn modern Irish because it would give them access to the grand old Saga literature; I have never forgotten the bale in his eyes when he read this and told me: 'That's a bloody lie, long after they know modern Irish, which they'll never know, they'll still be miles and miles from any power over the Saga.'[9]

Synge, of course, was right. He knew his older literature as well as the contemporary spoken tongue. Knowing how to speak argot English does not give you access to the tale of the green knight or the medieval Arthur. And yet, it was not as simple as that. He recognises the connection between the folktales he hears on Aran and the great stories of Europe. And because of his study at Trinity College and his attendance at the lectures of Renan and de

Jubainville at the Collège de France in 1898, 'more than any figure of his generation Synge was aware of the bearing, not to say overbearing, of Herder, Renan, the *Revue celtique*, and *Zeitschrift fur Celtische Philologie* on the local endeavours of Douglas Hyde, Tomás Ó Criomhthain, and others'.[10] In other words, he did realise that there was a connection between the writings of the past, the scholarship of the present and the living language. He did not want to admit it. Synge wished to keep a division between the life of the western peasant and the reality of modern life. Irish was fine as a peasant language, but he was suspicious of any broader cultural and political significance it might have. The Aran Islands and the west of Ireland and the Irish language were a cultural resource. Their reality was the present past and not the present future.

In the same way as exaggerated claims for the purity of the language were made, there were many Irish speakers who idealised the Gaeltacht and the islands. To be fair to Patrick Pearse, who most certainly was aware of the unsavoury aspects of the countryside, he admitted that his picture of the west and of its society 'was *intended* as an ideal picture'.[11] A closer inspection of Irish Gaelic literature of the time, however, will reveal bigotry, bigamy, wife-beating, murder, drunkenness, niggardliness, savagery and every vice that man or woman is capable of. And a brief perusal of Seán Ó Súilleabháin's *Handbook of Irish Folklore*,[12] which was designed as a guide for collectors in the field, will uncover questions about peasant behaviour which are not likely to be found in the sump of the brain of the most depraved moralist. One can only conclude that the Irish speakers who objected to *The Playboy* were not conversant with their own literature and folklore.

On the other hand Synge was guilty of the elevation of the spoken Irish of the peasant as a language of vigour and sap, while apparently degrading the printed word as a mere shadow and wisp. A contrast was set up between the authentic tongue of the countryman and whatever other variety lay beyond the heather and the bog. The debate flourished within Irish-speaking discourse, particularly in the celebrated confrontation between '*caint na ndaoine*' (the speech of the people) and '*Gaeilge Chéitinn*' (Keating's Irish) as competing models for a new Irish literature. This was a long-standing verbal war between those who claimed that the only authentic Irish was that spoken in the contemporary Gaeltacht and those who wanted to establish a prose style based more on the learned tongue which had last been most vibrant in the seventeenth century when Geoffrey Keating was at the height of his powers. There was therefore among cultural revivalists a suspicion of the book, of print, of learning. The best Irish was to be found, according to scholars and learners in pursuit of the most pristine unsullied tongue, not only among those monoglots who spoke no English, but also among those who could not read.

We find the same suspicion in George Moore railing against 'the pollution of Standard English by journalese', and especially in Yeats, who is 'indignant with those who would substitute for the ideas of folk life the rhetoric of the newspapers'.[13] It is even more explicit with Synge:

> Modern peasant Gaelic is full of rareness and beauty, but if it was sophisticated by journalists and translators – as it would certainly be sophisticated in the centuries I have spoken of – it would lose all its freshness, and then the limits, which now make its charm, would tend to prevent all further development. It is a different thing to defile a well and an inlet of the sea.   (CW II, 386)

We have it here. Irish is to remain a peasant language in case it becomes tainted with the modern world, with the filthy ink of journalese. In this he was as conservative and as anti-modernist as the most backward looking of the Gaelic League. But it is what he did with the language which he found before him that was profoundly radical.

It is true that we find what is most generally called the Anglo-Irish dialect of English in a prominently literary form in the novels of William Carleton. This dialect, often depicting the English of native Irish speakers like Carleton himself, is only prevalent in dialogue, and is marked more by the insertion of garbled Irish words than by idiom and syntax. It was George Moore who 'once wrote rather wickedly that Synge was responsible for the discovery that, if one translated Irish word for word into English, then the result was poetry'.[14] Synge himself would admit that it was Douglas Hyde in the first instance with his facing English translations to the Irish poetry in *Love Songs of Connacht* (1893) that prompted this discovery and, later, Lady Gregory's version of *Cuchulain of Muirthemne* (1902) which he read regularly. There is a background there, certainly, but it is not the whole story.

It is not easy, without a close textual analysis and with technical linguistic metrics to tease out exactly what it is that Synge does with his use of Irish and its transmogrification into English. Some of his plays have been translated 'back' into Irish and the effect is interesting.[15] They seem so natural on the ear, not really exotic, closer to a mundane reality – and yet not entirely so. It would be simple to argue that what is left over is the distillation of Synge, but this is not how works of art become alive. There is a short story by Pádraic Ó Conaire, 'M'fhile caol dubh' ('My slender dark poet') where the female narrator is brought to a play which by all hints must be *The Shadow of the Glen*. The romance she does not get from her disappointing poet is provided on the stage by the tramp who asks the woman to go with him:

'Téanam liomsa,' adeireadh sé, 'agus beidh muid ag imeacht de shiúl oíche faoi choillte dubha diamhra agus beidh réaltóga neimhe ag dearcadh anuas orainn.'

['Let us go,' he said, 'and we will be walking through the night through mysterious dark woods and the stars of heaven will be shining down upon us.'][16]

There is, of course, a Syngean echo here, but the original is much more like some of the seductive songs of the eighteenth century where the poet invites his lover to steal away to the woods and to sleep with him on a mossy knoll. It could also be translated into more standardised English than I have given, and lose even more of its poetic turn. The point is, that Irish writers saw Synge as a poet, as somebody whose beauty came from more than the language itself, and also associated him with their own romantic writers of the past.

Synge found something that already existed, but turned it into his own poetry. A glance at other celebrated translations from the Irish is worthwhile. In fact, one of the great difficulties in translating ordinary Irish speech into English at the present day is precisely to avoid Irish idiom. It is as if the example of Synge is so powerful in our minds that a species of non-standardised English forces itself upon us. Robin Flower alludes to these difficulties in his introduction to his translation of Tomás Ó Criomhthain's *An t-Oileánach* (1929) as 'The Islandman' (1934), and we sense he is referring to Synge although he does not say so explicitly. On his method of translation he says:

> Irish and English are so widely separated in their mode of expression that nothing like a literal rendering from the one language to the other is possible. It is true that there has come into being a literary dialect, sometimes used for translation from Irish or for the purpose of giving the effect of Irish speech, which in books or on the stage has met with considerable applause. And in skilful hands this mixture of Irish and English idioms has often an effect of great charm. It does not to my ear, however, convey the character of the language as naturally spoken by those to whom it is their only speech. There is always something slightly artificial about it, and often a suggestion of the pseudo-poetic.[17]

When we read Flower's translation he does seem to have a point, particularly when it comes to straightforward narrative or description: 'When we got home the island was full of wreckage. The White Strand was covered with beams of red and white deal, white planks, a fragment of a wrecked ship, a chair, a stool, apples and all sorts. The boat in which my father worked got twelve baulks.'[18] This is as close to standard English that you will find, and the substance of the book is written like this, apart from the occasional idiomatic turn. The passages in which he translated the direct speech of the islanders are very different, however. There are long quotes which could almost have been lifted from one of Synge's plays, but some unconnected sentences may suffice:

> 'God bless the souls of the dead! ... I never heard a proper account of their doings until to-day. They were a merciless, savage lot in those days. Thanks be to God, again and again, that that world is passed away!'; 'Sorrow on the day, I wish I had put your thigh out! ... for it's a long day before you'd bring a richer sack than that to my kitchen' ; 'I pray to God that no blot or blame may befall you till the year's end'; 'It's Pats Heamish who is not feeling very well. Since he left Dingle he's not had a bite to eat, and it's for a spoonful of whisky I've come'; if it hadn't been for whatever moved you to bring so much of it with you.'[19]

It has to be said that this sounds very familiar. But I think that Synge, consciously or less so, came across a fact not often alluded to: the written literary tradition for the normal Irish speaker in the nineteenth century was a distant and unattainable thing. They had folktales, of course, often the shards and detritus of a greater tradition. They had their beautiful songs, and song composition was still very much vibrant and creative. Their literacy in Irish for most of the century was virtually nil. As a result, they poured their creativity and invention into talk itself. Conversation became an art form. Banter and daring and bold chatter were raised above the mundane. It was often as if talk had become detached from its moorings and wandered away without reference to anything in particular. Even the maddest folktale has a drive and a narrative and ensures that continuous meaning is being alluded to. Tales, for all their fancy, are nailed to the ground. But chatter goes nowhere and is an end in itself.

One of the greatest examples of this is another of Tomás Ó Criomhthain's books *Allagar na hInise*, which has been translated into English as *Island Cross-talk*. It is a diary which he kept as a kind of apprentice writer, noting conversations and encounters in the daily life of the Great Blasket island. Although some of the entries are prose poems, most of them are apparently inconsequential chit-chat and banter, hence the invented translation 'cross-talk', as nothing quite matches what precisely *Allagar* is. An even better example of this *genre* is Arland Ussher's *Cainnt an tSean-Shaoghail*[20] which has never been translated, but which might be rendered as 'The Talk of the Old Life'. Folklorists from the middle of the nineteenth century, whether in Ireland or in Scotland, were a lot more interested in the big folktales, or, when not so distracted, local history often described as *seanchas*. What they were not determinedly interested in was just talk. And the talk of the normal Irish person, unmediated by literature, by story, by poetry, by local tale, unstructured by preordained moulds, went forever unrecorded. We have not the least clue what an Irish speaker spoke about in the nineteenth century, what a conversation sounded like, what it was that was going on. And the dearth, or near non-existence of drama in Irish, compounded this ignorance. So when we read a book like Arland Ussher's record of Tomás Ó Muirithe's talk and musings and gabble in *Cainnt an tSean-Shaoghail* we surmise that we are getting close to a way of thinking that is entirely uninfluenced by those pernicious newspapers that Synge and Yeats and George Moore loathed so passionately. It is difficult to describe what this world is about, but this is an attempt at a translation, but not entirely in the style of Synge:

> 'Well, you didn't connect with any woman of the house or with the dowry, did you not now?'
>
> 'I didn't connect, no.'
>
> 'Well, by this and that, I would walk Ireland and would turn back again and I would never see a hint of a man like you! You are looking for a woman for my memory and you didn't get her yet, and by my soul the cap does be on your head most sunshiningly. The stones of the road know you going on your old white horse every day, just as the Packer used to go away with the donkey and his little bag down on his shoulder and another little bag down on his tail!'
>
> 'Oh, you have your woman and your family and yellow money in your pocket and mockery boiling out of your eyes and I am going and returning with not enough in my pocket that would baptise a bee, and I will straighten away on the road and I will wait for the end of the rope.'[21]

What is this about? Did anyone speak like this? It appears that they did, and as Ussher's transcription came from the County of Waterford on the east coast, it must be that this art form of talk unhinged from context, talk for talk's sake, was something that Synge connected with and let rip in his drama and in his later poetry. It is no accident that Ussher agreed with Synge about the value of 'peasant' talk versus modern literature. He praises Synge for his authenticity:

> As for the expressiveness of the Gaelic folk-idiom, only the 'Irish-English' of Synge's plays can give strangers some idea of it. It is the language, if not of a race of poets (perhaps we are too poetical to be poets, as Wilde said), then at least of a race which has 'tired the sun with talking', a language of quips, cajoleries, lamentations, blessings, curses, endearments, tirades – and all very often in the same breath.[22]

At the level of dramatic art Synge's plays, like all plays, are about 'great talk'. His attempts at poetic drama were not hugely successful, but when he wrote prose they became poetry because of the rhythm of the sentences, of the cadence of the speech. They worked within the logic of the imaginative world he had created. His greatest poetry, at least that in translation, employs the same idiom. His translations from Villon, from Leopardi, from Muset, from Petrarch in this new language touch a chord which they could not do if rendered in more standardised English.

There are undoubtedly major unresolved issues. Terry Eagleton's argument that if one language inhered in the other anyway, then the issues are reduced to merely local colour, ignores the fact that the differences between languages have more to do than just the matching of idiom and syntax.[23] Sound and echo and taste and the ground of thousands of years of being bear more on the issue of language than surface translation. And there is no point in denying that Synge's plays cut close to the shore of the stage Irishman and woman, and that that stage Irishman and woman is the staple diet of playgoing and playwriting in Ireland in the twentieth and now into the twenty-first century. The Irish public loves its Martin McDonagh and its John B. Keane a lot more than it would ever accept Hugh Leonard or Bernard Farrell as emblematic of Ireland. Marina Carr's characters are more 'bogger' than anything Conor McPherson can throw up. It is not as if there wasn't a stage Irish character every bit as real as your drawing-room one, it is just that he or she is seen still as more authentic than those who didn't have the cultural advantage of being born on an island or in a field. And in his depiction of Irish speakers as being merely illiterate fluent spouters, Synge demeans a literate, learned, tradition which goes back to the coming of letters to Ireland. But his poetry, verve, invention, courage and character override any of the cultural arguments that we may wish to bring to our criticisms.

NOTES

1. Declan Kiberd, *Synge and the Irish Language* (London: Macmillan, 1993). As in the title of Kiberd's book, I use the word 'Irish' to describe the language throughout. This is historically correct and the use of 'Gaelic' should be shunned as far as possible. This is more properly used to describe the Irish language in Scotland. Synge himself uses both terms, but not consistently.
2. Kiberd, *Synge and the Irish Language*, p. 36.
3. Ibid., p. 92.
4. Stopford A. Brooke, *On the Need and Use of Getting Irish Literature into the English Tongue: An Address* (London: T. Fisher Unwin, 1895).
5. Kiberd, *Synge and the Irish Language*, p. 232.
6. Cited in Philip O'Leary, *The Prose Literature of the Gaelic Revival 1881–1921: Ideology and Innovation* (Pennsylvania, PA: Pennsylvania State University Press, 1994), p. 21.
7. O'Leary, *Prose Literature*, p. 21.
8. Ibid., p. 32.
9. Ibid., p. 226.
10. W. J. Mc Cormack, *From Burke to Beckett: Ascendancy, Tradition and Betrayal in Literary History* (Cork: Cork University Press 1994), p. 228.
11. O'Leary, *Prose Literature*, p. 123.

12. Seán Ó Súilleabháin, *A Handbook of Irish Folklore* (Dublin: Educational Company of Ireland, 1942).
13. Kiberd, *Synge and the Irish Language*, p. 221.
14. Ibid., p. 68.
15. See, for example, J. M. Synge, *Uaigneas an Ghleanna: agus Chun na Farraige Síos* (Dublin: Sáirséal agus Dill, 1972). This is the only published version of an Irish translation of his plays as far as I am aware. There have been many amateur productions of Synge's plays rendered into Irish by local groups which have remained unpublished.
16. For a discussion of this, see Pádraigín Riggs, *Pádraic Ó Conaire: Deoraí* (Dublin: An Clóchomhar 1994), pp. 70–2. The English translation is my own.
17. Tomás Ó Crohan, *The Islandman*, trans. Robin Flower (Dublin: Talbot Press, 1934), p. xiii.
18. Ibid., p. 110.
19. Ibid., pp. 67, 95, 186, 169, 182.
20. Arland Ussher, *Cainnt an tSean-Shaoghail. Do scríobh ó sheanchas Thomáis Uí Mhuirthe. Réamh-rádh le Tórna* (Dublin: Oifig an tSoláthair, 1942).
21. Ibid., p. 157. This is an entirely random choice out of a book of nearly 400 pages. It out-Synges Synge in its extravagance, but is not cut into any artistic shape or whole. The translation is my own.
22. Arland Ussher, *The Face and Mind of Ireland* (Old Greenwich, CT: Devon-Adair, 1950), pp. 146–7.
23. Terry Eagleton, *Heathcliff and the Great Hunger: Studies in Irish Culture* (London: Verso 1995). 'If Irish can be effectively rendered into English, then it cannot be entirely self-identical but must always have been intrinsically capable of this difference in itself. And if English can translate Irish, then this alien medium must be in some sense inherent in the Irish language itself' (268).

9

SUSAN CANNON HARRIS

Synge and gender

J. M. Synge was neither the first nor the last modern Irish playwright to run into gender trouble. His treatment of gender and sexuality is, however, credited with starting the most notorious theatrical controversy in the riot-studded history of Irish theatre.[1] Theories purporting to explain why Irish nationalists responded so violently to the premiere of Synge's *The Playboy of the Western World* in 1907 are as numerous as the stars in the sky; but Synge's contemporaries made it clear that they were protesting, among other things, his representation of Irish women. In particular, they were appalled by the spectacle of Irish women expressing and acting on their own sexual desires – or, as Synge's nemesis Arthur Griffith put it, 'contending in their lusts for the possession of a man who has appealed to their depraved instincts by murdering, as they believe, his father'.[2]

But *The Playboy*'s unusual romance was by no means Synge's only trans-gression. In fact, all of Synge's plays critique, indict, or undermine the pre-mises upon which nationalist constructions of 'Irish womanhood' were built. This essay will investigate what was at stake in the nationalist notion of 'Irish womanhood', will show how Synge's dramatic work dismantles that notion, and will suggest some of the forces that shaped Synge's own very different understanding of gender, sexuality and femininity.

To understand why Synge's women caused so much trouble, we must consider them as the product of Synge's approach to three things that always inform constructions of gender: the body, sexuality and reproduction. Any culture's gender norms – that is, its dominant beliefs about what a man or a woman is and what a man or a woman can or should do – are founded on that culture's understanding of the nature and purpose of sexual difference, which is in turn based on that culture's ideas about the nature and purpose of sex itself. Those attitudes are often codified in and perpetuated by religious doctrine; but religion does not single-handedly produce them. Though biology and theology have much to do with formations of gender and sexuality, so do economic conditions, political conflict, cultural history and literary tradition.

The experience of colonial rule has profound consequences for the development of gender and sexuality. Because dependence, submissiveness, passivity, self-denial and reluctance to use violence are constructed in most Western belief systems as feminine traits, the feminisation of the indigenous people is one of the more common tactics deployed by imperial discourse; and indeed, in the late nineteenth century the 'pseudo-science of ethnography characterised the Irish as a feminine people'.[3] It is also common for resistance movements to over-correct this disabling feminisation by representing the idealised national subject as 'hyper-masculine'.[4] In Ireland at the turn of the twentieth century that over-correction was legible in the masculinist discourse of the Gaelic League, which strove to overwrite the feminine, neurotic, pathologised Celt with their virile, healthy, athletic Gael.[5] Furthermore, because the colonising power often takes a lively interest in regulating the growth of the indigenous population, reproduction itself becomes politicised. Sexual intercourse can easily serve as a metaphor for both the violence of the initial conquest and the unchosen and intimate contact between coloniser and colonised that follows.

Ireland's colonial history, then, helped define the two roles that nationalist discourse most insistently prescribed for the Irish woman during Synge's lifetime: (1) woman as the idealised symbol of Ireland, and (2) woman as the real embodiment of an essential and 'pure' Irishness.[6] As Elizabeth Butler Cullingford has shown, Celtic fertility goddesses provided the foundation for nationalist tropes like the Shan Van Vocht (Poor Old Woman), Erin, or the *spéirbhean* – figures through whom Ireland was represented as a woman menaced by a foreign oppressor.[7] Though that threat was sometimes figured as rape, sex could also figure positively as a representation of Ireland's liberation and restoration through 'her' union with her rightful mate.[8] According to Cullingford, it was not until after the Famine of the 1840s that the 'intensification of the Catholic vision of woman as a creature of purity and innocence' led to the re-imagination of Ireland-as-woman as 'chaste'.[9]

This history accounts in part for the extraordinary investment in female chastity which is such a striking feature of the Irish nationalist response to Synge's work. (I use 'chastity' here and throughout in the sense of 'refraining from unlawful sexual intercourse', denoting marital fidelity as well as virginity and permanent celibacy.) Synge's hostility to this manifestation of 'Irish conservatism and morality' drives the plot of his first completed play, *When the Moon Has Set* (1902), in which the hero spends much of his time talking his love interest out of her commitment to celibacy (CW III, 160). Synge's critique of the Irish valorisation of female chastity becomes more sophisticated in *The Shadow of the Glen* (1903), in which a husband (Dan Burke) plays dead in order to catch his young wife (Nora Burke) with another man.

Though the play never definitely confirms Dan's suspicions, Nora does leave her husband – not with the young farmer her husband suspected, but with a silver-tongued tramp who has known her for less than an hour. This was too much for Arthur Griffith, who was largely responsible for perpetuating the controversy that followed. Griffith was the editor of the influential nationalist newspaper *United Irishman*, and devoted many column inches to arguing that Nora Burke was not Irish. No real Irish woman would ever do such a thing, Griffith maintained, because 'Irishwomen are the most virtuous in the world'.[10]

If we look at this response in the context of Griffith's political writing, we discover a more material basis for his attachment to the Irish woman's 'virtue'. Griffith, like many of Synge's most vigorous critics, adhered to the 'Irish-Ireland' strain of Irish nationalism. 'Irish-Irelanders' were defined by their belief that decolonisation was most effectively achieved by de-Anglicisation. They sought to restore a pre-colonial, authentic Irish culture by reviving the Irish language along with Irish music, Irish sports, Irish crafts, and Irish dress. During the years before *The Shadow*'s premiere, Griffith's writing emphasised two political goals that reveal the interdependence of Irish-Ireland nationalism and conservative gender politics: growing the Irish population and achieving economic independence from Britain.

Ireland had not yet fully recovered from the population crash triggered by the Famine. Griffith, who saw the Famine as a genocidal British conspiracy, believed that increasing the size of the Irish population was critical to resisting British imperialism.[11] This goal could not be accomplished without the labour of Irish women, who would have to bear the necessary numbers of Irish children. In addition, Griffith believed that Ireland's economic independence from England was as important as, and inextricable from, Ireland's cultural autonomy. It was understood that though the man of the house made the money, it was the woman who spent it. Therefore, convincing Irish women to 'buy Irish' – to consume products made in Ireland instead of England – was crucial to achieving both goals.[12] While supporting Irish industry, Irish mothers would turn their homes into Irish spaces within which their children would grow up saturated with Irish culture and committed to Irish nationalism.[13]

The Irish woman's dual reproductive responsibility – the demand that she reproduce not only strong and healthy Irish bodies but a pure Irish 'soul' – thus made her 'virtue' a political and economic problem. Her sexual purity was conflated with the cultural purity of the domestic space from which it was her job to exclude foreign products and foreign culture. By opening herself up to outside influence – whether that influence presents itself as a man to whom she is not married or as the hottest new fashion from England – the Irish woman, from this point of view, endangered not just her chastity and her home but the 'pure' Ireland to which all of her sexual, reproductive and economic activities should be dedicated.

The work Irish women did as mothers, homemakers and consumers was therefore indispensable to the project of national liberation as Griffith understood it. It was thus vitally important to keep the Irish woman in that home and doing that work. Griffith's efforts to promote the mother/homemaker role as the Irish woman's patriotic calling were assisted by other contributors, including several women.[14] Even Irish women whose own lives defied gender norms defined by the *United Irishman*'s home-and-hearth nationalism often reiterated those norms in their political writing.[15] The most prominent example was Maud Gonne, whose militant politics, radical activism and status as a 'secretly unwed mother' pushed her well beyond the boundaries of conventional femininity.[16] Yet Gonne's writing for the *United Irishman*, like the weekly column devoted to her organisation Inghinidhe na hÉireann (Daughters of Ireland), and like Mary E. L. Butler's series on 'Womanhood and Nationhood,' reproduced Griffith's focus on the national importance of 'women's life within the domestic sphere'.[17]

The Shadow of the Glen's conclusion calls into question not just the 'virtue' of Irish women, but Griffith's vision of national liberation. It's bad enough, from Griffith's point of view, that Nora abandons her home; but it's even worse that Nora's home has abandoned her. Nora is childless because economic pressures forced her to marry an old man who was 'always cold' to her (CW III, 35). Saddled with an impotent, spiteful, abusive husband, Nora cannot restore the Irish nation, the Irish economy, or the Irish home through the magical operation of her feminine 'virtue'; she has enough to do to keep herself sane. Nora's friendships with Patch Darcy, Michael Dara, and the Tramp are justified as her only means of surviving her captivity within the home – a home represented not as a cozy nest of Irishness but as a bleak and empty cell whose main ornament is a corpse.

Griffith does not seem to have appreciated the extent of Synge's critique, since he either failed to realise or refused to acknowledge that Nora does not leave home voluntarily. She is evicted by Dan, who commands her to 'walk out now from that door' while brandishing a stick with which he has long fantasised about beating her (CW III, 43). Clearly, Nora had no chance of making this house a home as long as Dan was living in it. The real threat *The Shadow* poses for Griffith's view of Irish nationalism is its suggestion that the Irish home simply does not and cannot function the way Griffith hopes it will – regardless of the chastity of the woman who is trapped inside it.

In fact, with the possible exception of Maurya from *Riders to the Sea*, none of Synge's leading women protect or are protected by the Irish home as

Griffith, Butler and Gonne imagined it. Like *The Well of the Saints*'s Mary Doul, the Travellers Sarah Casey and Mary Byrne of *The Tinker's Wedding* (1905) do not have homes to make.[18] *The Playboy*'s Pegeen Mike has been raised not in a private home but in a public house, where her 'virtue' is endangered by 'the harvest boys with their tongues red for drink, and the ten tinkers is camped in the east glen, and the thousand militia ... walking idle through the land' (CW IV, 63). For Deirdre of *Deirdre of the Sorrows* (1909), home always and only means captivity. It is by keeping Deirdre at home – in her isolated hut or in his palace at Emain Macha – that the aging Conchubor seeks to keep her bound to him. Conversely, Deirdre finds happiness only when wandering with Naisi through the woods of Alban.

Synge's plots do highlight the connection Griffith implied between the integrity of the home and the chastity of the Irish woman – but only to reveal chastity as a social construct which is meaningful only for women who can afford it. Marriage is represented not as a sacrament but as a social arrangement whereby a woman barters her youth, beauty and freedom for the home that promises security. Nora Burke describes her own marriage to Dan in those terms: 'What way would I live and I an old woman if I didn't marry a man with a bit of a farm, and cows on it, and sheep on the back hills?' (CW III, 49). Fortunately for Griffith and his blood pressure, Yeats and Gregory declined to produce Synge's *The Tinker's Wedding*, which dramatises the material basis of female chastity even more vividly.

Apart from the priest, all the characters in *The Tinker's Wedding* are Travellers. Precisely because these characters have no homes, they react to Sarah Casey's determination to marry her partner Michael Byrne as absurd – a lunatic whim which has possessed her 'since the moon did change' (CW IV, 7). The only motive Sarah articulates is a desire for respectability: 'no one will have a right to call me a dirty name' (CW IV, 35). Sarah understands that she is challenging the assumption that marriage and respectability are inseparable from the home: 'I've as good a right to a decent marriage as any speckled female does be sleeping in the black hovels above' (CW IV, 35) Even the priest is astonished that a woman without a home could want anything to do with marriage or decency: 'It's a queer woman you are to be crying at the like of that, and you your whole life walking the roads' (CW IV, 15). His insistence on being paid to perform the ceremony literalises the material basis of marriage and the 'virtue' it protects. As an institution whose function is to regulate the transfer of property, marriage is reserved for those who have property to transfer.

So much for chastity, marriage and the home. Motherhood fares no better. Apart from Nora Burke, none of the young women in Synge's universe seem at all interested in motherhood – even when they are technically mothers. Though engaged to Timmy the Smith, *The Well of the Saints*'s Molly Byrne is too taken up with vanity, flirting and mockery to think about children. In *The Tinker's Wedding*, Michael mentions Sarah 'rearing a lot' of children, but said children are nowhere to be seen and are never referred to again (CW IV, 7). When Pegeen Mike and Christy imagine their future in *The Playboy*, their vision of life together never includes children. In *Deirdre of the Sorrows*, Synge acknowledges the existence of Deirdre and Naisi's children, fearing perhaps that it was not credible that two such perfect specimens could make ardent love for seven years running without producing offspring. But Deirdre, who never mentions these children, appears to have forgotten that she ever had them; and in one draft, Naisi bluntly tells Lavarcham that 'we have put our children where they are well fostered, and we are leading the life of the woods that has no worry'. (CW IV, 226).

When he represents motherhood through older women, Synge burlesques the nationalist ideal of Mother Ireland by restoring to the suffering and saintly Poor Old Woman the bodily appetites and aggressive sexuality that characterised the Celtic figures on which she was based.[19] Mary Byrne is a parodic version of these 'great queens of Ireland' – a charismatic 'old drinking heathen' whose appetites are uncontainable, whose relationship with her son is more parasitic than nurturing, and who delivers a speech about the irrelevance of marriage while sitting astride a priest who has been bound, gagged and stuffed into a sack (CW IV, 25). In contrast to the Catholic ideal of motherhood modelled on the Virgin Mary, maternity in *The Playboy* intensifies female sexuality instead of purging it. As Stephen Tifft points out, both of the surrogate mother figures that Synge provides for Christy are also marital prospects, rendering motherhood a doubled Oedipal nightmare rather than a nationalist fantasy.[20] In Act II Christy recounts his father's attempt to marry him to the Widow Casey, 'a woman of noted misbehaviour with the old and young' who is old enough to be his mother – and actually nursed him as a newborn (CW IV, 101–3). The Widow Quin, who pursues Christy sexually, has 'buried her children and destroyed her man' (CW IV, 131). A mother and a murderer, Quin may also be a witch; Pegeen Mike accuses her of having 'reared a black ram at [her] own breast, so that the Lord Bishop of Connaught felt the elements of a Christian, and he eating it after in a kidney stew' (CW IV, 89). These bizarre breastfeeding references render the nurturing aspect of motherhood grotesquely corporeal and shockingly transgressive.

For motherhood, as for marriage, chastity and the home, *Riders to the Sea* is the exception that proves the rule. Set in the Aran Islands – a place beloved by Irish-Irelanders as the last reservoir of undefiled Irishness – *Riders* features a family whose female members have scrupulously obeyed Irish-Ireland gender norms. Maurya and her two daughters, Nora and Cathleen, live in a home built of authentic Irish materials. After bearing eight children to her husband, Maurya has certainly done her reproductive duty. Consumed by maternal anxiety and grief, Maurya does not appear to have any dangerous unfulfilled desires. Nora and Cathleen are wholly concerned with caring for their failing mother and their remaining brother. Both girls are good Irish homemakers; Nora knits, Cathleen spins and bakes bread in a turf fire. From an Irish-Ireland perspective, these women are perfect. Not coincidentally, *Riders to the Sea* is the one Synge play that was always respected by Irish audiences.

So, in *Riders*, Synge shows Irish women following all the rules – and the results are catastrophic. The next generation of Irish patriots will not emerge from this Irish home. Maurya's reward for her labour is the excruciating experience of watching her sons die. Maurya is struck by the cruel futility of motherhood as she has experienced it: 'In the big world the old people do be leaving things after them for their sons and children, but in this place it is the young men do be leaving things behind for them that do be old' (CW III, 13). This inversion of the generational process finally perverts Maurya's 'natural' maternal feelings. By the end of the play, Synge's only 'good' Irish mother welcomes her beloved son's death as the only thing that can release her from unbearable pain: 'It isn't that I haven't prayed for you, Bartley ... but it's a great rest I'll have now, and it's time surely' (CW III, 25). Though *Riders* poses no threat to the Irish woman's 'virtue', it does question the efficacy of maternity itself as a means of regenerating, restoring and reproducing Ireland. In that sense, *Riders* may be a more radical challenge to nationalist gender politics than any of Synge's other plays.

If Synge's understanding of gender and sexuality is not based on the chastity/marriage/motherhood/home nexus that supports the Irish-Ireland vision of national liberation, where does it come from? As with all questions of literary interpretation, this one admits of multiple answers; I will suggest only two, both relating to Synge's preoccupation with the vulnerability of the human body. As Ben Levitas observes, Synge's plays are informed by a materialism that links the economic and the sexual through its attention to the sensuousness of embodied experience; Synge dramatises the effects of poverty, exposure, age and disease as vividly as the desires of his characters.[21] Synge's fascination with tramps and travellers familiarised him with some of the realities of life beyond the margins of the middle class, and taught him among other things that for women whose poverty exposed them to harassment, humiliation and violence as well as the elements, Griffith's ideal of virtuous Irish womanhood could only be a cruel and bitter joke.

But Synge's understanding of gender and sexuality is also marked by a different form of materialism derived from the natural sciences. In his auto-biography, Synge describes his encounter with Charles Darwin's work in apocalyptic terms:

> When I was about fourteen I obtained a book of Darwin's. It opened in my hands at a passage where he asks how can we explain the similarity between a man's hand and a bird's or bat's wings except by evolution. I flung the book aside and rushed out into the open air – it was summer and we were in the country – the sky seemed to have lost its blue and the grass its green. I lay down and writhed in an agony of doubt ... It seemed that I was become in a moment the playfellow of Judas. Incest and parricide were but a consequence of the idea that possessed me.
> (CW II, 10–11)

As Mary King argues, Darwinian theory provided Synge with 'support ... for his rebellion against his mother's literalizing Christianity'.[22] By locating this memory at the beginning of his adolescence, Synge makes Darwin simultaneously catalyse his rejection of Christianity and his own sexual development.

Synge is probably referring to a passage from the end of the first chapter of Darwin's *The Descent of Man and Selection in Relation to Sex*.[23] *The Descent of Man*, in which human sexuality is explained by the same evolutionary forces that determine animal behaviour, provided Synge with the foundation for a sexual ethics based not on the will of God but on the dictates of nature. Though *The Descent of Man* replicates patriarchal assumptions about woman's inferiority, it does emphasise one idea which had profound consequences for Synge's female characters: the evolutionary importance of female desire and female agency. Darwin maintains that the 'exertion of some choice on the part of the female seems almost as general a law as the eagerness of the male' for sexual intercourse, and that males who 'allure or excite the female' are more likely to reproduce and thus pass on their traits. The process of evolution thus depends not only on the female's powers of discrimination but her freedom to choose the male best able to 'charm' her.[24]

Darwin's interpretation of female sexual desire and sexual agency as natural and necessary was one of many things that brought him into conflict with Catholic doctrine and Catholic sensibilities; and it is when the Darwinian foundation of Synge's gender politics becomes most visible that Synge's work excites the strongest opposition. In *The Shadow*, Nora Burke chooses a new partner based solely on his ability to 'allure and excite' her: 'you've a fine bit of talk, stranger, and it's with yourself I'll go' (CW III, 57). In *The Playboy*, sexual desire is rampant in all the play's female characters, and Pegeen Mike and the Widow Quin openly pursue the object of their obsessions. Several responses to the initial production explicitly identified *The Playboy*'s romance plot as an application of the 'doctrine of the survival of the fittest' to the Irish situation.[25] The competition between the village girls and women for Christy's attentions – not in spite of, but *because of* his reputation as a parricide and the strength, courage and passion it implied – read to these spectators as a parable about sexual selection which had unflattering implications not only for the 'virtue' of Irish women but for the fitness of the rural Irish men who cannot compete with Christy.

To account for the failure of maternity in Synge's dramatic universe, however, we must turn to the darker side of Darwinian theory. Synge was painfully aware that 'Darwin's arguments … concluded in a doctrine which predicted survival of the fittest only'.[26] This was a source of torment for Synge, who was convinced of his own unfitness at an early age. He reports in his autobiography that fear of heredity drove him to make his own vow of celibacy: 'I said, I am unhealthy, and if I marry I will have unhealthy children. But I will never create beings to suffer as I am suffering, so I will never marry' (CW II, 9).

This anxiety infects Synge's representations of the male body as well as his treatment of reproduction. The bodies of Synge's male characters are usually decrepit, often diseased, and not infrequently dead – or uncannily close to it. Young and healthy male characters are typically paired with and overshadowed by these not-quite-dead bodies, who represent their futures as old men. Nora refuses to marry Michael because she foresees his transformation into Dan: 'Why would I marry you, Mike Dara? You'll be getting old … and in a little while … you'll be sitting up in your bed – the way himself was sitting' (CW III, 51). In *The Playboy*, Christy is stalked not by the ghost but by the angry undead body of his wounded father. In *Deirdre of the Sorrows*, Owen insinuates that only death will keep Naisi from becoming 'as ugly and as old as Conchubor' (CW IV, 225). *Riders to the Sea* shows that 'fine men' still exist in the Aran Islands – but they appear to be facing extinction.

But though it replicates his fears about his own body, Synge's dramatic work also resists the doom he pronounced for himself as an adolescent, challenging some of the basic premises of evolutionary theory. Synge's contemporaries failed to realise how ambivalent and self-subverting Synge's use of Darwin was. Even *The Playboy* suggests that narrative trumps biology, as 'the power of a lie' transforms Christy from a 'dribbling idiot' into a 'likely man' (CW IV, 143). We can better appreciate Synge's complex engagement with Darwin if we compare Synge's first completed play, the unproduced *When the Moon Has Set*, with the last play he worked on, *Deirdre of the Sorrows*.

When the Moon Has Set rewrites the young Synge's unhappy love affair with Cherrie Matheson, translating evolutionary theory into a 'creed' which justifies and demands the devout heroine's submission to the irreligious protagonist's desires.[27] In his dialogues with Sister Eileen, Colm harps incessantly on the theme of fertility as woman's natural purpose: 'you know that motherhood, the privilege that lifts women up to share in the pain and passion of the earth, is more holy than the vows you have made' (CW III, 172). If she persists in defying 'the central order of the world,' Colm warns her, '[a] day will come when you will mourn over your own barrenness ... I do not blame you. I only blame the creed that has distorted the nature God made for you' (CW III, 168).

This veneration of fertility is the foundation of the religion into which Colm inducts Eileen – a form of nature worship derived as much from Wordsworth and the English romantics as from pagan Celtic mythology.[28] But while Colm represents their symbolic marriage rite as Eileen's 'emancipation', his language emphasises her submission to him: 'I, the male power, have overcome with worship you, the soul of credulous feeling' (CW III, 177). Forcing maternity on Eileen as mercilessly as Catholicism or Irish nationalism could, Colm's 'creed' does not grant Eileen any more agency than the one she rejects. It still requires 'a relinquishing of identity and a loss of personal freedom' as Eileen 'acquiesces will-lessly and wit-lessly' to Colm.[29]

But Synge's approach to female characterisation changes dramatically after *Moon* – partly because Synge rejects Colm's faith in fertility as the natural purpose of human sexuality. In no other play will Synge use pregnancy, childbirth or children to symbolise hope or the future. Sexuality remains both socially disruptive and powerfully life-affirming; but from *The Shadow* onward, reproduction is either pushed off-stage (as in *The Tinker's Wedding* and *Deirdre of the Sorrows*) or manifested as failed, dysfunctional, and/or morbid (as in *Riders* and *The Playboy*).

Mary King points out that *Deirdre of the Sorrows* recycles elements of *When the Moon Has Set*, including the oath with which Ainnle marries Deirdre and Naisi.[30] Many years and five plays later, however, Synge incorporates no discussion of fertility as the 'central order of the world', no celebration of motherhood as woman's holy privilege, and no attempt to browbeat the heroine with her perversity in choosing 'barrenness'. Not coincidentally, the balance of power between the lovers is reversed, with Deirdre pursuing and persuading Naisi. As Deirdre depicts it for Naisi, theirs is a love that has, as Lee Edelman might put it, no future; it leads not to birth but to death.[31] Though Deirdre bears Naisi's children, she remains convinced that 'great ruin' is the only future she has – or at least the only one she wants (CW IV, 211).

Lavarcham tries to persuade Deirdre to see her children as the guarantors of a better future:

> There's little hurt getting old ... Take my word and stop Naisi, and the day'll come you'll have more joy having the senses of an old woman and you with your little grandsons shrieking round you, than I'd have this night putting on the red mouth, and the white arms you have, to go walking lonesome byeways with a gamey king. (CW IV, 221)

Deirdre answers, 'It's little joy of a young woman or an old woman I'll have from this day' (CW IV, 221). Fergus tries the same tactic – 'You'll not be young always, and it's time you were ... getting in your children from the princes' wives' – and gets a similar response: 'It isn't pleasure I'd have while Conchubor is king in Emain' (CW IV, 226–7). To Deirdre, motherhood represents not the continuation of life but the end of any 'joy' or 'pleasure' she could take in it. Deirdre rejects this imagined future as mother and grandmother, and instead embraces death.

Synge's treatment of gender and sexuality is heretical, then, not just because of what he borrows from Darwin, but because of what he rejects. In its emphasis on reproduction, Darwin's account of human sexuality in *The Descent of Man* is – for once – in tune with Catholic doctrine, which legitimises sex only when it is potentially procreative. Synge conforms to this belief only to the extent that his universe excludes homosexuality; though 'queer' is a Syngean keyword, desire in Synge's universe is always and only heterosexual desire. What *is* queer about sex in Synge's world is its almost antithetical relationship to reproduction. For Deirdre and Naisi, as for all of Synge's lovers, sex matters for its own sake – not because it produces the future, but because it transfigures the ephemeral present, the 'short space only' during which human beings can ever know love, joy, or happiness (CW IV, 209).

For twenty-first-century audiences who find Madonna quaint and can gaze without flinching upon *Sex and the City*, Synge's representation of Irish women as willing and able to express and act on their own sexual desires is hardly controversial. But Synge's anxiety about reproduction – his suggestion that there may be no regeneration, but only degeneration – retains its power to shock. Dark as it is, Synge's pessimism releases his female characters from their reproductive obligations; and to suggest that maternity is neither woman's duty nor her destiny can still provoke intense opposition. Similarly, Synge's critique of marriage as an exclusionary and class-based social construct connects to contemporary debates about the definition of marriage. There are many arguments to be made about whether or how Synge's plays are feminist. What is clear is that the questions about gender and sexuality that Synge's plays engage with remain unsettled and unsettling, even a hundred years after his death.

NOTES

1. On the history of Irish theatre riots, see Helen Burke, *Riotous Performances: The Struggle for Hegemony in the Irish Theater, 1712–1784* (University of Notre Dame Press, 2003); Christopher Morash, *A History of Irish Theatre, 1601–2000* (Cambridge University Press, 2002); and Susan Cannon Harris, 'Clearing the Stage: Gender, Class, and the '"Freedom of the Scenes" in Eighteenth-Century Dublin', *PMLA*, 119 (2004), 1264–78, and 'Outside the Box: The Female Spectator, *The Fair Penitent*, and the Kelly Riots of 1747', *Theatre Journal* 57 (2005), 35–55.
2. Quoted in James Kilroy, *The Playboy Riots* (Dublin: Dolmen Press, 1971), p. 66. See also ibid., pp. 10–11, 13, 24, 70.
3. Elizabeth Butler Cullingford, *Gender and History in Yeats's Love Poetry* (Cambridge University Press, 1993), p. 61.
4. Ashis Nandy, *The Intimate Enemy: Loss and Recovery of Self Under Colonialism* (Delhi: Oxford University Press, 1983), pp. 50–52.
5. On the gendered discourse of the Gaelic League, see David Cairns and Shaun Richards, 'Tropes and Traps: Aspects of "Woman" and Nationality in Twentieth-century Irish Drama', in Toni O'Brien Johnson and David Cairns (eds.), *Gender in Irish Writing* (Buckingham: Open University Press, 1991), pp. 130–31, and Susan Cannon Harris, *Gender and Modern Irish Drama* (Bloomington, IN: Indiana University Press, 2002), pp. 30–33. On the feminisation/pathologisation of the Celt and Irish reactions against it, see Marjorie Howes, *Yeats's Nations: Gender, Class, and Irishness* (Cambridge University Press, 1996), pp. 16–43.
6. On woman as idealised symbol for Ireland, see Cullingford, *Gender and History*, pp. 55–62; Howes, *Yeats's Nations*, pp. 44–6; Cairns and Richards, 'Tropes and Traps', pp. 128–30. On woman as the concrete embodiment of 'pure' Irishness, see Harris, *Gender and Modern Irish Drama*, pp. 64–8.
7. Cullingford, *Gender and History*, pp. 55–9.
8. Ibid., pp. 57–8.
9. Ibid., p. 59.
10. Arthur Griffith, *United Irishman*, 24 October 1903, p. 2.
11. See Griffith's 'The "Economics" of Irish Famine', *United Irishman*, 6 December 1902, p. 5, and *How Ireland has 'Prospered' Under English Rule* and *The Slave Mind* (New York: Irish Progressive League [Donnelly Press], not dated).
12. See 'A Paper for Irishwomen', published under the pseudonym 'Lasairfhiona ni Shamraidin' in the *United Irishman*, 8 April 1905, p. 6.
13. I discuss this reasoning more fully in *Gender and Modern Irish Drama*, pp. 55–6, 61–8, and 74–6.
14. See Harris, *Gender and Modern Irish Drama*, pp. 61–8.
15. Karen Steele, *Women, Press, and Politics During the Irish Revival* (Syracuse University Press, 2007), pp. 72–80.
16. Ibid., p. 80.
17. Ibid., p. 74.
18. When not quoting Synge, I will use the term 'traveller' instead of the pejorative 'tinker'.
19. Stephen Tifft makes this argument about *The Playboy of the Western World* in 'The Parricidal Phantasm: Irish Nationalism and the *Playboy* Riots', in Andrew Parker et al. (eds.), *Nationalisms and Sexualities* (New York: Routledge, 1992).

20. Ibid., pp. 316–17.
21. Ben Levitas, 'Censorship and Self-Censure in the Plays of J. M. Synge', *Princeton University Library Chronicle*, 68 (2006/2007), p. 280.
22. Mary King, 'Text and Context in *When the Moon Has Set*', in Daniel J. Casey (ed.), *Critical Essays on John Millington Synge* (New York: G. K. Hall & Co., 1994), p. 65.
23. See Charles R. Darwin, *The Descent of Man and Selection in Relation to Sex* (London: John Murray, 1871), vol. I, pp. 31–2.
24. Darwin, *Descent of Man*, vol. I, pp. 273, 258, 279.
25. D. Sheehan, quoted in Kilroy, *The Playboy Riots*, p. 87. P. D. Kenny, the drama critic for the *Irish Times*, explicated the Darwinian aspects of *The Playboy*'s plot in his review ('That Dreadful Play', *Irish Times*, 30 January 1907, p. 9). In 'A Plea for the *Playboy*', one 'P.M.E.K.' laid out the Darwinian reading of *The Playboy* for the readers of Arthur Griffith's *Sinn Fein* (9 February 1907, p. 3).
26. W. J. Mc Cormack, *Fool of the Family: A Life of J. M. Synge* (London: Weidenfeld & Nicolson, 2000), p. 42.
27. On Matheson and *When the Moon Has Set* see Robin Skelton, *The Writings of J. M. Synge* (London: Thames & Hudson, 1971), pp. 16–19.
28. On the multiple origins of Synge's nature worship see ibid., pp. 12–16.
29. King, 'Text and Context', p. 71.
30. See King, 'Text and Context', pp. 60–61.
31. In *No Future: Queer Theory and the Death Drive* (Durham, NC: Duke University Press, 2004), Lee Edelman argues that we cannot 'conceive of a future without the figure of the child' (p. 11).

10

C. L. INNES

Postcolonial Synge

The declaration by W. B. Yeats that Synge 'seemed by nature unfitted to think a political thought' and 'long understood nothing … of the political thoughts of men'[1] for many years went unquestioned by scholars, producers and audiences. Appearing in an essay originally intended as a Preface for Synge's *Collected Works* but withdrawn when Yeats lost the battle to prevent the inclusion of Synge's 'Connemara' articles, Yeats's statement reflects his own withdrawal from a particular kind of nationalist politics rather than Synge's. It can also be seen as an attempt to counterbalance the political emphasis generated by Irish nationalist reactions to *The Shadow of the Glen* and *The Playboy of the Western World*.

Jack B. Yeats, who accompanied Synge on his tour of Connemara, described him as 'an ardent Home Ruler and Nationalist'.[2] Synge's series of twelve articles on Connemara published in the *Manchester Guardian* in 1905 make Synge's socialist and anti-colonialist politics unmistakable. In the final article ('Possible Remedies'), after suggesting various economic and social reforms, Synge concludes:

> Most Irish politicians scorn all merely economic or agricultural reforms … if Home Rule would not of itself make a national life it would do more to make such a life possible than half a million creameries. With renewed life in the country many changes of the methods of government, and the holding of property, would inevitably take place, which would tend to make life less difficult even in the bad years and in the worst districts of Mayo and Connemara. (CW II, 341–3)

Although Synge has long been a national icon, it is only in recent decades that critics such as Shaun Richards, Declan Kiberd, Gregory Castle and P. J. Mathews have fully addressed the significance of Synge's anti-colonialist politics to his drama, prose and poetry. In discussing Synge as a postcolonial writer, this essay seeks to build upon the work of such scholars and will also draw attention to his influence on and similarities with later postcolonial writers from Africa, Australia and the Caribbean. The term 'postcolonial' is here used more generally to refer to writers who, following the colonisation of their country, confront and are affected by the consequences of colonialism, consequences which are not only economic and social, but also cultural and linguistic. In Synge's case I will often refer to him more specifically as an 'anti-colonial' writer, since his drama and essays address the situation of a colonised Ireland seeking to free itself from physical and cultural domination by England.

When Synge resigned from the *Association Irlandaise* he explained to Maud Gonne, 'I wish to work in my own way for the cause of Ireland, and I shall never be able to do so if I get mixed up with a revolutionary and semi-military movement' (CL I, 47). 'Working in his own way' entailed writing plays, essays and poetry, as well as involvement in the construction and management of a national theatre. Nevertheless, like many anti-colonialist writers, he reveals in his work a degree of anxiety about the relative merits of words rather than military weapons as a means of liberation, an anxiety which is also reflected in his desire to balance 'realism' and poetry or 'joy'. Seamus Deane has remarked that Synge's plays are 'dateless, dislodged from history', and thus '"poetic" not "realistic" plays'.[3] But it is important to point out that historical specificity is at least partially present in some of the plays, and that those plays often dramatise or seek to reconcile the conflict between the 'poetic' and the 'realistic'.

Indeed the issue of authenticity and 'realistic' representation is central to much anti-colonial writing and appears as a central concern in the famous manifesto composed by Yeats, Lady Gregory and Edward Martyn announcing the aims of the Irish Literary Theatre. Similarly, the Nigerian author Chinua Achebe has said that what he set out to do with his first novel was counteract the misrepresentation of Africans by novelists such as Joseph Conrad and Joyce Cary, to tell their story 'from the inside', and to remind his readers that 'African peoples did not hear of civilization for the first time from Europeans'.[4] As the Martinican writer Frantz Fanon argues, the colonisation of the mind goes hand in hand with the physical occupation of a country, and it is the role of artists and intellectuals to decolonise the mind and restore a colonised people's belief in the validity of their own culture.[5] For Fanon, as for the founders of the Irish Literary Theatre, the Kenyan writer Ngugi wa Thiong'o and the Caribbean poet and playwright Derek Walcott, drama is seen as a particularly effective way of reaching the people and creating or recreating a nationalist community.[6] Moreover, drama can be not only a means of speaking directly to an audience and engaging it in a communal experience, but also a way of giving physical voice and bodily presence to those who have been marginalised by the metropolitan centre.

That has been the aim of the theatre workshops directed by Walcott and Ngugi, and by Athol Fugard in South Africa. In the case of the Irish Literary Theatre, and later the Abbey Theatre, the question of giving voice to marginalised or subaltern groups is a more thorny and controversial one, as demonstrated by the violent reaction to the first performances of *The Playboy of the Western World*, and later to Sean O'Casey's *The Plough and the Stars*. The hostile reactions by Irish audiences to these plays brought to the fore the core issues relating to representation in a colonial or postcolonial society: Who has the authority to represent the indigenous people? Who are to be recognised as representative of the nation and its people? In what language and through what media should they represent themselves?

Synge's writings offer a series of evolving responses to these questions. His 'Autobiography' records that soon after reading Darwin in his early teens and relinquishing 'the Kingdom of God I began to take a real interest in the Kingdom of Ireland. My politics went round from a vigorous and unreasoning loyalty to a temperate Nationalism, and everything Irish became sacred' (CW II, 13). His early notebooks record inscriptions in Irish from monuments and tombs, as well as his reading of *The Children of Lir* and the St John Gospel in Irish.[7] One might be reminded of the character Haines with his notebook and interest in Irish folklore, through whom Joyce presents in *Ulysses* a satiric view of imperialists in search of the primitive, but Synge's diaries reveal a deep and thorough pursuit of Irish literary traditions as well as contemporary spoken Irish.

Nevertheless, some of Synge's works, including *The Aran Islands*, draw on strategies and assumptions inherent in anthropological studies produced by colonialists in the nineteenth century. In writing about his quest for the most 'primitive' form of Irish society, as he leaves Inis Mór for Inis Meáin, 'where Gaelic is more generally used, and the life is perhaps the most primitive that is left in Europe' (CW II, 53), Synge reveals the contradictions which marked much of the Celtic Revival as well as cultural nationalist projects in other anti-colonial movements. As Gregory Castle remarks, the anthropological strategies employed by Synge and Yeats, with theories of cultural difference and the role of a distanced 'objective' observer, was 'at once complicit with and hostile towards a tradition of representation that sought to redeem Irish peasant culture by idealizing or essentializing its "primitive" social conditions'.[8] In other words, there is the danger of endorsing a Celticism comparable to the Orientalism analysed and denounced by Edward Said. Similarly, the Senegalese poet and statesman Léopold Sédar Senghor celebrated *négritude*, an essentialised view of African culture, influenced by the studies of the German anthropologist Frobenius, and through invocations of a simple pastoral world far removed from metropolitan France or Dakar.

Although one can discern the influence of nineteenth-century anthropological strategies and assumptions in Synge's decision to visit the Aran Islands and his observations about the customs, beliefs and stories he encountered there, his series of essays also challenges anthropological discourse. For whereas traditional anthropology deploys a discourse which assumes the mantle of objectivity and authority invested in an outside observer who describes a society frozen in time, Synge mingles autobiography with description, and reveals himself as a changing persona in a changing rather than a static society. Moreover, the difficulty in articulation and communication is shared by the author and his subjects alike, as Synge moves towards greater eloquence in Gaelic, and the islanders gain greater confidence in their ability to be heard and understood by him.[9] What emerges through the wealth of anecdotes and stories that Synge begins to hear and translate is almost the opposite of the dichotomy Seamus Deane analyses so persuasively in his essay, 'Dumbness and Eloquence', where the Irish language as the 'language of the real' is silenced, and the English language 'as the language of the possible' emerges as eloquence.[10] But that liberation into the 'reality and joy' of Irish is confined within the pages of *The Aran Islands*, and also confined within the English language. As Deane points out, the movement from dumbness to eloquence is itself the theme of some of Synge's most powerful plays, and particularly *The Playboy of the Western World*, where the realm of the real is suppressed, and the realm of the possible, where Christy is made a man 'through the power of a lie', is given full rein.[11]

The Aran Islands is remarkable not only for its concern to capture the voices of the islanders, but also for its refusal to sentimentalise them. It also famously provides the source for many of Synge's plays, and like them seeks to represent a quintessential 'Irishness' rather than a symbolic Ireland. Paradoxically that representation of 'Irishness' is linked to the specificity of place, a mapping of a particular area, whether it be each of the islands, or the evocation of Wicklow or Co. Mayo. As Edward Said points out, 'If there is anything that radically distinguishes the imagination of anti-imperialism, it is the primacy of the geographical in it.'[12] In anti-colonial poetry, drama and fiction the emphasis on the agrarian world, on the 'peasantry', is not merely an inheritance from Romanticism, although it is in the case of Yeats and Synge inflected by it, for what is being expressed is not simply a generalised relationship between man and nature, but a claim that a people and the land they inhabit or from which they have been dispossessed belong to one another. The unity between people and place is emphasised by Synge's Aran Islands essays through his detailed descriptions of their clothes, their movements, their livelihood, their landscape. In the plays it is the imagery of the local landscape and of agrarian life which links the people to the land,

and which enriches their speech. Similarly in their fiction and drama the language of Chinua Achebe's, Wole Soyinka's and Derek Walcott's characters expresses a consciousness which is fashioned by a way of life which is grounded in a particular place and climate within Nigeria or St Lucia. Throughout their speech the everyday similes, metaphors and proverbs they use draw on the vegetation and animal life specific to their location.

Here we may note the contrast between Synge's drama and that of Yeats (though not his poetry), a contrast which also relates to their concept of resistance to colonial domination and misrepresentation, and Yeats's concern to show Ireland as 'the home of an ancient idealism'. Whereas Yeats sought to dramatise 'noble' and 'heroic' figures such as Cuchulain and Deidre as equivalents to the knights and ladies poeticised in Tennyson's Arthurian *Idylls of the King*, Synge rejected what Stephen Mackenna termed 'a purely fantastic, unmodern, ideal, spring-dayish, Cuchulainoid National Theatre' (CL I, 74). Synge regarded the emphasis on martial heroics in the elevation of Cuchulain as a perpetuation of imperial values and constructions of masculinity, while also 'unmodern' and unrelated to 'the fundamental realities of life' (74). Edward Said has argued the relevance of Fanon's analysis of the necessity of violence in a liberation struggle to an understanding of the invocations of violence in poetry and drama by Yeats.[13] More relevant to Synge's staging of Irish society under the condition of colonisation, however, is Fanon's analysis of the tension, the dreams of muscular prowess, the aggression against one another which marks the 'natives' hemmed in by colonial powers. Compare Fanon's description of the colonised's psyche with Jimmy Farrell's celebration of Christy Mahon's achievements in *The Playboy*:

> ... and he after bringing bankrupt ruin on the roulette man, and the trick-o'-the-loop man, and breaking the nose of the cockshot-man, and winning all in the sports below, racing, lepping, dancing, and the Lord knows what! (CW IV, 133)

Fanon writes:

> The first thing the native learns is to stay in his place, and not go beyond certain limits. That is why the dreams of the native are always of muscular prowess; his dreams are of action and aggression. I dream I am jumping, swimming, running, climbing ... that I span a river in one stride ... During the period of colonization, the native never stops achieving his freedom from nine in the evening until six in the morning.[14]

Fanon believed that a violent rebellion could be cathartic, and indeed necessary. However, as Declan Kiberd argues, Synge was a pacifist who, like Sean O'Casey later, rejected the glorification of physical force embraced by Patrick Pearse and the Irish Republican Brotherhood or Maud Gonne's Irish League.

He reads *The Playboy* as both a realistic representation of the cruelty and brutality Synge observed in peasant societies and a mock-heroic version of the Cuchulain cycle, providing an ironic commentary on two aspects of the Celtic Revival – the glorification of 'a heroic past, which can have existed only in men's imaginations – the other dedicated to an equally spurious vision of the western peasant as a kind of secular Gaelic mystic'.[15]

Indeed the first two plays Synge wrote for the National Theatre Society may be understood as critical responses to the nationalist heroics and abstractions embodied in *Cathleen ni Houlihan*, written by Yeats and Lady Gregory, and performed to great acclaim in 1902. Whereas Cathleen ni Houlihan is a symbol of an abstract Ireland, an allegorical figure who calls upon young men such as Michael to sacrifice their lives in order to redeem her, Maurya in *Riders to the Sea* bitterly laments the loss of Michael and her other sons; she is a metonymical rather than a metaphorical character who is not redeemed and made younger by their deaths, but broken and made older. Her final words, 'No man at all can be living for ever, and we must be satisfied', are surely an ironic reminder and refutation of Cathleen ni Houlihan's promise, 'They shall be alive for ever.'[16]

The Shadow of the Glen also places a woman at the centre of the drama, and here too a young man called Michael is at first romanticised as her redeemer. But in this play it is a male stranger and homeless wanderer who enters the house and disrupts the constrained domestic security of Nora and her elderly husband, and it is Nora who makes the choice to leave the house and follow him to an early death in the open air, rather than suffer the indignity and suffocation of her present situation. Here Synge suggests that the liberation of Ireland will be meaningless for women unless it also involves liberation from an oppressively patriarchal society in which, for economic reasons, women are imprisoned by loveless and sexless marriages to older men.[17]

While Synge's early plays involve an implicit dialogue with the kind of cultural nationalism represented by Yeats in *Cathleen ni Houlihan* and *On Baile's Strand*, *The Playboy of the Western World* contains more explicit references to Ireland's situation as a colonised and occupied country. Pegeen speaks of her fear of the 'loosèd khaki cut-throats' (British soldiers) who roam the country, a phrase censored from the first production of the play together with all other phrases 'derogatory to the army'.[18] The play is set in Mayo, with specific references to Castlebar, Ballina and Crossmolina. Mayo was the birthplace of Michael Davitt and of the Land League, and there are also allusions to political crimes linked to opposition to landlords and evictions when Pegeen recalls 'the like of Daneen Sullivan knocked the eye from a peeler, or Marcus Quin, God rest him, got six months for maiming ewes' (CW

IV, 59). Mayo was also the birthplace of John MacBride, who contested a parliamentary by-election there while absent fighting in the Boer War, and there is an allusion to him when Philly suggest that Christy's crime may have been that he 'went fighting for the Boers the like of the man beyond, was judged to be hanged, quartered and drawn' (71). As Nicholas Grene points out, an earlier draft of the play made the reference more explicit: 'Maybe he went fighting for the Boers the like of Major MacBride, God shield him, who's afeard to put the tip of his nose into Ireland fearing he's be hanged, quartered and drawn.'[19] The play is thus historically and geographically located as a site of antagonism to colonialism, an occupied territory where the locals dream of escape and redemption. In such locations, Fanon writes, the people make heroes of those who are 'prosecuted by the colonial authorities for acts ... directed against a colonialist person or colonialist property'.[20]

For Synge, as for Yeats and Joyce, Ireland was 'the servant of two masters ... an English and an Italian'.[21] Pegeen and the drinkers at the shebeen where the play is set are as scornful of Shawn Keogh's subservience to Father Reilly and Rome as they are admiring of Marcus Quin and Daneen Sullivan. As in many anti-colonialist works, the plot resolves around an Oedipal conflict between father and son, or between father figures and a younger generation, in which the values of the father are seen as harsh, materialistic and sterile, and are in turn linked to the values of the colonising power. Such father/son conflicts recur, although with significant variations, not only in Yeats's drama such as *On Baile's Strand*, and Joyce's fiction, but also in Chinua Achebe's novels *Things Fall Apart* and *Arrow of God*, and Wole Soyinka's plays, *The Lion and the Jewel* and *Kongi's Harvest*. In all of these, as Seamus Deane remarks of *The Playboy*, 'the Law of the Father has been broken and then reinaugurated'.[22] These works stage not only an internal conflict but also resist the patriarchal authority of the coloniser's world view, his representation of the native as savage and inarticulate, and the weight of his literary and dramatic traditions.

In many anti-colonial works, including *The Playboy* and *The Shadow of the Glen*, the conflict also centres on a woman who becomes symbolic of the nation who is to be redeemed, the motherland. Eavan Boland has written of her need as a woman writer to combat 'the association of the feminine and the national – and the consequent simplification of both'.[23] But such an association of the feminine with the national is not limited to Irish literary and oral cultures. The Senegalese poets Léopold Senghor and David Diop, as well as many Ghanaian and black South African writers, assert their loyalty to a symbolic Mother Africa, portrayed as the embodiment of African tradition. In Derek Walcott's epic poem *Omeros*, Helen becomes symbolic of his native St Lucia, desired by coloniser and colonised alike.

But some postcolonial writers also reveal an ambivalence about the role of the son who is nourished by his community and then leaves it, in order to 'go romancing' and 'telling stories of the villainy of Mayo, and the fools is here' (CW IV, 173). The theme of the 'prodigal son' who deserts his home and becomes Christianised or Europeanised surfaces in the poetry of Senghor and Christopher Okigbo, the plays of Soyinka, Ngugi and Ama Ata Aidoo, and the novels of Achebe, Ayi Kwei Armah and Kofi Awoonor. Thus, like *The Playboy*, with its reconciliation of father and son at the end, Chinua Achebe's first novel, *Things Fall Apart* implies a similar reconciliation in that it is a celebration of the anti-poetic and inarticulate father and warrior Okonkwo by the poetic and articulate descendant of a convert akin to Okonkwo's son Nwoye. In this sense, both works reconcile 'reality' and 'joy', and Okonkwo, like Old Mahon, represents the 'reality which is the root of all poetry'. As I have argued elsewhere, that reconciliation is, of course, qualified by the ending of each work which leaves the lions thrown to the Christians. And in that qualified reconciliation is suggested the paradox of these and many other postcolonial works that it may be only when the sons have become alienated or Christianised that they can affirm the pagan culture of their fathers.[24]

The paradox of this affirmation of their traditional societies by the sons also involves the paradox that they write in the language of the coloniser, a language which as Stephen Dedalus famously remarked is 'his before it is mine',[25] and which has either been used to silence the indigenous language or to represent the native as inept and childlike in his deviation from the metropolitan standard. As a consequence language itself and the power to speak often become a significant focus of the work. Christy's movement from his father's definition of him as a 'dribbling idiot', too timid to speak to a woman, to a 'likely man' (143) who delights and woos Pegeen with his eloquence and 'poet's talking' (149) is foregrounded in *The Playboy*. Achebe's *Things Fall Apart* contrasts Okonkwo's reticence and dislike of talk with the pleasure other members of the community take in rhetoric, story-telling, and the proverbs said to be 'the palm oil with which words are eaten'.[26] The novel is an eloquent response to Conrad's silencing of Africans in *Heart of Darkness*.[27] Postcolonial writers like Achebe, Aidoo, Rushdie and Walcott have wrestled with the problem of making the English language 'carry the weight of [their] experience', creating 'a new English, still in full communion with its ancestral home but altered to suit its new … surroundings'.[28]

Synge's solution to the difficulty of giving voice and power to his Irish peasant characters, removing them from the inarticulateness or blarney of stage Irishmen, and making English 'carry the weight of their experience' has proved an influential model for later writers faced with similar problems. The Australian playwright and poet Louis Esson met Synge in Dublin in

1904, and with his encouragement returned to Australia to found eventually the Pioneer Players, the beginning of an Australian national theatre (CL I, 84). In his own plays Esson drew on Synge as a model for representing on stage the lives, language and idioms characteristic of the Australian rural and working classes.[29]

For African-American writers seeking in the 1920s to affirm the lives and culture of rural and poor black Americans, the Irish Literary Renaissance served as an inspiration for what has now became known as the Harlem Renaissance. In the Prefaces to his 1922 and 1931 anthologies, *The Book of American Negro Poetry*, the poet and academic James Weldon Johnson cited the example of Synge with particular reference to the creation of a language which moved away from the limitations and connotations of the kind of minstrel dialect which had in the past been used to represent African-American speech, a dialect which in his view had 'only two main stops, humor and pathos':

> What the colored poet in the United States needs to do is something like what Synge did for the Irish; he needs to find a form which will express the racial spirit by symbols from within rather than by symbols from without, such as the mere mutilation of English spelling and pronunciation. He needs a form which is freer and larger than dialect, but which still holds the racial flavor; a form expressing the imagery, the idioms, the peculiar turns of thought, and the humour and pathos too, of the Negro, but which will also be capable of voicing the deepest and highest emotions and aspirations, and allow the widest range of subjects and the widest scope of treatment.[30]

Johnson himself moved away from the dialect employed in his first collections of poems to 'a form freer and larger than dialect', but still holding 'the racial flavor' in his powerful collection of poems, *God's Trombones: Seven Negro Sermons in Verse*.[31] His Preface to this collection reiterates the points made and the example of Synge given in the Preface to his anthology.

Although not completely disowning his earlier dialect poems, Johnson gives reasons for eschewing dialect in *God's Trombones*. This collection seeks to convey the power and eloquence of traditional Negro sermons, which 'were all saturated with the sublime phraseology of the Hebrew prophets and steeped in the idioms of King James English .... It was really a fusion of Negro idioms with Bible English; and in this there may have been, after all, some kinship with the innate grandiloquence of their old African tongues.'[32] Here and in Johnson's quest for 'a freer and larger form' there is a potential comparison with Synge's invocation of the Elizabethan dramatist and other writers who live 'where the imagination of the people, and the language they use, is rich and living', allowing a writer 'to be rich and copious in his words, and at the same time to give the reality, which is the root of all poetry, in a comprehensive and natural form' (CW IV, 53). Synge's concern to capture 'a popular imagination' which will exist for only 'a few years more', before 'the harvest is a memory only' (54), is also comparable with Johnson's sense of the importance of encapsulating a world that will soon disappear. He concludes his Preface thus: 'The old-time Negro preacher is rapidly passing. I have here tried sincerely to fix something of him.'[33]

Synge's drama has also been a significant influence for the Caribbean poet and dramatist Derek Walcott. In a 1980 interview Walcott spoke of his identification with Irish writers:

> I've always felt some kind of intimacy with the Irish poets because one felt that they were also colonials with the same kind of problems that existed in the Caribbean. They were the niggers of Britain. Now with all that, to have those outstanding achievements of genius whether by Joyce or Beckett or Yeats illustrated that one could come out of a depressed, depraved, oppressed situation and be defiant and creative at the same time.[34]

Like Synge's first play, *When the Moon Has Set*, Walcott's early plays were written in a literary and elevated form of standard English, although he tended to choose historical figures such as Henri Christophe as his subject.[35] In later plays Walcott, like Synge, 'sought out the poor as an adventure, as an illumination, only to arrive where ... back in the bleached, unpainted fishing village streets everywhere seemed salted with a reek of despair, a life, a theatre, reduced to elementals'.[36] But this new subject also demanded a new language, a language that 'went beyond mimicry', a 'dialect which had the force of revelation as it invented names for things, one which settled for its own mode of inflection, and which began to create an oral culture of chants, jokes, songs, and fables; this, not merely the debt of history was his proper claim to the New World'.[37] In the interview with Edward Hirsch quoted above, Walcott went on to say:

> And then the whole question of dialect began to interest me. When I read Synge's *Riders to the Sea* I realized what he had attempted to do with the language of the Irish. He had taken a fishing port kind of language and gotten beauty out of it, a beat, something lyrical. Now that was inspiring, and the obvious model for *The Sea at Dauphin*. I guess I knew then that the more you imitate when you are young, the more original you become. If you know very clearly that you are imitating such and such a work, it isn't that you are adopting another man's genius; it is that he has done an experiment that has worked and will be useful to all writers afterwards. When I tried to translate the speech of the St Lucian fisherman into an English Creole, all I was doing was taking that

kind of speech and translating it, or retranslating it, into an English inflected Creole, and that was a totally new experience for me even if it did come out of Synge.[38]

First produced in 1954, *The Sea at Dauphin* is, like *Riders to the Sea*, a one-act tragedy. It is set near the St Lucian village of Dauphin, and is a play in which the ocean and poverty are antagonists faced with stoicism and dignity by the fishermen who mourn those who have been drowned at sea. Unlike Synge's play, *The Sea at Dauphin* foregrounds the words and activity of men rather than women; and accordingly the language is less lyrical, the temper more aggressive and bitter; for example in this speech by one of the main protagonists, a 40-year-old fisherman named Afa:

> And this new thing, compassion? Where is compassion? Is I does make poor people poor, or this sea vex? Is I that put rocks where should dirt by Dauphin side, man cannot make garden grow? Is I that swell little children belly with bad worm, and woman to wear clothes that white people use to wipe their foot?[39]

This is drama that is a response to Synge rather than an imitation or translation of him, marking not only the comparisons with Synge's representation of the Aran Islands, but also the differences between the language, histories and attitudes of the Irish and West Indian islanders. As Sandra Sprayberry remarks, Walcott is thus 'in dialogue with other texts that are themselves in dialogue with the colonizer'.[40]

Walcott's later plays, as well as his concept of the role and impact of the Trinidad Theatre Workshop he directed, continue to reveal the influence of Synge, although the dialogue becomes a conversation including other playwrights such as Genet, Soyinka and Brecht. *Ti Jean and His Brothers* dramatises a folktale which mingles African and European elements, drawing on the rituals of oral story-telling. *A Dream on Monkey Mountain*, like *The Playboy*, dramatises the movement from dumbness to eloquence, an eloquence made possible 'by the power of a lie'.

Another West Indian dramatist who has entered into dialogue with Synge is Mustapha Matura, who in 1984 wrote *The Playboy of the West Indies*. Matura was at this point already an established writer, the author of at least a dozen plays, and so he enters into dialogue with Synge at a different point in his career, and one for whom Synge's play works not so much as a formative influence as an analogy. (Like Brian Friel, he has also relocated Chekhov to his native island.) In an interview in the *New York Times* Matura explained that he wrote the play 'because I'm constantly trying to understand the character of Trinidad and the Trinidadians. They are enormously resilient: they will be down, but they will always tell you a joke or offer a drink.

That mirrors the Irish.'[41] His version of the play is almost a line-by-line translation into a West Indian patois, with the same storyline of a supposed parricide lionised by the deprived (and slightly depraved) patrons of a small Trinidadian village rum shop. Perhaps the most significant change is his refashioning of the Widow Quin into an obeah woman named Mama Benin, who challenges the playboy's story (he is called Ken in this version) mainly because it lacks authentic detail, and tells Ken, 'Yer not telling de story right yer no.'[42] As Tobias Döring argues, 'this battle for authorship and authenticity', together with the explicit references to the theatricality of the scenes and the two audiences on stage and in the theatre, emphasises the play's status as an adaptation.[43] Other critics have found the characterisation, especially of Mama Benin, all too stereotypical, and lacking in the depth and compassion with which Synge represents Pegeen and the community that Christy leaves bereft. Matura's comparison of Trinidadians and the Irish quoted above might lead one to accept such a critique. Döring, however, sees the use of such stereotypes or prefabricated images as a deliberate strategy, ironically playing with 'the common images in which West Indians, just like the Irish, have been captured and controlled. Instead of presenting Trinidad's society in its richness and diversity, the play partly transfers European clichés to the Caribbean text but marks them as such transfers.'[44]

Matura's *Playboy of the West Indies* was first written and performed for the Oxford Playhouse, and so for a largely white metropolitan audience for whom the comparisons between different sets of stereotypes constructed within England may be both distanced and recognisable. A more recent version of *The Playboy* by the Irish novelist Roddy Doyle and Nigerian-Irish dramatist Bisi Adigun was first staged at the Abbey Theatre in Dublin in 2007, marking the centenary of the first production of Synge's *Playboy*. In this version the translation is not so much in terms of two different colonised peoples – although Christy becomes a Nigerian refugee in Dublin – but in terms of rural and urban Ireland, and the contrast is between a remote rural society at the turn of the twentieth century and a globalised urban Dublin at the turn of the twenty-first century. And in this case a Dublin audience reacts not to the de-sentimentalised representation of Irish peasantry, but to a particular urban community and language already made familiar through Roddy Doyle's novels. Thus this translation was met not with shock or dismay but seeming recognition and delight, and the use of swear words so disquieting for the Abbey audience 100 years ago, merely produced giggles and titters from a twenty-first-century audience. Pegeen's final grief-stricken line 'Oh, my grief, I've lost him surely. I've lost the only Playboy of the Western World', is replaced in this updated urban adaptation with a brief and irritable 'Fuck off!', so ending the play comically rather than tragi-comically. Given the otherwise gritty realism of the portrayal of the characters, their language and their world in this version, some critics found implausible the ready acceptance of a Nigerian Christy in a white working-class neighbourhood, and condemned the relentless comedy in this adaptation for its failure to explore the tensions and prejudices faced by immigrant communities. At the same time it could also be argued that this latest adaptation effectively communicates and updates Synge's compassionate insight into the ways in which spirited young women in an impoverished community focus their thwarted ambitions for a fuller life on outside 'celebrities'.

Derek Walcott commended Synge for doing 'an experiment that has worked and will be useful to all writers afterwards'. For the Harlem Renaissance poets and for Walcott the most useful aspect was the experiment with language, the discovery of ways of making a subaltern group articulate and eloquent, and of disconnecting their language from the limiting and purely comic or sentimental connotations of stage Irish or minstrel dialect. Other writers such as Mustapha Matura and Roddy Doyle and Bisi Adigun have focused more on the plot, exploring the shared comic potential of the anecdote Synge dramatised (though he gave it a different and more serious ending). In so doing they have also foregrounded the issue of translation from one culture to another, making their audiences aware of the comparisons and contrasts between the West Indies and Ireland, or between past and present.

NOTES

1. William Butler Yeats, *Essays and Introductions* (New York: Macmillan, 1968), p. 319.
2. Quoted by Maurice Bourgeois, *John Millington Synge and the Irish Theatre* (London: Constable, 1913), p. 87.
3. Seamus Deane, *A Short History of Irish Literature* (University of Notre Dame Press, 1994), p. 154.
4. Chinua Achebe, 'The Role of the Writer in a New Nation', *Nigeria Magazine*, 81 (1964), p. 157.
5. Frantz Fanon, 'On National Culture', in *The Wretched of the Earth*, trans. Constance Farrington (New York: Grove Press, 1968).
6. See in particular Ngugi wa Thiong'o, *Decolonising the Mind: The Politics of Language in African Literature* (London: James Currey, 1986).
7. See Declan Kiberd, *Synge and the Irish Language* (London: Macmillan, 1979) pp. 22–3.
8. Gregory Castle, *Modernism and the Celtic Revival* (Cambridge University Press, 2001) p. 3.
9. See Castle, *Modernism and the Celtic Revival*, Chapter 3.

10. Seamus Deane, 'Dumbness and Eloquence', in Clare Carroll and Patricia King (eds.), *Ireland and Postcolonial Theory* (Cork University Press, 2003), p. 118.

11. Ibid.

12. Edward Said, 'Yeats and Decolonisation', in Terry Eagleton, Fredric Jameson and Edward Said, *Nationalism, Colonialism, and Literature* (Minneapolis, MN: University of Minnesota Press, 1990), p. 77.

13. Edward Said, *Culture and Imperialism* (London: Chatto & Windus, 1993), pp. 282–3.

14. Fanon, *Wretched of the Earth*, pp. 52–3.

15. Kiberd, *Synge and the Irish Language*, p. 114.

16. W. B. Yeats, *Collected Plays* (London: Macmillan, 1953), p. 56.

17. See P. J. Mathews's chapter on *The Shadow of the Glen* in *Revival: the Abbey Theatre, Sinn Féin, the Gaelic League and the Co-operative Movement* (Cork: Field Day / Cork University Press, 2003), pp. 117–45.

18. Maurice Bourgeois, *John Millington Synge and the Irish Theatre* (London: Constable, 1913), p. 201.

19. Nicholas Grene, *The Politics of Irish Drama* (Cambridge University Press, 1999), p. 97.

20. Fanon, *Wretched of the Earth*, p. 69.

21. James Joyce, *Ulysses* (Oxford University Press, 1993), p. 20.

22. Seamus Deane, *Strange Country* (Oxford University Press, 1997) p. 143.

23. Eavan Boland, 'Outside History', *PN Review*, 17:1 (September/October 1990), p. 24.

24. See C. L. Innes, *The Devils Own Mirror: the Irishman and the African in Modern Literature* (Washington, DC: 3 Continents Press, 1990).

25. James Joyce, *A Portrait of the Artist as a Young Man* (Harmondsworth: Penguin, 1974), p. 189.

26. Chinua Achebe, *Things Fall Apart* (London: Heinemann, 1980), p. 5.

27. Chinua Achebe, 'An Image of Africa: Racism in Conrad's *Heart of Darkness*', *Hopes and Impediments: Selected Essays 1965–87* (Oxford: Heinemann Educational Books, 1988), p. 6.

28. Chinua Achebe, 'The African Writer and the English Language', *Morning Yet on Creation Day* (London: Heinemann, 1975), p. 62.

29. See John McCallum, 'Irish Memories and Australian Hopes: William Butler Yeats and Louis Esson', *Westerly*, 34:2 (June 1989), pp. 33–40.

30. James Weldon Johnson, *The Book of American Negro Poetry* (New York: Harcourt, Brace & World, 1931), pp. 41–2.

31. James Weldon Johnson, *God's Trombones: Seven Negro Sermons in Verse* (New York: Viking Press, 1969).

32. Ibid., p. 9.

33. Ibid.

34. Quoted in Stewart Brown (ed.), *The Art of Derek Walcott* (Bridgend: Seren Books, 1991), p. 24.

35. See Derek Walcott, 'What the Twilight Says: An Overture', Preface to *Dream on Monkey Mountain and Other Plays* (New York: Noonday Press, 1970), p. 13.

36. Ibid., pp. 14–15.

37. Ibid., p. 17.

38. Derek Walcott, Interview with Edward Hirsch, *Contemporary Literature*, 20:3 (1979), pp. 288–9.

39. Walcott, *Dream on Monkey Mountain*, p. 53.

40. Sandra Sprayberry, 'Sea Changes: Post-Colonialism in Synge and Walcott', *South Carolina Review*, 33 (Spring, 2001), p. 117.

41. William Harris, Interview with Mustapha Matura, *New York Times*, 9 May 1993, Section 2, p. 21.

42. Mustapha Matura, *Playboy of the West Indies* (New York: Broadway Play Publishing, 1988), p. 13.

43. Tobias Döring, 'Dislocating Stages: Mustapha Matura's Caribbean Rewriting of Synge and Chekhov', *European Journal of English Studies*, 2.1 (1998), p. 89.

44. Ibid., p. 92.

11

GREGORY DOBBINS

Synge and Irish modernism

Samuel Beckett didn't often reveal his literary influences, yet his admiration for the writing of John Millington Synge is a matter of record. As Beckett's official biographer James Knowlson wrote in an early essay on the connections between Synge and Beckett:

> [I]n answer to a somewhat bold question relating to the most profound influences that he himself acknowledged upon his dramatic writing, Beckett referred me specifically to the work of J. M. Synge. Such an acknowledgement is relatively rare with Beckett and the nature and extent of his debt is therefore all the more worth pursuing.[1]

There are numerous biographical similarities between the two writers. Both grew up in affluent upper-middle-class sections of south Co. Dublin; both had a strict Protestant religious upbringing under the direction of somewhat repressive mothers; both were students at Trinity College Dublin, an institution with which each had an ambiguous relationship; most importantly, both discovered their mature literary styles through an intensive engagement with a language other than English. Each writer even found a supportive interlocutor in the artist Jack Yeats, perhaps Ireland's most important modernist painter. Yet despite all of these points in common, Beckett's identification of Synge as a profound formal influence initially seems odd when one compares the texts each writer produced. Early works by Beckett such as *More Pricks than Kicks* and *Murphy* are remote in their concerns from the Revival, and demonstrate an anti-traditional aesthetic very much opposed to the conventions of Irish writing at the turn of the century. *Murphy* in particular contains a parody of Synge's representation of mourning on the Aran Islands in *Riders to the Sea* and frequently parodies some of the more familiar rhetorical tropes of the Revival. While Synge's style frequently demonstrates the expressionist qualities of 'exaggerated realism', it is firmly anchored in realism nevertheless. Beckett's more experimental mature works, whether his prose or drama, seem even further removed from Synge's literary world in their minimalism, dearth of clear historical referents, and generally anti-realist qualities.

While the works of Samuel Beckett serve as an extreme example, their characteristics nevertheless underscore the distance between Synge's writing and the works of more typical Irish modernist writers like Joyce, Beckett, Flann O'Brien and others. Even in the case of W. B. Yeats, a figure who had a complex and ambiguous relationship to modernism and had a closer personal relationship to Synge than any other Irish writer, late poetic and dramatic works like *The Winding Stair and Other Poems* or *Purgatory* have more in common thematically and formally with those high modernist writers who emerged in the twenty-five or more years since the death of Synge than they do with anything Synge wrote. Thus, while Synge is often included in the list of names meant to identify the collective cultural project of Irish modernism, the connections he has to the other names on the list remains less clear. This is not to suggest that Synge lacked any connection to the writers, thinkers and movements that laid the foundation for the emergence of modernism. Synge's awareness of the works of such figures as Darwin, Hegel, Marx, Nietzsche and Spencer is well known, as is his familiarity with European literary movements like symbolism and naturalism. Early unpublished works such as the prose fragment 'Étude Morbide' (1899) and the play *When the Moon Has Set* (1901) demonstrate the extent to which symbolism and naturalism made an impact upon Synge's growth as a writer. The latter work in particular reads like an attempt to fuse Ibsen with the Comte de Villiers de l'Isle-Adam's *Axël* and relocate the resulting hybrid to rural County Wicklow. An awareness of Synge's culturally progressive interests, however, doesn't take into account two important matters. First of all, for the most part such observations are more relevant to Synge's earlier writing than to the mature works he remains best known for and which are more specifically identified with the Revival. More importantly, while those works demonstrate the degree to which Synge went well beyond his influences, they nevertheless still look very different from the more experimental texts that would typify Irish modernism in the years after his death.

Part of the reason for this has to do with the ambiguous relation the Revival had to modernism in the first place. Irish modernism, after all, emerged partly in response to the conventions of the Revival. In a sophisticated theoretical assessment of the singular characteristics of Irish modernism, Joe Cleary concedes the apparently 'archaic' character of the Revival in respect to a more international understanding of modernism:

> For many Irish scholars – whether liberal or leftist, republican or revisionist – the most embarrassing aspect of the Revival is its folkish idiom and its

nationalist tones, both of which seem to put Irish cultural production of this period completely out of step with contemporary European modernism usually viewed as the brashly iconoclastic and cosmopolitan or internationalist literature of new times, new cityscapes, new materials, new technologies.

Virtually all of the thematic and formal qualities Cleary cites, of which 'all seem to be distinctly at odds with the modernist currents of the time', can be found in abundance within Synge's writing.[2] One of the primary attributes of the west of Ireland that Synge was most attracted to concerned his sense that modernity had not yet arrived there and that it continued to exist in the organic condition of a much earlier era. Synge did not need to re-create artisanal practices which would stand as alternatives to the industrialised present as late-Victorian intellectuals like William Morris did; he merely had to spend time in Connemara. As he writes in *The Aran Islands*:

> Every article on these islands has an almost personal character, which gives this simple life, where all art is unknown, something of the artistic beauty of mediaeval life. The curaghs and the spinning-wheels, the tiny wooden barrels that are still much used in the place of earthenware, the home-made cradles, churns, and baskets are full of individuality, and being made from materials that are common here, yet to some extent peculiar to the island, they seem to exist as a natural link between the people and the world that is about them. (CW II, 58–9)

Both *The Aran Islands* and *Riders to the Sea* register a community defined by a whole way of life seemingly oblivious to the passage of time in 'the big world'. Daily life in such conditions is indistinguishable from an aesthetic conception of reality since the distinction between utility and luxury does not exist there. By representing this version of the west in prose and on stage in the more metropolitan context of the Dublin-based Revival, Synge offered a seemingly alternative conception of the present that did not appear remarkably different from the past but was very distinct from the processes of modernisation identified with both capitalism and colonialism which prevailed within more developed parts of Ireland.

Synge regarded such supposedly 'pre-modern' qualities as the lack of industrial development or widespread urban growth as advantages to the Irish writer. In his introduction to *The Playboy of the Western World*, one of the texts in which he articulates his aesthetic goals most clearly, Synge discusses the distinction between the modern influences of symbolism and naturalism on the one hand, and his impressions of rural Irish society on the other:

> In the modern literature of towns, however, richness is found only in sonnets, or prose poems, or in one or two elaborate books that are far away from the profound and common interests of life. One has, on one side, Mallarmé and

Huysmans producing this literature; and on the other Ibsen and Zola dealing
with the reality of life in joyless and pallid words. On the stage one must have
reality, and one must have joy, and that is why the intellectual modern drama
has failed, and people have grown sick of the false joy of the musical comedy,
that has been given them in place of the rich joy found only in what is superb and
wild in reality ... In Ireland, for a few years more we have a popular imagination
that is fiery and magnificent, and tender; so that those of us who wish to write
start with a chance that is not given to writers in places where the springtime of
the local life has been forgotten, and the harvest is a memory only, and the straw
has been turned into bricks.   (CW IV, 53–4)

In Synge's view naturalism foregrounds the joyless alienation of modernity
while symbolism generates an imaginative realm which joyfully seeks to
escape it. Compared to either case – and in distinction from the lower
aesthetic aims of popular culture – Irish drama has the capacity to represent
the integration of what naturalism and symbolism lack in each other precisely
because the alienation of modernity has not completely arrived yet in Ireland.
To Synge, pre-modern social conditions provide the condition of possibility
for the expressionist qualities of the language of his writing. While Synge's
mature plays certainly do not idealise underdevelopment – with the exception
of the mythical *Deirdre of the Sorrows*, all of his plays are unstinting in their
representation of the social and economic impoverishment he witnessed first-
hand while compiling the prose records of his travels throughout rural
Ireland – aside from an occasional contextual reference or authorial indication most of them take place in a more or less unspecified time prior to the
development and the arrival of a recognisable form of modernity.[3] Synge's
focus on the past aligns him with the conventions of the Revival in general
and positions him away from the more urban focus of writers like Joyce,
Beckett and O'Brien. The nature of Yeats's enthusiasm for Synge re-affirms
his apparent difference from a modernist project oftentimes critical of the
values of the Revival. In the mythology of the Revival Yeats constructed in the
decades after it ended Synge stood as its central figure, the writer he identified
in his Nobel Prize acceptance speech as most committed to 'bring[ing] the
imagination and speech of the country, all that poetical tradition descended
from the Middle Ages, to the people of the town'.[4] Given such a backward-
oriented gaze, it is no surprise that it becomes difficult to link Synge's writing
to the more avant-garde forms of modernism that began to emerge not
long after his death. Yeats's version of Synge –'that rare, that distinguished,
that most noble thing, which of all things still of the world is nearest to being
sufficient to itself, the pure artist', who 'seemed by nature unfitted to think
a political thought'– evidently made the apolitical autonomy of the aesthetic
a primary value of his writing, just as many other modernists did. Yet the

apparent commitment to the revitalisation of the archaic within the context of the modern space of the city Synge (or at least Yeats's version of him) emphasised in his work suggested that his project was different in its aims.[5]

Yet recent scholarship asserts that Yeats's version of Synge has more to do with the reactionary turn of his own thinking in the decades after independence than it does with any position Synge actually took himself and that it has seriously limited a more complete understanding of Synge's writing.[6] Moreover, while Yeats may have re-fashioned Synge in order to fit him into his own personal pantheon, there is also the matter by which the once controversial writer became acceptable to a conservative Catholic audience after independence through the work of critics like Daniel Corkery.[7] In addition to post-independence revivals of Synge's plays that tended to mute some of the more radical qualities of his writing, the process by which Synge was assimilated into the canon of twentieth-century Irish writing made his plays safe for consumption.[8] Yeats's valorisation of Synge's ability to bring the various characteristics of Irish tradition to the attention of an early twentieth-century urban audience deserves closer attention. Crucially, there seems to be an important difference between Yeats and Synge regarding the relationship the past has to modernity. While Yeats found a preferable alternative to the utilitarianism and rationalism of modernity in the past, Synge's understanding of that relationship was more ambivalent than Yeats let on in his writing about Synge. The representation of the past – often in collision with a dramatically different present – is not as conservative or reactionary in itself as theorisations of modern Irish writing which hold that it stems from 'an archaic avant-garde' would have it.[9] As Cleary argues:

> The embrace in modernist hands of the archaic pre-modern worlds of aristocracy, epic past, and rural countryside or that of the metropolitan city and technology can be equally reactionary. From a political standpoint, what is decisive is not whether a modernist writer embraces the archaic or the modern elements, the country or the city, on this spectrum, but rather how the dialectic between the two is actually elaborated.[10]

In Synge's case, a connection to Irish modernism, a loosely defined tendency linked by a commitment to forms of cultural production distinct from those of the Revival, depends not so much upon the fact that his work demonstrates the conventions of that moment in literary history but rather on the values he attached to those conventions. Joep Leerssen, who regards Synge as 'the great forerunner of Joyce' in the history of Irish modernism, argues that Synge made use of the trope of tradition in his writing but did so for radically different purposes than other writers identified with the Revival. While Yeats and company celebrated the resurrection or rebirth of the elements of traditional culture as a means to nullify the reality of modernity as a central value to the Revival:

> Synge's treatment of the revival or rejuvenation theme insistently tended the other way … [Synge's] revivals are by no means the escape from history, the glorious phoenix-like rebirths that the audience was used to. On the contrary, revivals in Synge are not rejuvenations but a reassertion of the power of the old over the young … Synge's handling of the terms of youth, old age and revival goes squarely against standard patterns of the time. Therein lies what we may call his originality, or his creative genius; therein lies certainly the deeper reason why he outraged his audience.[11]

By restaging the elements of tradition in a modern context, Synge's writing has something in common with any of the other significant works of literature in the Revival. But by reversing the value of that practice, Synge's writing implicitly calls for something new which will negate the fetishisation of the past; in doing so, it anticipates the more radical modernist positions that would follow.

Synge's work is at once the source of many of the Revival's most familiar characteristics but is also implicitly critical of its central ideological positions; it is formally more conservative than any number of Irish modernist works but nevertheless complicit with the critique of the construction of tradition found in later texts. Consequently, Synge should be considered what Fredric Jameson would call 'the vanishing mediator' of Irish literary history.[12] Jameson's concept of the vanishing mediator accounts for the manner in which historical change occurs by postulating 'the hypothesis of some central mediatory figure or institution that can account for the passage from one temporal and historical state to another one'. In order for one historical period to succeed another, there needs to be some type of interim that enables the transition to happen; the vanishing mediator 'is thus in the strictest sense of the word a catalytic agent that permits an exchange of energies between two otherwise mutually exclusive terms'; once the historical change has occurred, however, the vanishing mediator 'has no further reason for being and disappears from the historical scene'.[13] In literary terms, the vanishing mediator would refer to a writer, movement or series of texts that would share most of the typical formal or thematic attributes of a given cultural period, but would also bear newer characteristics that would act to negate those previously dominant values. In this sense, Synge's writing may have been at the core of the Revival through its engagement with the dominant stylistic and thematic tropes of that movement, but it also introduced precisely those values and positions which would ultimately supplant the Revival. If the characteristics of Synge's plays seem aesthetically conservative compared to some of the more experimental modernist works which followed, it is only because the sorts of changes it anticipated culminated in the arrival of a completely different framework of literary value. Since the vanishing mediator creates the conditions for a rearrangement of the dominant values of a given period, the work in question will not lack controversy.

In Synge's case, controversy was inextricably bound up with the category of the stereotype. Early hostility to the production of virtually all of Synge's plays often resulted from the perception that he was yet another example of a privileged Anglo-Irish Protestant focusing upon some supposed characteristic of the rural peasantry (sexual repression, sexual promiscuity, drunkenness, the lack of masculinity, blasphemy, the authoritarian nature of the Catholic Church, lawlessness, violence) that was either a negative stereotype of Irishness or the antithesis of valorised forms of Irish identity. Ultimately, Synge's writing does not participate in the construction of stereotypes as much as it attempts to find value in the concept of recalcitrance towards modernity in general. But the fact that each of these supposed characteristics of rural Irishness evident in Synge's writing was regarded as a stereotype in the first place goes right to the heart of the central contradiction of the parallel projects of the Revival and emergent forms of Irish nationalism. As Homi Bhabha and a host of other postcolonial theorists have argued, the content of a given colonial stereotype is not at issue as much as its status as an ambivalent discursive representation that at once registers both the presumption of superiority and the intrinsic paranoia of colonial ideology.[14] Since the derivative discourse of anti-imperialist nationalism seeks to initiate a form of sovereignty represented by the colonial nation-state within its own specific local terms, cultural nationalism, whatever form it might take, must necessarily engage with the stereotype. For the most part, Irish nationalism responded to colonial stereotypes in one of two ways: it either disavowed the stereotype altogether, or through a process of transvaluation it re-classified it in positive terms and re-articulated it as an index of Irish difference resistant to colonial norms.[15] Whether or not a particular stereotype might be useful for the rhetorical clothing of nationalism – however distorted the characteristic in question may have been – had to do with temporality, as the distinction Seamus Deane draws between 'the character of nations' and 'national character' makes clear.[16] Deane refers to the tension between the character of nations, that progressive 'explanatory element in the story of a progression from the narrow ambit of the new territory or space of the state' and national character, that seemingly static or backward 'controlling voice in a recalcitrant community narrative that refuses, with decreasing success, to surrender its particularities, to yield itself either to the state or to any comparable transnational, or "universal" goal or condition'.[17] Cultural nationalism thus faced a contradictory dilemma that proves to be one of its own conditions of possibility: in order to bring about the acceleration of that process which will allow the character of nations to unfold into the onset of a modernity typified by statehood, it must repress those aspects of the national character – many of which, in exaggerated or distorted form, are the basis for various stereotypes – which prevent progress. Yet in order to maintain an iteration of the character of nations that is not wholly derivative of that model imposed by colonial violence, cultural nationalism must retain as many facets of national character as possible in order to signal the particularity of local difference.

In order to achieve its political goals, cultural nationalism must either develop or appropriate new narrative forms that can allow for the simultaneous presence of national character and the progressive logic which drives the character of nations.[18] Since the specificity of local national tradition must be accounted for at all costs, representational forms and genres must depart to at least some extent from the models provided by the culture of the coloniser. In the period leading up to the struggle for independence, the Revival served as that crucial moment in which the exploration of new representational forms occurred. The specific texts may have varied, but they shared a common project of delineating those aspects of the national character which would help enable an imaginative construction of the nation that could become a reality through enough hard work. Importantly, the Revival substituted the concept of tradition for the actual traumatic history of the more recent past. The intellectuals of the Revival not only evaded the consideration of certain historical events (such as the Famine or the Land War) which might have provided evidence of attributes of the national character contrary to the progressive drive towards nationhood, but converted the past into a more general concept suitable for the teleological narrative required by nationalism.[19] Though Yeats may have had misgivings about the concept of modernity as well as some of the more ethnocentric forms of Irish nationalism that emerged in this period, the work-ethic and texts of the Revival he was an important part of crucially cleared the imaginative space for the Irish version of modernisation enacted by state-centred nationalism.

To a certain extent, all of this is true of Synge's writing as well. Synge's plays contributed some of the most vital formal characteristics of Revival drama, ranging from set design to the prominence of colloquial, Gaelicised dialogue, and in this regard the work of the vanishing mediator coincides with the dominant aesthetic values of the period. Yeats's understanding of Synge's importance, in which the 'poetical tradition' of rural Ireland emerges in the context of the city, is essentially diachronic in that the juxtaposition it creates initiates a teleological link between the elements of national character identified with the past and the re-fashioned qualities of the modern character of the Irish nation. For those various movements committed to the project of the delineation of the character of the new nation and the ultimate goal of statehood, the attributes of tradition prominent in a given literary work should ideally comprise in embryonic form values and characteristics suitable to modern conceptions of citizenship. Yet in his positive representation of such central characters as the Tramp in *The Shadow of the Glen*, Martin and Mary Doul in *The Well of the Saints*, Sarah Casey in *The Tinker's Wedding*, and Christy Mahon in *The Playboy of the Western World*, Synge placed an emphasis on those aspects of the national character most problematic to the teleology of progressive modernisation. As the visceral reaction to so many of his plays demonstrates, the presence of such figures, each of them unassimilable to the modern ideals of propriety, morality and development, contributed to the scandalous reputation of his writing. Rather than representing idealised values of the past that contribute to an ongoing progressive temporality which unfolds into modernity, Synge's plays emphasise the centrality of a recalcitrance which serves as an obstacle to progress.

The critique of progress evident in so much of Synge's writing provides the most significant instance of how he internalised the radical intellectual influences of his youth; it also introduces a position that will mark one of the most important distinctions between the cultural projects of the Revival and the modernists. Synge's tragedies find their power not in some traumatic moment or cataclysmic change which presents an irrevocable fate for their protagonists, but in the fact that events have occurred exactly as anticipated. Maurya accepts her fate at the end of *Riders to the Sea* precisely because it is an expected dimension to life in a place outside of history governed by the condition that 'in the big world the old people do be leaving things after them for their sons and children, but in this place it is the young men do be leaving things behind for them that do be old' (CW III, 13). In *Deirdre of the Sorrows*, Conchubor can do nothing that will prevent the fulfilment of the prophecy of Deirdre's fate. Deirdre, upon meeting Naisi, willingly embraces the certainty that her anticipated death will come soon – and is better than aging – by asking 'isn't it a small thing is foretold about the ruin of ourselves, Naisi, when all men have age coming and great ruin in the end?' (CW IV, 211). Both plays take place in a mythic setting in which events occur but time never really passes into an unpredictable future. Synge's comedies are slightly different in that they represent situations in which central dramatic events pose the possibility of a future not anticipated in advance that in conventional terms offers an improvement upon present conditions. Yet in each of these plays the protagonists reject proper decorum or stability by choosing nomadic lives, recalcitrant to acceptable modern values. Whether it be the acquisition of property in *The Shadow of the Glen*, religious devotion and responsible work in *The Well of the Saints*, the institution of marriage in *The Tinker's Wedding*, integration into a community through a combination of all of these things in *The Playboy*, or social respectability in all of these works, Synge's primary characters consistently refuse to sacrifice something of themselves in order to attain those qualities which mark a sense of character conducive to citizenship by choosing an alternative modernity that defies propriety and comfort. On the one hand, the communities or situations represented in these plays are not especially vibrant, so they don't exactly serve as emblems of aggressive modernisation. On the other hand, the values and institutional arrangements necessary for the forms of progress celebrated by the nationalist movement do characterise the settings of each of these plays, and if there is a gap between such ideological positions and the social reality they mask it is because Synge found something wrong with both.

Temporality proves to be a vexed concern in Synge's writing. On the one hand, his tragedies, full of sorrow, loss and death, suggest that change for the better is impossible in the deterministic pre-modern world of the past they represent. On the other hand, his comedies suggest that heroism is the province only of those who reject convention by living according to those values which the ongoing process of modernisation is committed to eradicating. Synge's plays do not fetishise tradition in the way Yeats's writing does. As Leerssen argues, the hold of the past upon the present is a sinister matter in Synge's writing; it either indicates the return of tragedy or it maintains a repressive status quo that prevents the possibility of radical innovation.[20] Yet the corrupt and impoverished world of the present, most evident in his comedies, hardly presents an improvement upon the past. What *is* most apparent about Synge's writing is his opposition to a hallmark of modernity: the alienation which results from the division of labour, a condition which all of the different manifestations of recalcitrance evident in the plays respond to. Conventional forms of labour serve as the basis for oppression and exploitation in Synge's writing. The Douls in *The Well of the Saints* would rather live in indigent blindness than have to work for a living; as Martin Doul states at the end of the play:

> We're going surely, for if it's a right some of you have to be working and sweating the like of Timmy the smith ... I'm thinking it's a good right ourselves have to be sitting blind, hearing a soft wind turning round the little leaves of the spring and feeling the sun, and we not tormenting our souls with the sight of the grey days, and the holy men, and the dirty feet is trampling the world. (CW III, 149)

The abject position of Christy Mahon – according to his father, 'a lier on walls, a talker of folly', who does 'the devil a work' (CW IV, 121) – before *The Playboy* begins is partly due to his father's exploitation of his labour, and if employment in Michael James's pub is attractive, it is only because it's:

> a fine place to be my whole life talking out with swearing Christians in place of my old dogs and cat, and I stalking around, smoking my pipe and drinking my fill, and never a day's work but drawing a cork an odd time, or wiping a glass, or rinsing out a shiny tumbler for a decent man.   (CW IV, 95)

The source of Synge's wonder concerning the people he encounters on the Aran Islands does not arise out of the confirmation of a preconceived notion of the mythical past, but rather from the fact that within modernity they prove to be the exception:

> It is likely that much of the intelligence and charm of these people is due to the absence of any division of labour, and to the correspondingly wide development of each individual, whose varied knowledge and skill necessitates a considerable activity of the mind … His work changes with the seasons in a way that keeps him free from the dullness that comes to people who have always the same occupation. The danger of life on the sea gives him the alertness of a primitive hunter, and the long nights he spends fishing in his curagh bring him some of the emotions that are thought peculiar to men who have lived with the arts.   (CW II, 132–3)

The islander is complete in every respect because the variety of work that he performs does not cause him to become alienated from his own labour. Crucially, the most important consequence of that situation to a writer like Synge is that the aesthetic sensibility has not been severed from a practical orientation to daily life. Unlike in 'the big world' of late colonial modernity, in which the intellectual labour of cultural production was distinct from socially respectable forms of employment which drove development, in Synge's view art and work presented different facets of the same unified life on the Aran Islands. In poems like 'Adam's Curse', Yeats praised precisely the same unification of art and labour, but lamented the fact that it was a characteristic of the past that had disappeared as a possibility. To Synge, this whole way of life was not to be found in the past of tradition, but within the present in the alternative modernity he encountered on Inis Meáin.

The integration of art and life has long been the goal of a variety of aesthetic movements throughout the history of culture at large, and modernism was no exception. Synge's valorisation of this possibility presents another point in common. Yet the majority of Synge's plays do not attempt to re-create the integrated life he discovered on the Aran Islands. Instead, they deal more directly with situations in which that possibility is absent due to the conventions of a more familiar conception of modernity. Synge's innovation lay not so much in the transcendence of the material conditions which inspired his writing but in his construction of what Raymond Williams would have called the 'residual', in order to provide a substitute for the missing integration of art and work Synge wrote about in *The Aran Islands*. If the Aran storyteller presented a contemporary incarnation of the type of artist whose work is a valued part of the community's collective labour, the *filí*, the traditional Gaelic bardic poets who persisted up into the eighteenth century, presented for Synge representative examples of that figure from the past.[21] Colonisation and development – the twin forces of modernisation in Ireland – contributed to the death of the social structure which sustained the *filí*, however, and poets Synge had an interest in like Aodhagán Ó Rathaille and Eoghan Rua Ó Súilleabháin (a poet Pegeen compares Christy to in *The Playboy*) presented the last gasp of that tradition. Yet Synge's plays presented an exception; if the modern world had no use for the *filí*, it is no wonder that they inhabit the position of tramps, travellers, wanderers, beggars and fugitives in the 'exaggerated realist' world Synge represents on stage. Recalcitrance is closely tied to eloquence in Synge's drama, and is the reason that Synge's emphasis on those elements of the national character resistant to the values of the modern state do not ultimately participate in the reaffirmation of Irish stereotypes. Synge's plays neither reproduce the figure of the stage-Irishman nor do they attempt to resurrect the long-departed *filí*. Instead, they focus on a non-alienated form of cultural production once widespread in the past but now residual – yet persistent – within the margins of Irish society. Eloquence is the compensation for an impoverished life outside of social convention and is contrary to the logic of work, as Timmy the Smith frequently reminds Martin Doul in *The Well of the Saints*. It is the source of the Tramp's romantic appeal to Nora in *The Shadow of the Glen* and the basis for Pegeen's attraction to Christy in *The Playboy of the Western World*; it even causes Molly Byrne to momentarily consider as dissolute a figure as Martin Doul as an attractive man. Yet each of these character's 'fine bit of talk' (CW III, 57) is something more than a way to pass the time or a tool of seduction. It is both an immediate, spontaneous form of quotidian oral art as well as an act of work in its own right not made corrupt or detached from the social sphere by the division of labour. While this form of aesthetic work, comparable to the once prominent labours of the *filí*, is not necessarily regarded as a refined form of cultural production within the world in which Synge situates it in his plays, in its recalcitrant origins it provides a critique of a dominant conception of modernity in which the injustice that arises from the division of labour and the institution of private property continues.

Ultimately Synge's greatest link to modernism was thematic rather than formal even if the expressionist qualities of his dialogue had an impact upon Irish writing in general. The link Synge establishes between alternative forms of aesthetic labour not marked by alienation and those aspects of the national character recalcitrant towards modernisation ultimately proves to be the most important connection Synge had to the emergence of Irish modernism. It is what distinguishes him from other writers associated with the Revival and presents the primary value he brought in his role as vanishing mediator to the next period in literary history. Joyce would launch a thoroughgoing interrogation of the relationship between literary representation and the critique of the temporality of modernisation. Many different manifestations of recalcitrance would become the means in works like *Ulysses* and *Finnegans Wake* to explore the lengths to which stylistic eloquence could provide something different from the social conditions which were the basis of his writing. Beckett and O'Brien would take the critique of work even further, suggesting in works like *Murphy* and *At Swim-Two-Birds* that idleness could become a means to refuse the obligation of arduous labour. O'Brien's writing in particular juxtaposes the pleasures of idle talk as a form of cultural production identified with the recalcitrant past against a stifling form of postcolonial modernity defined by propriety and responsibility. While the modernists committed to the formulation of an innovative literary practice that responded to the immediate past of the Revival and the contemporary reality of post-colonial independence, Synge's crucial role in the genealogy of that project was obscured. As modernism itself recedes further from view into literary history, one should not neglect the impact Synge's formulation of the radical qualities of recalcitrance towards modernity made upon the formation of its values.

NOTES

1. 'Beckett and John Millington Synge', in James Knowlson and John Pilling, *Frescoes of the Skull* (New York: Grove Press, 1980), p. 260.
2. Joe Cleary, *Outrageous Fortune* (Dublin: Field Day, 2006), pp. 89–90.
3. Synge notes that *The Well of the Saints* takes place 'one or more centuries ago' (CW III, 69), and *The Playboy of the Western World* refers to the Boer War which broke out in 1899. The temporal setting of the other plays is unspecified.
4. W. B. Yeats, 'The Irish Dramatic Movement', in *Autobiographies* (New York: Scribner, 1999), p. 417.
5. W. B. Yeats, 'J. M. Synge and the Ireland of his Time', in *Essays & Introductions* (New York: Macmillan, 1961), pp. 323, 319.
6. W. J. Mc Cormack's biography seeks to counter a version of Synge mediated by 'the mythology broadcast through Yeats' autobiographies and poems'; see *Fool of the Family* (New York: New York University Press, 2000), p. 388.

7. Though Corkery's book on Synge is best known for its critique of 'Anglo-Irish' literature, Synge represents a 'portent' of the coming national culture who 'stands apart from all his fellow Ascendancy writers'. See *Synge and Anglo-Irish Literature* (Cork: Mercier Press, 1966), p. 27.

8. See Declan Kiberd, *Inventing Ireland* (London: Jonathan Cape, 1995), p. 175.

9. See Terry Eagleton, 'The Archaic Avant-Garde', *Heathcliff and the Great Hunger* (London: Verso, 1995), pp. 273–319.

10. Cleary, *Outrageous Fortune*, p. 91.

11. Leerssen, *Remembrance and Imagination* (Cork: Field Day / Cork University Press, 1997), pp. 222–3.

12. Jameson develops the concept of the vanishing mediator in the essay 'The Vanishing Mediator; or, Max Weber as Storyteller', in *The Ideologies of Theory: Essays 1971–1986: Volume 2* (Minneapolis, MN: University of Minnesota Press, 1988), pp. 3–34. W. J. Mc Cormack makes somewhat different use of the concept in a discussion of Synge; see *From Burke to Beckett* (Cork University Press, 1994), pp. 247–53.

13. Jameson, 'The Vanishing Mediator,' pp. 22–5.

14. See Homi Bhabha, *The Location of Culture* (London: Routledge, 1994), pp. 81–2.

15. See David Lloyd, 'Counterparts: *Dubliners*, Masculinity and Temperance Nationalism', in Derek Attridge and Marjorie Howe (eds.), *Semicolonial Joyce* (Cambridge University Press, 2000), pp. 131–3.

16. See Seamus Deane, *Strange Country* (Oxford University Press, 1997), pp. 49–99.

17. Ibid., p. 49.

18. Ibid., p. 54.

19. See Deane's discussion of 'the remarkable feat of ignoring the Famine and rerouting the claim for cultural exceptionalism through legend rather than through history', Ibid., pp. 50–51.

20. See Leerssen, *Remembrance and Imagination*.

21. On the debt Synge and Yeats had towards the *filí*, see Kiberd's essay, 'Synge, Yeats and Bardic Poetry', in *The Irish Writer and the World* (Cambridge University Press, 2005), pp. 70–90.

PART III

Synge on Stage

12

NICHOLAS GRENE

Synge in performance

Unpopular playwright

It began as it was to continue, with conflicts and controversies. Synge's first performed play, *The Shadow of the Glen*, precipitated a split in the Irish National Theatre Society that staged it. At the play's premiere on 8 October 1903 in the Molesworth Hall in Dublin, two of the company walked out in protest, along with the recently resigned Vice-President of the INTS, Maud Gonne. Arthur Griffith led a strong editorial campaign against it in his paper *United Irishman*. Even though Synge had based the one-act comedy on a folk-story told him in the Aran Islands of a man pretending to be dead to expose his wife's infidelity, the play was judged to be unIrish, and Synge was accused of decadent foreign influences. His play was 'a corrupt version' of the 'Widow of Ephesus' and 'no more Irish than the Decameron'. Irishwomen, Griffith claimed, 'are the most virtuous in the world'; however loveless an Irish rural marriage might be, the housewife, unlike Nora Burke in Synge's play, does not go off with a Tramp.[1] In spite of the enthusiastic promotion of Yeats, in part because of it, Synge's plays were suspect from the start.

And they were never to become popular in Ireland in his lifetime. Even *Riders to the Sea*, his one play later to attract respectful admiration from Dublin audiences, was regarded with dismay when first produced on 25 February 1904. 'The long exposure of the dead body before an audience may be realistic, but it certainly is not artistic,' complained the *Irish Times*. 'There are some things that are lifelike, and yet are quite unfit for presentation on the stage, and we think that "Riders to the Sea" is one of them.'[2] *Shadow* was not true to life; *Riders* was too true to life to be staged. The originality of Synge's work, its failure to conform to theatrical or political expectations, left audiences doubtful or resistant. When *The Well of the Saints*, Synge's first three-act play, opened at the Abbey Theatre on 4 February 1905, it was to another hostile reaction. W. G. Fay, the play's director, who also played the lead role of Martin Doul, had been worried by the fact that 'every character in the play from the Saint to Timmy the Smith was bad-tempered' and that 'all this bad temper would inevitably infect the audience and make them bad-tempered too'.[3] Certainly the *Freeman's Journal* declared that Synge was not 'in sympathetic touch with the people from whom he purports to draw his characters' and the *Evening Herald* thought the characters were all repulsive and therefore caricatures of Irish people.[4] A complimentary letter to the *Irish Times* from that loose cannon of the Irish literary scene, George Moore, cannot altogether have helped. 'Mr Synge has discovered great literature in barbarous idiom as gold is discovered in quartz.'[5] This aestheticist eulogy, with its reference to the language of Irish peasants as a 'barbarous idiom', would have only confirmed suspicions of Synge as a European decadent misrepresenting the people.

All this provided the context for the premiere of *The Playboy of the Western World* on 26 January 1907, the most famous single event in the history of Irish theatre. That night has been subjected to repeated analysis focused on the performance, the audience, and the social and political motives for the violent response to the play with the 'riots' that followed in the week of its run.[6] Reviewers of virtually any latter-day theatrical revival feel obliged to refer back to its stormy opening. The play has come to be defined by, inseparable from, the reaction against it. What were the issues and what was the immediate background?

Synge had spent two and a half years working on the play since he first conceived the idea in 1904. By 1907 he was (with Yeats and Lady Gregory) one of the three Directors of the Abbey Theatre, and a new full-length play by him was therefore a major event. Yeats and Gregory, having read the text, were concerned that the amount of profanity in it would cause offence and were disposed to cut the number of oaths. But neither of them was directly involved in the production, and Synge himself was little inclined to bowdlerise his own script. A measure of the anxiety about the effect of the play and the likelihood of adverse advance publicity was the secrecy in which rehearsals were conducted.

The company was anxious, and it turned out with good reason. But there was no planned opposition to the play on its opening night. The audience, including many of Dublin's best-known social and literary figures, were well disposed. *Riders*, staged as curtain-raiser to the new play, was watched in respectful silence. Right through the run of *The Playboy*, indeed, even at the height of the disturbances, *Riders* was received with enthusiasm, as though to make clear that there was no general prejudice against Synge's work. Even the first act of *The Playboy* itself seemed to do well and was applauded, so that Gregory sent off a telegram to Yeats, who was away lecturing in Scotland, to announce the play's success. A very premature announcement it turned out to be. For in the second act, the audience began to grow hostile from the appearance of Old Mahon, the supposedly dead father, as one witness remembered: 'That scene was too representational. There stood a man with horribly-bloodied bandage upon his head, making a figure that took the whole thing out of the atmosphere of high comedy.'[7] And when, in Act III, Christy actually attacked his father and re-entered, apparently having succeeded in killing him, it was more than the spectators could bear. They erupted into loud protests so that the rest of the play could hardly be heard.

It has often been pointed out that the audience in the theatre were exactly repeating the reactions of the characters on the stage. As the Mayo villagers turned from admiration for the young man who claimed to have killed his father to violent revulsion against him, so the Abbey crowd veered round from approving applause to riotous revolt. They too may have learned the truth of Pegeen's dictum: 'there's a great gap between a gallous story and a dirty deed' (CW IV, 169). After all, viewing the play for the first time, the audience would not have known that Christy's second attempt on his father's life had been as unsuccessful as his first. They had come to see a 'comedy in three acts'; they had laughed happily at what was evidently a comic situation in Act I, but the change into a totally different theatrical mode in the course of the remainder of the play was deeply unsettling. The hostile response to *The Playboy* can be compared to the outrage provoked by Luigi Pirandello's *Six Characters in Search of an Author* twelve years later in Rome. In both cases, the provocation came from the challenge to expected dramaturgical norms. These were plays such as no audience had ever seen before, and their estranged bewilderment vented itself in angry reaction.

The first-night audience at *The Playboy* may have been genuinely disturbed by the strange originality of the play. But thereafter politics unquestionably came into operation. At the second performance, and even more at the third, there were people who came deliberately to voice their disapproval – and a contrary claque of students from Trinity College Dublin commissioned by Lady Gregory to oppose the objectors. At one stage the political polarities in the auditorium were marked by the loyalist 'God Save the King' sung by one group in the expensive stalls seats, the nationalist 'God Save Ireland' chanted from the cheaper pit.[8] Insult was added to injury, from the nationalist point of view, when the management summoned in police to arrest the protestors. It was lamentable that the Abbey, claiming to be Ireland's national theatre, should persist in staging a play offensive to national feeling. It was outrageous that they should use a colonial police force to hale those justifiably offended before what were regarded as British courts of law. Joseph Holloway, the architect of the Abbey Theatre, inveterate playgoer and theatrical diarist, spoke for many when he declared: 'Synge is the evil genius of the Abbey and Yeats his able lieutenant.'[9]

There were three main sources of objection to the play: its profanity, its obscenity and its misrepresentation of the Irish people. Synge's fellow-directors had been right to worry about the number of times the name of God was taken in vain in the text; in later performances of the play the oaths were notably thinned down. This was after all still seven years before Eliza Doolittle's 'Not bloody likely!' in Bernard Shaw's *Pygmalion* was to cause a stir on London's West End stage. As for the play's obscenity, the infamous word 'shift' used by Christy Mahon in Act III, an old-fashioned word for a woman's chemise regarded as coarse by middle-class Dubliners, seems to have triggered the riot, but it was symptomatic of a sexual indelicacy detected throughout.[10] Again the Directors toned down the coarseness of the language and cut the offending line about the 'shift'. But there was nothing that could be done about the basic storyline of the play, and it was to this above all that the objectors objected. The country people of the West of Ireland, hallowed heartland of the nationalist imaginary, were represented hero-worshipping a man who claimed to have killed his father; the parricide won the admiration of the men, the devotion of the women, for his deed. This was a travesty of the truth, a misrepresentation of Irish life worse than any stage Irishman the British had ever conceived.

The controversy over *The Playboy* was a row over the real. Synge affirmed the genuineness of his language in his programme note to the original production, subsequently in the Preface to the published text: 'In writing *The Playboy of the Western World*, as in my other plays, I have used one or two words only, that I have not heard among the country people of Ireland, or spoken in my own nursery before I could read the newspapers' (CW IV, 53). A devout nationalist like Joseph Holloway vehemently denied this claim: 'I maintain that his play of *The Playboy* is not a truthful or just picture of the Irish peasants, but simply the outpouring of a morbid, unhealthy mind ever seeking on the dunghill of life for the nastiness that lies concealed there.'[11] What is disputed here is not verisimilitude but authenticity. Both Synge and his opponents claimed the authority of the real to authenticate or de-authenticate the truth of the drama. For later generations arguments about whether Mayo people were likely to hero-worship a parricide, or about the literal accuracy of Synge's peasant dialect might come to seem literal-minded and irrelevant to an appreciation of the play. But for a national drama at a time of anti-colonial self-definition this need for authenticity was of the essence.

National canon: staging styles

By the time of his death in 1909, Synge's plays, unpopular as they had been with their initial Dublin audiences, were established as part of the standard repertory of the Abbey. *Shadow* and *Riders* were both regularly used as curtain-raisers or billed with other one-act plays. The performance of Sara Allgood as Maurya in *Riders* was to become legendary in Irish theatre. She had already taken on the role in 1906 when she was 27, and she was to go on playing it into the 1920s. Something of her power in the part can be seen in the otherwise indifferent film of the play made by Brian Desmond Hurst in 1935. *Well* was one of the works showcased by the Abbey on their 1911 tour of the US, where it does not seem to have attracted anything of the hostility that *The Playboy* did. There was poignancy in the posthumous premiere of the unfinished *Deirdre of the Sorrows*, staged in January 1910, with Molly Allgood, Synge's fiancée, for whom the play was written, in the title role, though it was seldom revived afterwards.

The most remarkable change in Synge's reputation in Ireland after 1909 came with his rehabilitation in the nationalist community and an altered reception of *The Playboy*. Patrick Pearse at the time of the *Playboy* riots had denounced the play as a 'brutal glorification of violence, and grossness, and the flesh'. But by 1913 he had recanted:

> When a man like Synge, in whose sad heart there glowed a true love of Ireland, one of the two or three men who have in our time made Ireland considerable in the eyes of the world, uses strange symbols which we do not understand, we cry out that he has blasphemed and we proceed to crucify him.[12]

Synge in death is on his way to becoming a Christ / Pearse figure. What probably helped audiences to understand Synge's 'strange symbols', to facilitate the transformation of *The Playboy* from execrated travesty of Irish life to national classic, was a change in playing style. When the play was revived after Synge's death, the realism that had been so much a part of the original production was adjusted.

> Originally that excellent actor W. G. Fay was in the part of the Playboy. He made the role a little sardonic, and this … took from the extravagance of the comedy. Afterwards the Playboy's father was made a less bloody object, and the part of the Playboy in the hands of another actor was given more charm and gaiety, and there was no trouble with the audience.[13]

The actor in question who succeeded W. G. Fay in the part was Fred O'Donovan, who was to go on to a career in the cinema, and a photograph of him in the part in 1910 makes it clear the sort of conventional juvenile lead the role became. In later productions *The Playboy* was played fast as a comedy, whereas 'when it was given for the first time it was played seriously, almost sombrely'.[14] In other words, the play was returned to the stock forms of comedy that Synge had so daringly subverted in his original text.

The Playboy soon became one of the Abbey's most popular plays – and has remained so. With a repertory company, which depended on short runs of well-known pieces for one or two weeks, Synge's masterpiece was revived more or less annually. The parts of Christy and Pegeen were the acknowledged property of the leading man and woman of the company, however little suited they might be. So, for instance, in the 1920s, Sara Allgood who had created the part of Widow Quin, played Pegeen even though she was in her 40s and quite stout. One actor, Brid Lynch, remained in possession of Pegeen from 1942 to 1953, while Cyril Cusack played Christy for almost twenty years, culminating in a performance with his own company in Paris in 1955 at the First International Theatre Festival.[15] Siobhán McKenna, the leading Irish woman actor of her generation, was apparently a notable Pegeen Mike in her time. It is unfortunate that the only record of McKenna's playing of the part is the 1962 film (also directed by Desmond Hurst) in which she was cast opposite the conventionally handsome English actor Gary Raymond. The film as a whole is an exercise in the Irish picturesque, making much use of the wild west of Ireland scenic locations. McKenna as Pegeen, perfectly coiffed and dressed in a beautiful red flannel dress, is the winsome Irish colleen throughout.

Recurrent efforts have been made over the last thirty years in Ireland to rescue the play from its stereotypical presentation as 'Irish classic'. A metatheatrical staging at the Abbey in 1971, the centenary of Synge's birth, directed by Colin George and designed by Brian Collins, used cinematic images, beginning with a background of projected newspaper clippings relating to the *Playboy* riots, as a framing device to foreground the play's history.[16] However, within the naturalistic dramaturgy called for by the play's text it has proved difficult to achieve significant stylistic variation. One radical alternative was the production by Blue Raincoat in the Peacock, the Abbey's studio space, in 2001. Blue Raincoat, based in Sligo, led by Niall Henry, is relatively unusual among Irish theatre companies in being movement-based. Henry directed a very untraditional, balletic *Playboy*, with no representational set and Mikel Murfi as an acrobatic Christy appearing first mysteriously through a previously unopened trap high in a sidewall, somersaulting into the action as though newly born into this new world of the Mayo pub. The publican Michael James, the barflies Jimmy and Philly, even the cowardly Shawn Keogh, normally played as broadly comic figures, were sombrely costumed in suits to emphasise their conformism by contrast to the outsider Christy. The contest for Christy between a very sexy Widow Quin (Cathy Belton) and a much older Pegeen (Olwen Fouéré) was played as a stylised movement sequence, as was the final attempted 'lynching' of Christy.

The most significant challenge to what had become the orthodoxy of Abbey productions of the play came with the Druid Theatre staging of

1982. Druid was set up in 1975 in Galway by the director Garry Hynes with actors Marie Mullen and Mick Lally, and as an innovative provincial company represented in itself an alternative to the dominance of Dublin and the Abbey as national theatre. Hynes's production of *The Playboy*, staged originally in Druid's tiny theatre in Galway, was neo-realist in style. The set design was a convincingly rough country pub of the period, with a picture of the Sacred Heart prominently displayed in ironic juxtaposition to an Edwardian cigarette advertisement. Acting and costuming were painstakingly naturalistic. After a prolonged silence in which Brid Brennan as Pegeen busied herself round the empty pub, she sat to write the letter ordering her trousseau with the slow deliberateness of the near-illiterate, spelling out each word, stopping to scratch a fleabite as if to validate the Widow Quin's description of her 'itching and scratching, and she with a stale stink of poteen on her from selling in the shop' (CW IV, 127). Maeliosa Stafford, playing Christy, was equally unprepossessing at first entrance, grimy and fearful, gnawing his turnip by the fire. The violence of the play was unrestrained, with the tall and commanding figure of Mick Lally a terrifying Old Mahon. This was a version of the play that rediscovered much of what must have been its original shock value, the grotesque mixture of realism and fantastic comedy. The play toured very widely in Ireland, including a visit to Inis Meáin in the Aran Islands where Synge heard the source story, was acclaimed at the Edinburgh Festival and hailed by the critics when it played for four weeks in the Donmar Warehouse, London in 1985.[17] Broadcast on British Television by Channel Four in 1986, it became the most influential production of modern times.[18]

For much of the twentieth century Synge was made to appear a one-play playwright, the history of Synge staging in Ireland being a series of more or less conventional productions of that well-loved classic comedy *The Playboy*. As curtain-raisers and composite theatrical programmes became less common, the one-act plays largely became the property of amateur companies, the radio (where they were often played) and occasionally television. *The Well of the Saints* also, though a three-act play, was relatively rarely revived, in part because too short on its own to fill a full night show. An Abbey production directed by Hugh Hunt in 1969, which transferred to the Old Vic in 1970, was preceded by George Fitzmaurice's one-act *The Dandy Dolls*. Tom Murphy's experimental staging at the Abbey in 1979 was combined with the playwright's own tribute to Synge, 'Epitaph under Ether'. Patrick Mason's 1994 revival was quite exceptional in staging *The Well of the Saints* on its own. With its innovative breach of fourth-wall naturalistic conventions – pious processions of villagers followed the Saint through the auditorium – and its blend of timeless archetype and contemporary edge, this was a landmark production, under-appreciated in Ireland but lavishly praised at the

Edinburgh Festival. It is unusual, however, in Irish theatre history as a stand-alone staging of a Synge play that is not *The Playboy*.

On the whole, it has taken special occasions to give the opportunity for more of Synge's work to be seriously produced. The centenary of Synge's birth in 1971 was one such. Apart from the metatheatrical *Playboy*, the Abbey mounted its first ever production of *The Tinker's Wedding*, in Synge's lifetime judged 'too immoral for Dublin' (CL I, 148), in a double bill with *Riders*, as well as a production of *Deirdre* in the Peacock. A 'Synge season' on RTÉ in 1999 included radio versions not only of all the previously staged works but the early prentice piece, *When the Moon Has Set*. However, the first, and so far only, opportunity to see the entire Synge canon staged at once came in 2005–6 with DruidSynge.

Druid Theatre had a long-standing engagement with Synge; the 1982 *Playboy*, discussed earlier, was one of their many re-stagings of the play. Plans for the marathon production of all six plays as a single event were developed over years. *The Playboy*, *Well* and *Tinker's Wedding* were all mounted by Druid in 2004; and in 2005 these plays (re-directed) were joined by productions of *Riders*, *Shadow* and *Deirdre* to make up the performance branded as DruidSynge. It was to be seen either in a series of evening two-play programmes, or on a number of occasions in an all-day production lasting eight and a half hours. The production of the plays together in this way, bound by Francis O'Connor's single set of dirty green walls and turf-covered dirt floor representing both interiors and exteriors, allowed audiences to experience the imaginative unity of Synge's theatre. In its all-day version, it began with *Riders* and ended with *Deirdre*. Hynes substituted for the keeners at the conclusion of *Riders* a chorus of black-clad women who beat the walls in choreographed mourning and brought them back to lament the deaths of Deirdre and the sons of Usna. The white boards bought by Maurya to bury her drowned son Michael in *Riders* remained on stage throughout the six plays to represent the omnipresence of death in Synge's vision. Yet they served also to remind spectators of the comic games the playwright could play with the theme in the mock death of Dan Burke in *Shadow*, the double resurrection of Old Mahon in *The Playboy*. And if the single set composed the production in an overall unity, Kathy Strachan's eclectic costuming released the plays from a conventional period idiom. The travellers of *Tinker's Wedding* in modern punk gear clashed with a Priest in full traditional black soutane. The timeless moral fable of *Well* was placed historically by 1960s costuming. What DruidSynge enabled audiences to see across the six plays was Synge's tragic and comic variations on certain essential human themes: life against death, Christianity against paganism, the struggle of the individual to express himself or herself within a collective community.

DruidSynge was a huge theatrical success, not least because of the outstanding performance of three actors, including the virtuoso Marie Mullen, each of them in five different roles. The show won awards and acclaim in Ireland and then at the Edinburgh Festival in 2005, at the Tyrone Guthrie Theatre in Minneapolis and the Lincoln Center in New York in 2006. It has done a great deal to raise again the international profile of Synge's work, to rescue some of the less well-known plays from obscurity, and to reveal new aspects to his drama. But as a single monolithic event it has not necessarily provided a way forward for future Irish productions of Synge. The problem of how to re-invigorate the plays, to recover them from the condition of revered but neglected national canon, has to be left again for future directors and producers.

International productions, translations, adaptations

Though Synge was so unpopular in Ireland in his own lifetime, and *The Playboy* produced such an explosive reaction at the time of its first production, his work in general, and that play in particular, were very successful outside the country from the earliest times. Though the Directors took care not to stage *The Playboy* in cities with large Irish immigrant populations in Britain, such as Liverpool or Birmingham, it was well received in Oxford, Cambridge and London on the Abbey tour of 1907, the year of its premiere. No doubt in part because of the controversy, it was specifically requested as part of the Abbey's repertoire by Liebler's, the theatrical agents arranging the 1911–12 North American tour, and in fact outside New York and Philadelphia, the contentious cities where the Irish-American opposition was active, it met with a warm welcome. It continued to be regularly included in tours abroad by the Abbey for the rest of the century. Throughout the English-speaking world it remains a frequently revived part of the theatrical canon. Though not produced recently in Australia, between 1961 and 1985 there were at least six stagings in Western Australia, Queensland, Melbourne and Sydney.[19] It has been popular in Canada, with a 1996 production at the Shaw Festival in Niagara-on-the-Lake (Canada's second biggest theatre) revived in 1997. Ironically, where originally *The Playboy* was regarded as too dangerous to stage in cities with large Irish diasporic communities, it is now just such communities that have produced specialist theatres in which it is a natural part of the repertoire. So, for instance, it was an obvious choice for the New York Irish Repertory Company for a two-month summer run in 2002, and for the opening production by the newly formed New Gate Celtic Theatre Company of Cincinnati in 2003. In such productions the exoticism of the Irish peasant setting has proved part of the marketable theatrical attraction.

And there has been a similar attitude towards the play's picturesqueness in British stagings of the play. The 1975 production by the British National Theatre in London, directed by Bill Bryden, was a major event, if only because the play had always been so closely identified with Ireland's national theatre, and it proved highly successful, being repeatedly revived in repertory over the next two seasons. It helped to establish the reputation of Stephen Rea, who played Christy, opposite the imposingly tall English actor Susan Fleetwood. More than one reviewer was aware of the relevance of the play's concern with the heroisation of violence at one of the worst periods of the Troubles in Northern Ireland and IRA bombing in Britain. Relevant but not relevant:

> the casual attitude to life and death, the glorification of the criminal because he has got away with his crime – we see these things reported every day in the Press, and they are not for laughter. Well, *The Playboy* is for laughter anyway, for laughter and pathos and poetry and sympathy, and I doubt if there is a happier evening to be had in the London theatre anywhere at this moment.[20]

The most recent revival of the play at the National, directed by Fiona Buffini in 2001, was harder edged, with Derbhle Crotty playing a Pegeen Mike moving from listless depression to a full-throated despair at the end, Patrick O'Kane a fierce Christy, and the eruption of violence in the crowd scenes of the final act genuinely frightening in the small Cottesloe Theatre. But the set and costuming were close to standard Irish kitsch, and as one reviewer put it: 'The play's intense Irishness teeters on the brink of Oirishness.'[21] The play that so challenged stereotypical representations of Irish life in its own time seems all too frequently now to be confined by received ideas of its Irishness.

Synge achieved European recognition surprisingly early with translations into Czech and German even within his own short lifetime. A version of *Well* was performed at the Deutsches Theatre in Berlin in 1906.[22] The record of Synge's work on the Czech stage is especially interesting because it was sustained over such a long period. Karel Mušek, Synge's first Czech translator, actually visited Dublin in 1906 and met Synge, who was clearly intrigued by the similarities between the Bohemian National Theatre in Prague and their own Abbey, though struck by the vastly greater resources available to their European counterparts (CL I, 181). Mušek eventually translated *The Playboy* as *Hrdina Západu* and it was produced for the first time in Prague in 1916. Since then there have been no fewer than sixteen other Czech stagings of the play in three different translations.[23]

Martin Hilský, the play's most recent translator, comments on the difficulties and the opportunities presented by the play. Mušek had used a Moravian dialect of Czech:

Mušek's strategy was to give a flavour of the peasant language to his translation and to dramatize the difference between the standard Czech and the peasant dialect. It also served an important cultural purpose: it integrated the language of *The Playboy* into the tradition of the Czech rural drama at the turn of the century.[24]

By the end of the twentieth century, however, that had become exactly the drawback of any such strategy: 'Any Czech or Moravian dialect would invite a contemporary spectator or reader to perceive *The Playboy* as a late-nineteenth-century regional play or romantic exercise in local colour.'[25] Hilský's solution was to use a standard form of the language but to seek to match the texture of Synge's style, its characteristic rhythmic units and turns of phrase, where it was often possible to find Czech equivalents to fit the original. The 1997 production of Hilský's translation at the National Theatre in Prague adopted a theatrical idiom to correspond to this linguistic style. While the costuming and acting were suggestive of the peasant setting, the *mise-en-scène* was non-representational and there was no attempt made to reproduce the specificities of the Irish original as such. What such European versions of *The Playboy* have definitively demonstrated is that this is not a play that is dependent on its original context for success, and that its theatrical power can transfer and translate to other languages, other dramatic idioms. Indeed, what has become something of a liability within the English-speaking world, the inheritance of its Irishness, the history of the riots it first provoked, clichéd styles of representation, may be transcended by vital and imaginative re-creations in theatres less saturated with such traditions.

From early on, Synge's work, particularly *Riders*, provided the model for other plays and adaptations, including D. H. Lawrence's one-act mining tragedy *The Widowing of Mrs Holroyd* (1914) and Bertolt Brecht's 1937 Spanish Civil War based play *Señora Carrar's Rifles*. Vaughan Williams in 1927 created his opera by setting virtually the entire play text of *Riders* to music. Mustafa Matura's 1984 Trinidadian transplantation of *The Playboy*, *The Playboy of the West Indies*, is discussed elsewhere in this volume. Two recent stagings of the play are suggestive both of the opportunities and the challenges of translating/adapting Synge. The 2006 Chinese production of *The Playboy*, staged by Irish theatre company Pan Pan, re-located the play to a hairdressing salon/brothel on the outskirts of Beijing with Christy a refugee from the provinces. It produced something of a scandal for the shortness of the miniskirts worn by the girls when premiered in Beijing, but was very well received when it transferred for a week's run to Dublin. The balletic style of the performance and the extraordinary skills of the actors gave the production a new non-Western theatrical life. On the other hand, the projected surtitles giving the Mandarin text translated back into English seemed like an uneasy compromise between Synge's original Hiberno-English dialect and a contemporary Chinese urban argot. The 2007 staging of the play by the Abbey, in a specially commissioned adaptation by Roddy Doyle and Bisi Adigun, was also problematic. Set in contemporary Dublin, Christy was re-cast as a Nigerian asylum-seeker on the run. The collaborating writers sought not only to connect the play to modern multi-ethnic Ireland with its new influx of immigrants, but to find in the criminal celebrity culture of Dublin's urban gangland a correlative for Synge's Mayo with its hero-worship of the parricide. It was an inventive idea, making effective comic capital out of the parodic distance between Synge's rural original and its latter-day metropolitan counterpart. However, the language again proved a problem with a mismatch between a deliberately unpoetic Dublinese for most of the characters and a self-consciously different Nigerian English for Christy and his father. The equivalents between original and adaptation made for some good gags – the girls and Christy's father watching on mobile phones the recorded gang fight which substituted for the play's offstage mule-race – but they did not add up to a coherent reinterpretation of *The Playboy*. Synge's drama continues to have a theatrical life well into the twenty-first century, to inspire directors and playwrights inside and outside Ireland to attempt to re-create the energies and significance of his work in new productions, translations and adaptations. However, it is the very specificities of his drama, in language, setting and dramaturgical idiom, which make such attempts at once problematic and imaginatively productive.

NOTES

1. Quotations from *United Irishman*, 17 October and 24 October 1903, cited in Antoinette Quinn, 'Staging the Irish Peasant Woman: Maud Gonne versus Synge', in Nicholas Grene (ed.), *Interpreting Synge: Essays from the Synge Summer School 1991–2000* (Dublin: Lilliput Press, 2000), pp. 128–9. For the wider political context for the controversy, see P. J. Mathews, *Revival: The Abbey Theatre, Sinn Féin, the Gaelic League and the Co-operative Movement* (Cork: Field Day / Cork University Press, 2003), pp. 137–45.
2. *Irish Times*, 26 February 1904.
3. Quoted in David H. Greene and Edward M. Stephens, *J. M. Synge, 1871–1909* (New York: Collier Books, 1961), p. 181.
4. Ibid., p. 185.
5. *Irish Times*, 13 February 1905.
6. James Kilroy, *The 'Playboy' Riots* (Dublin: Dolmen, 1971) provided a full documentary narrative. See also, Nicholas Grene, *The Politics of Irish Drama: Plays in Context from Boucicault to Friel* (Cambridge University Press, 1999), pp. 77–109; Christopher Morash, *A History of Irish Theatre 1601–2000* (Cambridge University Press, 2002), pp. 130–38; Ben Levitas, *The Theatre of Nation: Irish*

Drama and Cultural Nationalism 1890–1916 (Oxford: Clarendon Press, 2002), pp. 115–36; Paige Reynolds, *Modernism, Drama, and the Audience for Irish Spectacle* (Cambridge University Press, 2007), pp. 38–75.

7. Padraic Colum, quoted in Nicholas Grene, *Synge: a Critical Study of the Plays* (London: Macmillan, 1975), p. 144.

8. See Morash, *A History of Irish Theatre*, p. 135.

9. Robert Hogan and Michael J. O'Neill (eds.), *Joseph Holloway's Abbey Theatre* (Carbondale, IL: Southern Illinois University Press, 1967), p. 81.

10. For a fuller analysis, see Grene, *The Politics of Irish Drama*, pp. 80–84.

11. Hogan and O'Neill, *Joseph Holloway's Abbey Theatre*, p. 81.

12. Quoted in Declan Kiberd, *Synge and the Irish Language* (London: Macmillan, 1979), pp. 253, 259.

13. Padraic Colum, cited in Grene, *Synge: a Critical Study of the Plays*, p. 145.

14. Ibid., citing Maire Nic Shiublaigh, one of the early Abbey Theatre company.

15. Cyril Cusack, 'A Player's Reflection on *Playboy*', in Thomas R. Whitaker (ed.), *Twentieth Century Interpretations of* The Playboy of the Western World (Englewood Cliffs, NJ: Prentice-Hall, 1969), pp. 49–55.

16. See Seamus Kelly, ' "The Playboy" at the Abbey', *Irish Times*, 20 April 1971.

17. See Jerome Hynes (ed.), *Druid: the First Ten Years* (Galway: Druid Performing Arts and Galway Arts Festival, 1985).

18. For a detailed account of its impact see Nicholas Grene, 'Two London Playboys: Before and After Druid', in Adrian Frazier (ed.), *Playboys of the Western World: Production Histories* (Dublin: Carysfort Press, 2004), pp. 74–86.

19. For this information I am grateful to Julie-Ann Tapper of Sydney University.

20. B. A. Young, 'The Playboy of the Western World', *Financial Times*, 30 October 1975.

21. Alastair Macaulay, ' "Playboy" has the charm of the Oirish', *Financial Times*, 22 February 2001.

22. Greene and Stephens, *J. M. Synge 1871–1909*, p. 190.

23. I am grateful to Professor Ondrej Pilny of Charles University, Prague, for this information.

24. Martin Hilský, 'Re-imagining Synge's Language: the Czech Experience', in Grene, *Interpreting Synge*, p. 151.

25. Ibid., p. 154.

13

BRENDA MURPHY

J. M. Synge in America

Americans were well prepared for the first US tour of the Abbey Players in 1911 by those intrepid advance men, William Butler Yeats and Lady Augusta Gregory. In August, before the departure of the Players for their 16 October opening in Boston, both of the theatre's directors were giving publicity interviews to American reporters, which were carefully couched to address anticipated objections to two of the plays in the repertory, G. B. Shaw's *The Shewing-up of Blanco Posnet* and J. M. Synge's *The Playboy of the Western World*. In an interview for a South Carolina newspaper, Yeats told the story of the 1907 *Playboy* riots. Expressing outrage that 'violence' had been used against the 'chief work of the chief dramatist of Ireland', Yeats explained that although some 'dislike' had been expected for 'a fantasy so strange and full of mischief', violence that was 'intended to prevent others from hearing and judging for themselves' could only have been dealt with by calling in the police. Yeats exulted that the Abbey Players had won their fight before the week was out, and not only did the curtain fall to 'thunders of applause' at Dublin performances, but *The Playboy* continued to be presented in Dublin to 'enthusiastic and crowded audiences – some of the rioters sitting there and applauding', and in England and on the continent, 'the play had won not only for Synge but for the Ireland that produced him, admiration and respect'.[1]

Yeats went to the USA with the troupe, and stayed about a month, continuing to reiterate the themes that those who disturbed *The Playboy*'s performances were unfairly keeping others from judging for themselves, and that subsequent performances had confirmed Synge's place as Ireland's major dramatist and *The Playboy* as his masterpiece. He characterised Synge as a genius capable of wild imaginative flights of fantasy while he 'brought the real mind of Ireland on to the stage', emphasizing Synge's experience of living among the peasants he wrote about and learning their speech directly from their mouths. Anticipating the charge that Synge portrayed the peasants of Ireland in a false light, which indeed did come, Yeats compared him to Cervantes and Shakespeare, saying that these objections were 'as though contemporary Spain had risen up against Cervantes and said: How dare you represent the gentlemen of Spain by that crack-brained knight!'[2]

Lady Gregory stayed with the troupe throughout the tour, enlisting the support of the elite in the major cities where the Players appeared: the Boston brahmins, the Philadelphia blue bloods, and celebrities such as John Dewey and former president Theodore Roosevelt in New York. Lady Gregory maintained a public demeanour of calm good humour throughout the tour, attributing the disturbances, protests and riots the troupe faced to 'misunderstandings, and to something that might be called "race sensitiveness"'.[3] This effort was aided by sympathetic newspapers like the *New York Times*, which printed an editorial supporting the Players and a review of the American edition of *The Playboy*, which said it was 'based on an idea and understanding of life to test the powers of a genius in the drama; and in this comedy Synge unquestionably is a genius'.[4]

The Abbey Players were not the only ones preparing audiences, however. As Paula Kane has noted, the American protests 'were orchestrated in advance by Irish-American societies that targeted local theatre owners and city censorship agencies', and some of the groups seem to have been incited directly by agitators in Ireland.[5] On 9 October, before the American premiere in Boston on 16 October, and well before the New York opening on 23 November, the *New York Times* reported that a meeting of the United Irish-American societies in New York passed resolutions condemning the play 'by G. N. Synge, "The Plowboy of the Western World"', stating that the play 'is immoral and not true to Irish character, and that it makes a hero of a parasite'. It was said at the meeting that 'an effort would be made to prevent the production of this play in New York'.[6] Some of the protesters at the New York opening identified themselves as members of the Philo Celtic Club, and the first man to rise at the raucous Philadelphia opening was identified as Joseph McLaughlin, National Vice-President of the Ancient Order of Hibernians, who called out, 'I protest against this play. It is a shame! Why don't you present Irish character as it really is?'[7]

The preparations from both sides established that protests, and perhaps riots, against Synge's play were to be expected. Nowhere did the objectors succeed in suppressing the play, and the violence of the response varied from city to city. In Boston, where Lady Gregory had garnered support both from the social and cultural elite and from the powerful Irish-American political machine run by John Francis ('Honey Fitz') Fitzgerald, the grandfather of President John F. Kennedy, the protest was minimal. The premiere was attended by Boston cultural leader Isabella Stewart Gardner, the mayor's daughter Rose Fitzgerald, and a bloc of Harvard students to whom Lady Gregory had distributed tickets. While the protesters made a good deal of noise, the play went on without major incident in Boston. Providence and New Haven were more troublesome, with riots erupting in New Haven, where the police chief had ordered cuts in *The Playboy*, not realising that the play he had seen was Shaw's *Blanco Posnet*.[8]

The *New York Times* suggested that these disturbances were 'as prayer meetings' compared to the reception *The Playboy* got at its 23 November opening in New York. As soon as the curtain rose, the audience was prepared with eggs and various vegetables, as well as foul-smelling asafoetida capsules. When Fred O'Donovan, playing Christy, announced for the first time that he had killed his father, cries of shame and showers of vegetables erupted from the audience. The report of the *New York Times* had a decidedly ethnic bent, emphasising that the first missile that came through the air was a potato, and that a potato that had struck Eithne MaGee (Pegeen) on the head rolled into the wings and was picked up by Lady Gregory, who said she would 'keep it as a token of her visit to this country'.[9]

Two things that stand out in the *Times* report are the violence of the ejections from the theatre and the putative Irishness of the whole proceeding. Twenty policemen and all of the detectives on hand at the West Thirtieth Street Police Station came on a run at news of the disturbance but, before they arrived, audience members were being summarily ejected by employees of the theatre. According to the *Times*, they grabbed everyone they could and hustled them towards the doors, and the scene that followed was like the slapstick of a Keystone Cops comedy:

> Everyone that got there was thrown out and followed until he became a rolling ball that thumped and thumped down the stairs, [and when they reached the bottom] a big man caught them and threw them out without bothering to open the swinging doors first. They crashed through with enough momentum to carry them out in the middle of the street.

When the police arrived, 'no questions were asked, but they reached for every man who was on his feet and dragged him to the stairs, where willing hands helped him to the street'.[10]

In an editorial on 29 November, the *Times* deplored the fact that 'a few quarrelsome Irish patriots, who claim American citizenship, though obviously they do not value it, declare that the posture of events, the characterization, and some of the text of "The Playboy" misrepresents Ireland, which they hold to be a land devoid of crime and violence, free from evil passions, and full of brotherly love and virtue'. These patriots 'invade the theatre, pelt the actors with missiles, and try to howl down the performance. Whereupon Irish-American policemen arrest them, and arraign them before an Irish-American magistrate while the performance proceeds.' The editorial suggested that 'the delightful Hibernianism of it all is obvious, but the incident may not be dismissed as a joke', concluding, 'Synge's "Playboy" may or may not misrepresent the character of the Western Irish peasantry, but it is quite clear that the howlers and egg-throwers have grossly misrepresented the great body of law-abiding American citizens of Irish birth and descent.'[11]

In preparing for the opening in Philadelphia on 15 January, the Irish-American societies had done their work well. Joseph McLaughlin's opening salvo, demanding 'why don't you present Irish character as it really is?' was featured prominently in the reports of the Philadelphia *Ledger* and the *New York Times*, establishing the ground of the protest. One man called from the balcony, 'As one born and bred in Ireland, I protest!' and another began a prepared speech, 'From time immemorial ...', but was not allowed by the police to get any further.[12] On the second night, a man began reading from a manuscript, 'In the name of County Down', but was immediately silenced by one of what were reported to be thirty uniformed policemen and forty detectives in the theatre. On the first night, as had been decided at the meeting, the demonstrations were confined to hissing, and nothing was thrown at the actors. On the second night, however, there were reports of programmes, eggs and pie being thrown, and a total of fourteen men were arrested, all of whom gave their birthplace as Ireland. The Ancient Order of Hibernians was represented in court by an Assistant District Attorney, who got the protesters released before the performance was over.

In Philadelphia, the Players faced their biggest obstacle, as Joseph Garrity, a businessman with many interests who was identified in the *New York Times* as 'a local liquor dealer' swore out a warrant against them and had them arrested for violating a state law against producing an immoral play. Although they had to appear in court, this amounted to nothing materially, as the players were never actually put in jail, and were freed on a writ of *habeas corpus* by a magistrate who made no comment on the character of the play, and a week later refused an appeal to re-open the case and ordered that their bail bond be returned. Nevertheless, the incident generated a good deal of publicity, provoking George Bernard Shaw, whose *Mrs. Warren's Profession* had suffered the same fate in 1905, to remark that 'the occurrence is too ordinary to be worth any comment. All decent people are arrested in America.' Shaw went on to say that he had warned the Players that 'America is being governed largely by a mysterious race, probably one of the lost tribes of Israel, calling themselves American Gaels. It is a genuine country for genuine Irishmen and Irishwomen. American Gaels are the real playboys of the Western World.'[13] This note of cultural superiority is one that had been sounded by Yeats in response to the Boston criticisms of the Players. 'The Irish-Americans,' he said, 'should be very careful how they criticise the drama of the Irish players ... they should not form hasty judgments about things upon which the Irish of Ireland had already given a favorable opinion.'[14]

A major subtext of the opposition between the protesters and the Players was, in fact, the question of who were the more fake Irishmen. Comments like these by Shaw and Yeats may be seen as calculated responses to the insistence on their Irish identity by many of the protesters, and charges that Synge was not presenting the Irish peasant authentically. They were answered in turn by dismissals of Yeats, Synge and Lady Gregory as foreign and un-Irish. A letter to the *Kansas City Star*, for example, asserted that 'Synge's school was not the hills and valley of Mayo, but the slums of Paris; his characters are not typical of the Connaught peasantry, but children of the imagination.'[15]

During the New York run, Seamus MacManus was quoted as saying that, as Yeats had been offered a pension by the British government in the previous year, 'Ireland has lost Yeats; Yeats has lost Ireland.'[16] *The Gaelic American*, a Fenian newspaper which carried on a non-stop attack on the Players throughout their six-month tour, said of Lady Gregory and *The Playboy*, 'a woman with a foreign title was patroness of the vile thing'.[17] In New York, former Member of the UK Parliament Michael Conway was wildly cheered and carried out of a Knights of Columbus debate about *The Playboy* on the shoulders of the crowd after calling Yeats 'a cheap pensioner of the hated British crown'. The play, the players and their defenders were declared, 'amid the wildest applause of the audience, "the bribed tools of the British in an effort to make Irish Nationalism look silly and ridiculous, and to satirize it out of countenance before its demands are pressed too far in Parliament"'.[18]

In the long run, the culture war was won by the Players. Despite the charges of false representation of the Irish peasantry, of vulgarity and immodesty, of attacks on Catholicism and Nationalism, of the 'foreignness' of its playwright and producers, after the first couple of days in each of the cities, *The Playboy* was performed without incident to appreciative audiences in full houses. So successful was the tour that its original schedule was doubled in length. The Players went on from Philadelphia to a Midwest tour that concentrated on such college towns as Richmond, Bloomington, Lafayette, Crawfordsville, and Terre Haute, all in Indiana, and Champaign and Bloomington in Illinois before it got to Chicago, where, after a premiere that was 'as peaceful as an afternoon tea',[19] they played for a month despite a failed attempt to keep *The Playboy* off the stage.[20]

Yeats and Lady Gregory were, of course, masters at channelling and exploiting the perceptions and responses that surrounded the protests. And subsequent events confirmed the material value of the publicity to the Players. The 1911–12 tour was an immense success financially, to the extent that Lady Gregory, who by then had essentially assumed sole directorship of the Irish

National Theatre, thought that English patronage could in future be replaced by American tours as a way of keeping the theatre financially secure. A second tour in 1912–13 made money, but less than the previous year, and a third tour in 1913–14 actually lost money, an outcome that Lady Gregory blamed on Lennox Robinson, who was managing the company, but is at least partially attributable to the fact that the Irish Players were an old story in North America now, and there were no fresh riots to whet the interest of American audiences.[21]

The protests and the political issues that occasioned them had driven not only the American audience's response to *Playboy*, but its understanding of both the play and the Players. There were some in the audience who chose to focus on more aesthetic issues, however, particularly realism as practised by the playwright and the actors. While the simplicity and 'naturalness' of the actors was generally praised, there was some dissent. An early review suggested that Fred O'Donovan:

> knows by far the most about the art of acting. And for that very reason he seems far more real than any of the others, most of whom, indeed, are as artificial as their wigs and make-ups. Again a little more art would result in less monotony, for there is too much reading of lines on one key and with one inflection.[22]

Reviewing the 1913 tour, Andre Tridon complained that 'in their attempt to depict simple folk, the players presented a distressing conglomeration of half-witted individuals ... Some were cheerful idiots, some sinister idiots, but half-witted they all were ... driveling idiocy is not synonymous with realistic simplicity.'[23] Despite objections like these in 1911 and 1913, it was the Players' realism that was to prove most influential on the American theatre, and particularly on the young generation of writers who were just beginning to discover the drama as the most exciting form in which to develop their talents while participating in the nascent movement towards the modern in all the arts that was concentrated in New York's Greenwich Village. Two of these writers, Eugene O'Neill and Djuna Barnes, who were to become significant playwrights for the Village's Provincetown Players, gratefully acknowledged the influence of Synge and the tours of the Irish National Theatre on their work.

O'Neill was to become one of the United States's most significant play-wrights, the only one to win the Nobel Prize for literature. In 1911, the 23-year-old O'Neill had not yet begun to write plays, and was living a transient life in New York, subsisting mainly on handouts from his father, the famous matinée idol, James O'Neill. Eugene evinced little interest in following his father into the theatre at this point, but he made a point of seeing all of the productions of the Irish National Theatre in New York. O'Neill's biographer notes that he discussed the plays and *The Playboy* row enthusiastically with his friend Jimmy Byth, and 'was scornful not only of the humorless Irish whose sensibilities had been outraged by the comedy but of the critics who failed to realize that the Dubliners were pioneers of a new style of acting, honest, true, without the familiar tricks'.[24] In an interview in 1923, O'Neill explained that he had revolted against the theatre in his youth because of his experience with 'the old, ranting, artificial romantic stage stuff' he had seen so much of in his father's performances, and 'it was seeing the Irish Players for the first time that gave me a glimpse of my opportunity. The first year that they came over here I went to see everything they did. I thought then and I still think that they demonstrated the possibilities of naturalistic acting better than any other company.'[25]

Perhaps not surprisingly, it was *Riders to the Sea* rather than *The Playboy* that seems to have had the deepest effect on O'Neill. The Irish actor Eileen Curran told O'Neill at the rehearsals for his 1921 *Anna Christie* that she was constantly reminded of Synge's tragedy, and said, 'you've written about the conflict between a man and the sea just as Synge wrote of the conflict between an old woman and the sea', quoting Maurya's line, 'they're all gone now, and there isn't anything more the sea can do to me'. O'Neill looked at her and said, 'it would take someone who was Irish to feel that'.[26] In fact, when O'Neill began his self-directed course of play-reading while he was in a tuberculosis sanatorium in 1913, the works of Synge, Yeats and Lady Gregory were at the top of his list.

As is evident from the exchange about *Anna Christie*, Synge's plays had their deepest effect in providing O'Neill with a theatrical idiom for expressing the profound truths about the human condition and the human spirit that he saw in the experience of the simplest and least pretentious of people, particularly the sailors he had met when he briefly went to sea in his early twenties. O'Neill's experience with the sailors was similar to Synge's with the peasants in the west of Ireland. He had lived with them, listened to them, tried to understand them, and was welcomed among them, although there was never any question that he was one of them. In writing the one-act plays about sailors that began his career at the Provincetown Playhouse, O'Neill made use of Synge as his model for representing their lives and experience with a realistic simplicity and dramatic seriousness. O'Neill did not have Synge's gift for lyricism, or his access to the rhythms of the Irish language on which to build his dialogue, but he tried to avoid the conventions of ethnic stage language that pervaded the theatre and to find a dialogic idiom that conveyed the true quality of the speech his characters would use.

In his first attempts in the sea plays, O'Neill consciously created the ethnic microcosm that he had found among the sailors through vernacular speech that was a rather crude approximation of the different ethnic versions of English he was trying to suggest. In *The Moon of the Caribbees* (1918), for example, Driscoll says:

> A chanty is ut ye want? I'll bet me whole pay day there's not wan in the crowd 'ceptin' Yank here, an' Ollie an' meself, an' Lamps an' Cocky, maybe, wud be sailors enough to know the main from the mizzen on a windjammer. Ye've heard the names av chanties but divil a note av the tune or a loine av the words do ye know. There's hardly a rale deep-water sailor lift on the seas, more's the pity.[27]

By the time he wrote *The Hairy Ape* (1922), his technique had improved, and he was able to approach something of the lyrical quality of Synge's dialogue in Paddy's nostalgic paean to the age of sail by avoiding the dialect markers and concentrating on syntax and rhythm:

> Oh, to be back in the fine days of my youth, ochone! Oh, there was fine beautiful ships them days – clippers wid tall masts touching the sky – fine strong men in them – men that was sons of the seas as if 'twas the mother that bore them. Oh, the clean skins of them, and the clear eyes, the straight backs and full chests of them! Brave men they was, and bold men surely![28]

By 1922, O'Neill had fully digested another lesson from Synge. In the context of the play, the lyricism of the dialogue is not simply decoration. It has a thematic purpose in conveying Paddy's dedication to a romantic ideal in the past as opposed to Yank the stoker's embracing of the harsh realities of the present, which is also reflected in his speech. O'Neill was to make the Irish peasant his own in his classic depiction of Irish-American rural characters, Phil and Josie Hogan, in *A Moon for the Misbegotten* (1947). While the conception of these New England farmers is deeply indebted to Synge's conception of the rural Irish, it is original in its re-imagining of the Irish character in an American context.

Djuna Barnes was even more outspoken than O'Neill about Synge's influence. When she was part of the Provincetown Players in the 1910s, Barnes was quite different from the sophisticated, acerbic modernist writer who is associated with her masterpiece, *Nightwood*. At this time, Barnes made her living as a journalist, particularly popular for her celebrity interviews and the stunt pieces she did, such as getting into a cage with a baby gorilla, or being force-fed in order to report on hunger-striking suffragettes from direct experience. She also published a good deal of her own creative writing in the newspapers, including several plays, and she had three plays produced by the Provincetown Players in the 1919–20 season, *Three from the Earth*, *Kurzy of the Sea* and *An Irish Triangle*.

Barnes had not been able to go to the theatre during the tours of the Irish Players, but she expressed her deep admiration for Synge in a newspaper piece entitled 'The Songs of Synge'. She had discovered Synge through reading *Deirdre of the Sorrows*, and she wrote that Deirdre's dialogue was 'the first song that had come into my ears to stay ... to me there is nothing in the English language that sets my whole heart to singing as his lines, "the dawn and the evening are a little while, the Winter and Summer pass quickly and what way would you and I, Naisi, have joy forever?"'.[29] Apart from his dialogue, however, Barnes felt a deep affinity with the writer who 'realized that grim brutality and frankness and love are one, the upper lip is romance, but the under is irony, and he knew "there is no timber that has not strong roots among the clay and worms"'.[30] As her biographer notes, with the exception of Joyce, Barnes never again paid such a tribute to a literary forebear.[31]

Barnes's debt to Synge is obvious in two of her plays that were produced by the Provincetown Players, *Kurzy of the Sea* (1919) and *An Irish Triangle* (1920), as well as several short plays that saw only newspaper publication, such as *At the Root of the Stars* (1917), *Maggie of the Saints* (1917) and *The Death of Life* (1916). *Kurzy* owes a good deal to *The Playboy*. In it, Molly and Pat McRace become willing dupes in a scheme that will get their dreamy son Rory married off and out of the house when Kurzy, a barmaid from a neighbouring town, claims to be a mermaid Pat has scooped up in his fishing nets. Rory is overcome by what he takes to be Kurzy's supernatural hold on him until he throws her in the ocean as a test, and finds out that she is an ordinary human girl with a bathing suit on under her petticoat, and she swims off, telling him that he will have to learn long-distance swimming to catch her. Like Christy Mahon, Rory becomes empowered when a young woman displays her attraction to him, and he goes off, having shaken off his seeming enchantment by romantic stories, determined to win Kurzy as his wife.

All of the 'Irish' plays display Barnes's attempt to replicate the dialogue of Synge that she so admired. But having only read Synge's plays, Barnes had not even O'Neill's advantage of having heard the words as well as seeing them. Her Irish dialogue is clearly imitative and its 'poetic' effects are forced:

It's a great change the world has taken on since last it dropped down its leaves and the hares were running. And there's a rare mighty change come over the things John does be putting his eyes on, for there's not a hare this side of the hills that doesn't be sitting tight on its tail and showing pleasure only, when John does be stepping down into the bogs.[32]

These plays were all apprentice work, but like O'Neill's they were precursors of a truly original Irish-American character, Dr Matthew O'Connor. In her classic modernist novel *Nightwood*, Barnes transforms the elements of 'Irishness' that she saw in Synge's work into a uniquely conceived character who embodies both his Irish and his American backgrounds.

While subsequent productions of Synge's plays in the USA did not have the dramatic impact of the first Abbey tour, Synge's work has had a steady presence on the American stage since the early twentieth century. His most prolific producer has been the Abbey, which returned to the USA for the first time after the lacklustre 1914 tour in 1932, when the company travelled the country from New York to Walla Walla, Washington, producing *The Playboy*, *Riders to the Sea* and *The Shadow of the Glen*. The Abbey performed *The Well of the Saints* in 1934 and *Playboy* in 1934, 1937, 1990 and 2004. In recent years, the Druid Theatre Company has been an acknowledged rival of the Abbey as interpreter of Synge for Americans. As early as 1986, Garry Hynes directed a well-received production of *The Playboy* in Purchase, New York. In 2006, DruidSynge received universal acclaim when it was produced at the Lincoln Center Festival in New York.

Americans have not been shy about producing Synge themselves. *Riders to the Sea* was produced by the American Negro Theatre in 1949, and it and *The Shadow of the Glen*, *The Tinker's Wedding*, *The Playboy* and *The Well of the Saints* have all been produced off-Broadway. In 1971, New York's Lincoln Center produced *The Playboy* in celebration of Synge's centenary. *The Playboy* has been produced in many regional theatres from Boston to Los Angeles, and Synge remains a staple of university theatre, where his plays are regularly studied in drama and theatre courses. The USA has also seen the 'Dancing *Playboy*' (1979) with the Irish Ballet Company and The Chieftains, the musical *Christy* (1975), and Mustapha Matura's *Playboy of the West Indies* (1989). All of this activity attests to Synge's living presence in the American theatre, and the impact of his plays, particularly *The Playboy of the Western World*, on American culture.

NOTES

1. Nora M. Williams, 'Emerald Isle Grows Crop of Dramatists', *The State* (Columbia, SC), 13 August 1911, p. 10.
2. Ibid.
3. 'Lady Gregory Here with Irish Players', *New York Times*, 20 November 1911, p. 11.
4. 'The Genius of Synge's "Playboy"', *New York Times*, 1 October 1911, p. RB584.
5. Paula M. Kane, 'Boston Catholics and the New Irish Drama', in Patrick O'Sullivan (ed.), *The Irish World Wide*, vol. 5: *Religion and Identity* (London: Leicester University Press, 1996), p. 115.
6. 'Object to an Irish Play', *New York Times*, 9 October 1911, p. 2.
7. 'Irish Play Row in Philadelphia', *New York Times*, 16 January 1912, p. 8.

8. Lady Augusta Gregory, *Our Irish Theatre: A Chapter of Autobiography* (New York: Oxford, 1972), p. 105.

9. 'Riot in Theatre over an Irish Play', *New York Times*, 24 November 1911, p. 1.

10. Ibid.

11. Ibid.

12. 'Irish Play Row in Philadelphia', p. 8.

13. 'Shaw Scores Philadelphia', *New York Times*, 20 January 1912, p. 3.

14. 'Poet Yeats Defends the Irish Players', *New York Times*, 12 October 1911, p. 9.

15. 'The "Playboy" a False Picture', *Kansas City Star*, 29 January 1912, p. 5.

16. 'Seamus M'Manus Raps "The Playboy"', *New York Times*, 27 November 1911, p. 11.

17. Quoted by Lucy McDiarmid, 'The Abbey and the Theatrics of Controversy, 1909–1915', in Stephen Watt et al. (eds.), *A Century of Irish Drama: Widening the Stage* (Bloomington, IN: Indiana University Press, 2000), p. 65.

18. 'Synge's Defender Jeered', *New York Times*, 24 January 1912, p. 20.

19. 'Irish Play Only Evoked Titters', *Grand Forks Herald*, 8 February 1912, p. 2.

20. For the schedule, see Ida G. Everson, 'Young Lennox Robinson and the Abbey Theatre's First American Tour (1911–1912)', *Modern Drama* (May 1966), pp. 88–9.

21. For accounts of the tours, see Peter Kavanagh, *The Story of the Abbey Theatre* (New York: Devin-Adair, 1950), pp. 96–9; Lennox Robinson, *Ireland's Abbey Theatre: A History* (London: Sidgwick & Jackson, 1951), pp. 95–9; Lady Augusta Gregory, *Our Irish Theatre*, pp. 97–135.

22. 'Irish Players in Three Short Plays', *New York Times*, 21 November 1911, p. 9.

23. Andre Tridon, 'The Truth About the Irish Players', *New Review* 1 (1913), p. 255.

24. Louis Sheaffer, *O'Neill: Son and Playwright* (Boston: Little, Brown, 1968), p. 205.

25. Charles A. Merrill, 'Eugene O'Neill, World-Famous Dramatist, and Family Live in Abandoned Coast Guard Station on Cape Cod', *Boston Sunday Globe*, Editorial and News Feature Section, 8 July 1923, p. 1.

26. Sheaffer, 'O'Neill', p. 205.

27. Eugene O'Neill, *The Moon of the Caribbees*, in *Seven Plays of the Sea* (New York: Vintage, 1972), p. 9.

28. Eugene O'Neill, *The Hairy Ape*, in *The Plays of Eugene O'Neill*, vol. I (New York: Modern Library, 1982), p. 213.

29. Djuna Barnes, 'The Songs of Synge: The Man Who Shaped His Life as He Shaped His Plays', *The Morning Telegraph*, 18 February 1917, p. 8.

30. Barnes, 'Songs of Synge', p. 8.

31. Phillip Herring, *Djuna: The Life and Work of Djuna Barnes* (New York: Penguin, 1995), p. 123.

32. Djuna Barnes, *An Irish Triangle: A Play in One Act*, in Barbara Ozieblo (ed.), *The Provincetown Players: A Choice of the Shorter Works* (Sheffield: Sheffield Academic Press, 1994), pp. 236–7.

14

ANTHONY ROCHE

Synge and contemporary Irish drama

Synge's plays have not faded from the Irish stage, unlike the work of so many other playwrights of the Irish Dramatic Movement. His own works continue to merit regular production, particularly *The Playboy of the Western World*, and attract some of the most outstanding interpreters of the contemporary Irish stage. Yet the subversive originality of Synge's work is often more apparent nowadays in the profound impact and influence he continues to exert on contemporary Irish drama. Michael Billington, theatre critic of the *Guardian*, welcomed the DruidSynge staging by director Garry Hynes of Synge's six canonical plays in July 2005 as offering 'a rare chance to assess the man who did so much to shape modern Irish drama', and went on to note how Synge had been a 'fount of inspiration for other Irish writers'.[1] Of the contemporary dramatists, Billington cites Martin McDonagh and Conor McPherson and could well have added the names of Brian Friel, Tom Murphy and Marina Carr, all five of whom will be discussed in this chapter.

When Friel – the most outstanding of contemporary Irish playwrights and arguably Synge's modern inheritor – spoke at the reopening of the 'Synge cottage' on Inis Meáin in 1999 he acknowledged Synge's influence not only on his own formidable body of work but on that of every other Irish playwright: 'On this occasion, on this island, it is very important to me to acknowledge the great master of Irish theatre, the man who made Irish theatre, the man who reshaped it and refashioned it, and the man before whom we all genuflect.'[2] As Friel openly acknowledged, Synge laid out the template of what an Irish theatre might be. The situations he developed in his scenarios, the language he fashioned for his characters, the issues he raised in his works, have in turn been taken on and responded to by the playwrights who came after him in a century-long dialogue which shows no signs of ending.

The two great contemporary Irish playwrights Brian Friel and Tom Murphy began their writing careers in the late 1950s by needing to distance themselves from the anxiety of Synge's still culturally proximate influence. An early short story by Friel, 'Mr. Sing My Heart's Delight', shows this clearly.

Synge's name resounds throughout the text and, while the spelling may be different, the pronunciation is the same. Friel's Mr. Sing is a 'packman' or travelling salesman from the Punjab marooned in Donegal. The narrator's grandmother responds by exclaiming: "'Man, but that's a strange name. Sing. Sing", she said, feeling the sound on her tongue ... "I'll call you Mr. Sing My Heart's Delight! That's what I'll call you – a good, big mouthful. Mr. Sing My Heart's Delight!"'[3] The Indian protests that he doesn't speak English too well, but as it turns out neither does she: 'A constant source of fun was Granny's English. Gaelic was her first tongue and she never felt at ease in English.'[4] The English spoken by Granny is closely modelled on the Irish language ('let the sleep come over you for an hour') and resembles most of all the Hiberno-English syntax and structure of Synge's dramatic speech. In the plays he was to go on to write, Friel opted for a syntactically restrained, relatively neutral speech in which the Irishisms are carefully placed. This is most evident in *Translations* (1980), where the only Irish words in the text are the highlighted place names.

Tom Murphy has always claimed that he was uninfluenced by Irish theatre, finding anything Irish 'a pain in the arse [including] O'Casey and Synge', and has instead stressed the impact on his early writing of the great American playwrights Eugene O'Neill, Arthur Miller and, above all, Tennessee Williams.[5] But a photograph in the programme for the 2001 season of Murphy plays at the Abbey Theatre shows an extremely youthful Tom Murphy clad in a jockey's outfit and hoisted aloft by a cheering throng. The photo was of a young Murphy playing Christy Mahon in a production of *The Playboy* by the amateur dramatic company of his home town Tuam in County Galway. When Murphy and his friend Noel O'Donoghue resolved one Sunday after Mass that they would write a play, they did so in words that declared outright opposition to the drama associated with the Abbey Theatre tradition: 'One thing is sure – it's not going to be set in a kitchen.'[6] At the outset of their careers, Brian Friel and Tom Murphy needed to clear their own ground in relation to a potentially overbearing precursor. It was only when they had authoritatively established their own distinctive idiom and dramaturgy that they were prepared to take Synge on.

Friel's 1979 masterpiece, *Faith Healer*, has suggested more than one Syngean parallel. In an influential reading, Declan Kiberd has argued that Friel's play is a modern-day version of Synge's *Deirdre of the Sorrows*.[7] This works best at the level of structural parallel, with the long exile in Scotland (Alban) followed by the fatal return home to Ulster; but the dramatis personae do not line up revealingly. More suggestive for my argument is Richard Kearney's remark that *Faith Healer* can be read as a sequel to Synge's *Playboy*, showing how Pegeen Mike 'might have mused to herself had she left her homeland of Mayo and taken to the roads with her story-telling playboy'.[8] That life is far from romantic. The play's third character, the manager Teddy, recalls 'the bitterness and the fighting and the wettings and the bloody van and the smell of the primus stove and the bills and the booze and the dirty halls and that hassle that we never seemed to be able to rise above'.[9] It more accurately resembles the life predicted by Synge's Nora in response to the Tramp's evocation of their shared life on the roads: 'I'm thinking it's myself will be wheezing that time with lying down under the Heavens when the night is cold, but you've a fine bit of talk, stranger, and it's with yourself I'll go' (CW III, 57). The three women, Nora Burke, Pegeen Mike and Grace Hardy, are wooed by the promise inherent in the 'fine bit of talk' offered by the wanderer who has entered into and disrupted their orderly lives. If Grace leaves with her playboy for a life on the roads, she too comes to lose him, and her twelve-page monologue amplifies the most famous closing line in the Irish dramatic canon: 'O my God I'm in such a mess ... how I want that door to open – how I want that man to come across that floor and put his white hands on my face and still this tumult inside me ... O my God I don't know if I can go on without his sustenance.'[10] The title characters of Synge's and Friel's plays have a good deal in common. Christy Mahon works his own brand of faith-healing amidst the physically and psychically maimed community of County Mayo. Frank Hardy's faith-healing and Christy's story-telling are 'a craft without an apprenticeship, a ministry without responsibility, a vocation without a ministry',[11] and, one might add, a religion in need of believers, a theatre in search of an audience. Both plays ask whether Frank and Christy are liars and charlatans or quasi-religious truth-tellers. This troubling question is bound up with the intense and self-conscious theatricality of *The Playboy* and *Faith Healer*. The fiction of the stage space repeatedly gives way before the actuality of performance. The Friel play is structured as a succession of monologues, in which Frank, Grace and Teddy confront the audience with their versions of what occurred and ask in turn to be believed. Synge's play makes of its cast of characters an on-stage audience who listen to Christy's narrative claims with increasing credulity, until those claims are tested in succeeding acts. The question posed by both plays is: how much faith do we invest in the truth of theatrical story-telling?

Friel's most overtly 'Syngean' play is his most acclaimed, *Dancing at Lughnasa* (1990). In his account of 1930s Ireland, Friel shows a thin veneer of Christianity or, more specifically, Catholicism covering a more permanent paganism. Synge's *The Aran Islands* contains a memorable account of the keening which accompanied the burial of one of the islanders: 'Each old woman ... seemed possessed for the moment with a profound ecstasy of grief, swaying to and fro, and bending her forehead to the stone before her, while she called out to the dead with a perpetually recurring chant of sobs' (CW II, 74). This is the same wild ecstasy that is released in the five Mundy sisters during their celebrated dance. When the dance ceases, Kate urges them to act and think with 'propriety'; during the dance itself, she has finally succumbed by *'suddenly leap[ing] to her feet, fling[ing] her head back, and emit[ting] a loud "Yaaaah"'*.[12] Synge was frequently charged with wilfully ignoring the deeply held Catholicism of the islanders and playing up the paganism. Friel is liable to the same charge since, of the five Mundy sisters, Kate is the only one who manifests the conservative Catholicism that would have been pervasive in the Ireland of the 1930s. But the position of the lapsed Protestant playwright in the late nineteenth century seeking common ground with the Catholic natives of the Aran Islands matches up with the lapsed Catholic playwright of the late twentieth seeking to connect with a more pious previous generation. When Friel left the seminary at Maynooth and a priestly vocation, he attributed it to his 'paganism',[13] and this metaphor of dissidence serves to link the two playwrights. While the Reverend Alexander Synge came to the Aran Islands in 1851 to convert the islanders to Protestantism, his nephew John travelled there fifty years later to be converted. The reversal is not unlike what has happened to the missionary Father Jack in *Lughnasa*; and young Johnny caused no less grief to his loving evangelical mother for going over to the Irish nationalists, as she saw it, than Father Jack does to his sister Kate by his admiring talk of the Ryangans and their rituals.

In 1994 Brian Friel produced *Molly Sweeney*, which drew intertextually on Synge's *The Well of the Saints*.[14] What is central to both dramatic narratives is the profoundly ironic contrast between the optimism that attends the 'miraculous' cure and the profound disillusion that the protagonists experience when their sight is restored. Molly is more isolated than the Synge couple; her husband Frank is more like the seeing community, displaying a limited good will that ultimately turns self-interested as he abandons her. Instead, Molly confides her view of the world to the audience, which thereby comes to share and participate in her vision. (Like *Faith Healer*, the play is structured as a succession of monologues.) The most disturbing aspect of the two plays, in their meditation on illusion and reality, is the third state at which the protagonists arrive in the final act. The 'recovery' from disillusionment is achieved by Martin and Mary Doul when they embrace what Timmy the smith unsympathetically but accurately describes as 'a wilful blindness' (CW III, 143). But where their earlier state can be described as innocence, since they believed in the literal truth of their visions, what they are describing now is a way of seeing, one which Martin defends at the end of the play in terms of rights: 'if it's a right some of you have to be working and sweating ... and a right some of you have to be fasting and praying ... I'm thinking it's a good right ourselves have to be sitting blind, hearing a soft wind turning round the little leaves of the spring and feeling the sun' (CW III, 149). Molly Sweeney, in her last speech, confirms that she sees nothing at all now and describes herself as living in her 'borderline country', a place she described earlier as occupying 'a borderline between fantasy and reality'.[15] As in the Synge play, the final vision is radically subjective and disturbing in its assertion of the truth of fable against the lies of the everyday. Friel was to go on from these plays of the 1990s to a decade-long renewal of his creative engagement with the plays of Anton Chekhov in translations, versions and free adaptations. But his profound engagement with the plays of John Millington Synge at the heart of some of his greatest plays deserves more sustained attention.

If Tom Murphy sought to flee the influence of Synge at the outset of his career in 1958, by 1979 he was willing to re-engage by agreeing to direct a production of *The Well of the Saints* at the Abbey Theatre. He also provided a curtain-raiser in a piece he devised from the writings of Synge entitled *Epitaph Under Ether*. The title refers to a prose work by Synge, 'Under Ether: Personal Experiences During an Operation', a Poe-like phantasmagoria of the visions he experienced while anaesthetised during one of his operations. Murphy used this to dramatically frame the various other writings he drew on, with Synge re-experiencing his life as if it were a dream. A keynote for Murphy's production of *The Well of the Saints* was provided by the last line of 'Under Ether': 'The impression was very strong on me that I had died the preceding day and come to life again, and this impression has never changed' (CW II, 43). In his director's notes scribbled on his copy of the programme, Murphy has written in relation to the opening of Act III: 'Death – Act 3. Light on church comes up as morning spreads across stage.'[16] The moment is the most bleak and desolate in the play. Mary Doul enters, *sola*, '*blind again, grop[ing] her way in on left*' (CW III, 125). The two blind people are further apart than ever and the return of Mary's physical darkness is accompanied by the onset of isolation and dread. Tom Murphy directed actress Marie Keane to play Mary Doul's opening lines in this Act 'as if she were dead':[17] 'Ah, God help me … God help me, the blackness wasn't so black at all the other time as it is this time' (CW III, 125). There can be little question of Murphy's profound engagement with Synge's play when he came to direct it, and since this interest clearly preceded the invitation to direct, one looks to Murphy's earlier plays to see whether any of them bear the marks of such interest and influence.

The Morning After Optimism (1971) comes immediately into the critical foreground. Murphy viewed *The Well of the Saints* as a fairy story:[18] it not only has a miracle but also the disastrous consequences of a wish being granted. The same could be said of the fairy-tale forest of *Optimism* into which Murphy's odd couple, James and Rosie, have fled, pursued by unnamed but threatening forces. Both of them are old and their worldly experience is signified by their occupations: he is a pimp, she is an (aging) whore. In the forest they encounter idealised representations of their younger selves, who disconcert them with the contrast of what they have become, to the point that each kills his other. Rosie is as concerned by James's obsessive talking about 'young girls', as Mary is with Martin Doul, and in time James makes as determined an effort to seduce the young, beautiful Anastasia as Martin does Molly Byrne, though with no greater success. There is a sharp contrast in the play between the realistic language of the older couple, especially when they deliberately 'talk dirty', and the idealised sentiments of the younger couple; but the most dramatically effective speech is when James and Rosie move between their slangy idiom and a more lyrical vein, exhibiting the same verbal range and contrast as in Synge's play. But it is in the taunts and accusations directed at each other that their disillusionment is most acute and their affinity with the 'cured' Martin and Mary Doul the greatest:

> JAMES: Get your supporting harnesses on, your teeth out of the cup, princess!
> ROSIE: The princess that this corseted ponce dragged into filth and scum, until she became filth and scum –!
> JAMES: You said it! – You said it! –
> ROSIE: From *his* touch![19]

The director of the premiere of Murphy's *The Morning After Optimism* on the Abbey main stage in 1971 was Hugh Hunt, who had restored Synge's *The Well of the Saints* to the Abbey repertoire in a luminous production two years earlier. Rarely was the connection between the most innovative contemporary work of the Irish stage and that of the theatre's founders more evident or persuasive than in the conjunction of these two visionary productions.

In 1985, Tom Murphy established a two-year writer-in-association relationship with Garry Hynes and Galway's Druid Theatre Company. This collaboration bore fruit in the staging of *Bailegangaire* (from the Irish, 'town without laughter') in December 1986 with the actress Siobhán McKenna in her last role as the ferocious patriarch, Mommo. If this was something of a homecoming to Galway for Murphy, it was also a further reckoning with Synge. For long before the staging of the DruidSynge cycle in 2005, Synge had been something of a 'house dramatist' for the Druid Theatre Company: their 1982 staging of *The Playboy* was lauded for its rediscovery of the violence and realism of Synge's classic. In his play Murphy engages most with Synge's *Riders to the Sea*, the one play in the canon set in the Galway locale. *Bailegangaire* takes place in the Galway of 1984 but this is not apparent from the setting: '*a country kitchen in the old style*',[20] stylised to underscore the fact that this is the traditional rural setting of the Abbey Theatre tradition. The rural interior is dominated by a massive bed in which a senile old woman tells a rambling, never-completed story of a laughing competition which came to a grief-stricken end. Coping with Mommo are her two grand-daughters, as Synge's Maurya has her two daughters, Nora and Cathleen. The affinity is further accentuated by the absence of male figures in the lives of both women. The terrible secret which shadows the laughing contest is revealed as the inadvertent death by fire of the young grandson, Tom, while awaiting his grandparents' belated return home. Mommo's tragic status is confirmed as she goes on to articulate the fate of all her male children:

> Her Pat was her eldest, died of consumption, had his pick of the girls an' married the widdy again' all her wishes ... Oh she made great contributions, rollcalling the dead ... An' for the sake of an auld ewe was stuck in the flood was how she lost two of the others, Jimmy and Michael.[21]

This cannot but recall Maurya's great speech enumerating the roll call of the dead men in *Riders*. The same dramatic condensation is evident in both. The foregrounded death serves to implicate and unfurl all of the others in the monologues through which the two old women outline the fate of each of their sons. Mommo's stance, however, differs from the stoic acceptance of Synge's Maurya in its more spirited defiance of the angels of destruction, kept at bay if not defeated by the howls of laughter: 'driving bellows of refusal at the sky through the roof. Och hona ho gus hah-haa.'[22] The phonetic notation of Mommo's laughter with which this speech concludes is only one example of the extraordinary range of sounds uttered in *Bailegangaire*. Mommo's story bears along in its verbal torrent frequent scraps of Irish-language dialogue. In this, Murphy goes Synge one better in a continuous aural reminder of Ireland's joint linguistic inheritance.

Synge has proved no less an influence on younger contemporary Irish play-wrights such as Conor McPherson, Marina Carr and Martin McDonagh. They quote much more explicitly from his work, in a postmodern and inter-textual way. To this newer generation of playwrights he is a cultural resource available to be appropriated – along with a proliferating range of references in other media (notably television and cinema) – rather than an intimidating historical presence to be faced up to. What links Synge most profoundly to McPherson, and especially to his most acclaimed play *The Weir* (1997), is the fact that the latter regards himself as a story-teller. This self-perception has resulted in plays which are frequently monologues, where the primary engagement is between the actor and the audience. McPherson believes it is no accident that the monologue form was favoured in the 1990s and the new millennium not only by himself but in acclaimed work by other younger playwrights like

Mark O'Rowe's *Howie the Rookie* (1999) and Eugene O'Brien's *Eden* (2001).
They were written during a period of uncertainty and trauma in the light of
political and clerical scandals: 'Irish drama went "inside" because our stories
were fragile, because everything was changing.'[23] These monologue plays were
frequently accused of being untheatrical, more akin to displaced prose narrative, because they did not avail of the usual theatrical resources of a cast of
characters engaged in dialogue. But it might well be argued that Irish theatre
had its origins as much in the communal art of the *seanchaí*, the act of oral
story-telling, performed in a person's home or in a public house, as in a
formal metropolitan venue. In fact, Synge's prose narrative of *The Aran
Islands* contains many stories, subsequently drawn on for his plays, which
are presented by a story-teller to an audience which included Synge.

With *The Weir*, McPherson decided to write a play with five characters
rather than one, for them to gather in a familiar locale (a pub in the Irish
countryside) and engage in dialogue. But McPherson's distinctive handling of
monologue remains central: four of the characters in turn tell a story which
draws on folklore beliefs and which plays and preys on fear of the irrational
in human behaviour. The play recognises the extent to which traditional
Irish story-telling has always drawn on the cluster of beliefs surrounding the
fairy folk, the 'others', those who enjoy a continued existence after death
and frequently return to confront the living. Of the writers of the Revival, it
was Synge who made the greatest dramatic capital of such stories, drawing
on what he witnessed of the impact of such beliefs in the lives of the Aran
Islanders. His plays are a complex exploration of truth and fiction in story-
telling, from Maurya's account of the vision of her dead son at the well in
Riders to the Sea to Christy Mahon's many versions of his father-slaying
in *The Playboy of the Western World*. In *The Weir* the three older men tell
stories of the reappearance of the dead. At one level they are trying to impress
if not scare Valerie, the young city woman who has recently moved in to this
desolate and windswept area, with its dark nights and isolation. Their stories
all tell of a rural life which is passing away, and enact the trauma of displacement, of the psychic disturbance caused by the inroads of social progress on
traditional custom. Valerie responds with her own story, set in an urban
environment but even more disturbing, about the recent death by drowning
of her young daughter and a communication from beyond the grave. The
question raised by its impact on the men – is Valerie's story true? – radiates
outward to everything that has been said in the course of the evening. There is
nothing, finally, but the words as spoken on the stage, not even the degrees of
verification allowed by Synge's *Playboy* and Friel's *Faith Healer*.

Although Greek tragedy has been much discussed in relation to the plays of
Marina Carr, the engagement with Synge is no less central to her dramatic

achievement. I have written elsewhere of how her breakthrough play, *The Mai* (1994), can be linked with *The Shadow of the Glen* through its exploration of the liminal figure of a woman on the threshold.[24] And *The Playboy of the Western World* permeates all of Carr's work. But it is on *By the Bog of Cats* (1998) that I wish to concentrate here, both because it is one of her most accomplished plays and because it is centrally engaged with a play by Synge which has not yet featured in my argument. Had the title not already been used by him, Carr might as readily have entitled her play *The Tinker's Wedding*. Its dramatic action centres on a marriage between Carthage Kilbride, Oedipally dominated by a ferocious mother, and Caroline Cassidy, the weak daughter of a strong farmer. The omens for their marriage are not good; but they are seriously complicated and rendered tragic by the presence at the wedding of the play's central character, Hester Swane, the woman with whom Carthage has lived for over ten years and who is not willing to disappear from his life with their young daughter, Josie. Hester is categorised and anathematised by those who oppose her, especially Carthage's mother, as a tinker: 'I warned him about that wan, Hester Swane, that she'd get her claws in, and she did, the tinker.'[25] In writing a programme note in the 1990s for an Abbey production of Synge's *Playboy*, Marina Carr drew on Augustine Martin's distinction between two categories of character in Synge's drama: the 'settled men, householders' and 'the people of passion and poetry'.[26] Her own play develops and complicates the distinction.

Hester Swane occupies two dwellings, the caravan by the Bog of Cats in which she was reared by her mother, and the house she has shared with Carthage and her daughter. Much is made in the play by the householders of the legal procedures by which Hester has signed over her rights in the property. Like a latter-day Antigone, Hester insists with a stubborn personal authority on her right to dwell by the Bog of Cats, whether in a housed or un-housed condition. In that opposition lie the seeds of tragedy. But preceding that is the high comedy of Act II where three potential brides present themselves at the wedding from hell: Caroline, the disconsolate intended; her mother-in-law, who has insisted on decking herself in white; and the spurned Hester Swane, who makes her entrance '*in her wedding dress, veil, shoes, the works*'.[27] The unmarried Hester attends the wedding with Josie, the daughter she has had with Carthage ten years earlier. Synge's unmarried tinkers make passing mention of the fact that they already have children: 'You to be going beside me a great while, and rearing a lot of them, and then to be setting off with your talk of getting married' (CW IV, 7). And in his earlier drafts of the play Synge supplied Michael and Sarah Casey with a son and a daughter. In Carr's play Hester's disruptive presence reveals the lack of any true union at its core. The same critique is offered at the close of *The Well of the Saints*, when the marriage of Timmy the smith and Molly Byrne is secured by the scapegoating and expulsion of the two blind tramps. In Marina Carr's, as in Synge's drama, the social order is not confirmed by a wedding, but exposed and ripped apart.

The most postmodern of these 1990s playwrights, and the one who has most explicitly appropriated the work of Synge, is Martin McDonagh. His name evokes an eerie resonance because Synge lodged in the McDonagh cottage on Inis Meáin and was taught Irish by their son, Martin. The contemporary London playwright is the son of Irish parents who emigrated to England, a Sligo mother and a Galway father. McDonagh had tried writing plays set in London and the US, but without success; it was when he recalled the setting and conversations from his summer visits as a child to the parental west of Ireland that he found his dramatic idiom. In interviews, McDonagh has always claimed to be influenced by English playwrights like Harold Pinter and the American David Mamet rather than the more traditional playwrights of the Irish Literary Revival. Further, critics of his work were quick to make comparison of the casual cruelty of McDonagh's plays with the films of Quentin Tarantino. But the evidence of the plays themselves belies McDonagh's claims, particularly in relation to Synge. The title of the third play of what has become known as 'the Leenane trilogy', *The Lonesome West* (1997), is itself a direct and far-from-obvious quotation from *The Playboy of the Western World*: when the Mayo villagers are taunting the craven Shaun Keogh for his fear of Father Reilly, Pegeen's father holds up Shaun's coat and proclaims: 'Well, there's the coat of a Christian man. Oh, there's sainted glory this day in the lonesome west' (CW IV, 65). And the key moment in the middle play, *A Skull in Connemara* (the title itself deriving from Lucky's speech in Beckett's *Waiting for Godot*) is provided by the young gravedigger crawling back on stage after apparently having been killed with a spade driven into his skull. The type and diversity of McDonagh's borrowings have been seen as postmodern, but there is no doubt that Synge is central to the enterprise.[28]

For those critics who take a positive view of both Synge and McDonagh the close kinship and continuum between the two writers is clear. Michael Billington wrote in the *Guardian* in 1997 of the 'Leenane Trilogy': 'McDonagh is not the first writer to tell us that the travel-poster Ireland conceals dark impulses: Synge, to whom he remains deeply indebted, made the point back in 1907. But McDonagh's great strength is that he combines a love of traditional story-telling with the savage ironic humour of the modern generation.'[29] But the same mix of traditional story-telling with ironic humour is no less characteristic of Synge. For those who take a negative view of McDonagh, the criticisms sound remarkably like those made a hundred years ago concerning

Synge. Both are outsiders to the culture they represent – an Anglo-Irish Protestant from an Ascendancy background, a streetwise Londoner – appropriating real places in the west of Ireland to claim authenticity for what is in effect Stage Irish stereotype, a reliance on characters of limited intelligence and psychopathic tendencies. The involvement of respected theatre professionals such as director Garry Hynes and her Druid Theatre Company served only to give a gloss of authenticity to plays which were not Irish. If Irish audiences turned out in great numbers and responded with laughter to what they saw, it only served to show how thoroughly colonised they were.[30] What was so striking a feature of the Irish audiences McDonagh drew was that many of them were young and few of them would be characterised as 'regular theatregoers'. His plays work with a calculated cunning, and an utter lack of sentimentality, towards the Irish theatrical canon as much as anything else. My own feeling is that the smash-and-grab theatrics of Martin McDonagh have altered the Irish dramatic landscape irrevocably. Their influence on our reading of Synge, and on how Synge's plays are interpreted in the cultural present, is notable. What the 'McDonagh effect' does most in relation to *The Playboy of the Western World* is to foreground the pervasiveness of violence in the normative, everyday lives of the characters. When Nicholas Grene writes that 'the high colour of violence throughout is a feature of the grotesquely fantastic version of reality which the play presents',[31] his remarks may refer to *The Playboy* but could just as well be read as an account of McDonagh's 'Leenane Trilogy'. The irony is that Grene's book accords McDonagh's plays one dismissive sentence.[32] The two playwrights cannot be quarantined from each other in this regard. For the creative interchange between Synge and contemporary Irish drama is two-way and remains ongoing.

NOTES

1. Michael Billington, 'Synge for Your Supper', *Guardian*, 19 July 2005.
2. Brian Friel, in TG4 documentary, *Synge agus an Domhan Thiar* (dir. MacDara Ó Cuirraidhín, 1999).
3. Brian Friel, 'Mr. Sing My Heart's Delight', *The Saucer of Larks* (New York: Doubleday, 1962), pp. 176–7.
4. Friel, 'Mr. Sing My Heart's Delight', p. 170.
5. See Nicholas Grene (ed.), *Talking About Tom Murphy* (Dublin: Carysfort Press, 2002), p. 94.
6. Cited in Fintan O'Toole, *The Politics of Magic: The Work and Times of Tom Murphy* (Dublin: Raven Arts Press, 1987), p. 20.
7. Declan Kiberd, '*Faith Healer*', in William A. Kerwin (ed.), *Brian Friel: A Casebook* (New York and London: Garland Press, 1997), pp. 211–25.
8. Richard Kearney, 'Language Play: Brian Friel and Ireland's Verbal Theatre', in ibid., p. 88.

9. Brian Friel, *Faith Healer*, *Plays: One* (London: Faber & Faber, 1996), p. 367.
10. Ibid., p. 353.
11. Ibid., p. 333.
12. Brian Friel, *Dancing at Lughnasa*, *Plays: Two* (London: Faber & Faber, 1999), p. 36.
13. Attributed in the script by playwright Thomas Kilroy for the TV documentary *Brian Friel* (dir. Sinead O'Brien, Ferndale Films, 2000).
14. See Carole-Anne Upton, 'Visions of the Sightless in Friel's *Molly Sweeney* and Synge's *The Well of the Saints*', *Modern Drama*, 40.3 (1997), 347–58.
15. Brian Friel, *Molly Sweeney*, *Plays: Two*, pp. 509, 500.
16. Copy kindly supplied by Tom Murphy.
17. Interview with Tom Murphy, Santa Barbara, California, April 1981.
18. 'I certainly saw it as [a] fairy tale, a morality tale.' Interview, April 1981.
19. Tom Murphy, *The Morning After Optimism*, *Plays: Three* (London: Methuen, 1994), pp. 55–6.
20. Tom Murphy, *Bailegangaire*, *Plays: Two* (London: Methuen, 1993), p. 91.
21. Murphy, *Bailegangaire*, pp. 163–4.
22. Ibid., pp. 164–5.
23. Conor McPherson, 'Will the Morning After Stop us Talking to Ourselves?', *Irish Times*, 3 May 2008.
24. Anthony Roche, 'Woman on the Threshold: J.M. Synge's *The Shadow of the Glen*, Teresa Deevy's *Katie Roche* and Marina Carr's *The Mai*', *Irish University Review*, 25.1 (Spring/Summer 1995), pp. 143–2.
25. Marina Carr, *By the Bog of Cats*, *Plays: One* (London: Faber & Faber, 1999), p. 279.
26. See Augustine Martin, 'Christy Mahon and the Apotheosis of Loneliness', in Anthony Roche (ed.), *Bearing Witness: Essays on Anglo-Irish Literature* (Dublin: University College Dublin Press, 1996), pp. 32–43.
27. Carr, *By the Bog of Cats*, p. 311.
28. See Shaun Richards, '"The Outpouring of a Morbid, Unhealthy Mind": The Critical Condition of Synge and McDonagh', *Irish University Review*, 33.1 (Spring/Summer 2003), p. 210.
29. Michael Billington, review of Druid's production of the trilogy, *Guardian*, 28 July 1997.
30. See Victor Merriman, 'The Theatre of Tiger Trash: Decolonisation Postponed', *Irish University Review*, 29.2 (Autumn/Winter 1999), pp. 305–17.
31. Nicholas Grene, *The Politics of Irish Drama: Plays in Context from Boucicault to Friel* (Cambridge University Press, 1999), pp. 94–5.
32. Grene, *The Politics of Irish Drama*, p. 262.

SELECT BIBLIOGRAPHY

Primary Works

J. M. Synge Collected Works (4 vols.), gen. ed. Robin Skelton.
Vol 1, *Poems*, ed. Robin Skelton (London: Oxford University Press, 1962).
Vol 2, *Prose*, ed. Alan Price (London: Oxford University Press, 1966).
Vol. 3, *Plays: Book 1*, ed. Ann Saddlemyer (London: Oxford University Press, 1968).
Vol. 4, *Plays: Book 2*, ed. Ann Saddlemyer (London: Oxford University Press, 1968).

Photographs

My Wallet of Photographs: The Collected Photographs of J. M. Synge, ed. Lilo Stephens (Dublin: Dolmen Editions, 1971).

Synge Manuscripts

The Synge Manuscripts in the Library of Trinity College Dublin: A Catalogue Prepared on the Occasion of the Synge Centenary Exhibition 1971, compiled by Nicholas Grene (Dublin: Dolmen Press, 1971).

Biographical Sources

J. M. Synge, *Collected Letters of John Millington Synge, vol. 1, 1871–1907*, ed. Ann Saddlemyer (Oxford: Clarendon Press, 1983).
Collected Letters of John Millington Synge, vol. 2, 1907–1909, ed. Ann Saddlemyer (Oxford: Clarendon Press, 1984).
Letters to Molly, John Millington Synge to Maire O'Neill 1906–1909, ed. Ann Saddlemyer (Cambridge, MA: Belknap Press of Harvard University Press, 1971).
Kiely, David M., *John Millington Synge: A Biography* (Dublin: Gill & Macmillan, 1994).
Mc Cormack, W. J., *Fool of the Family: A Life of J. M Synge* (London: Weidenfeld & Nicolson, 2000).
Masefield, John, *John M. Synge: A Few Personal Recollections with Biographical Notes* (Dundrum: Cuala Press, 1915).
Mikhail, E. H. (ed.), *J. M. Synge: Interviews and Recollections* (London: Macmillan, 1977).
Stephens, Edward, *My Uncle John*, ed. Andrew Carpenter (London: Oxford University Press, 1974).

SELECT BIBLIOGRAPHY

Books on J. M. Synge

Bickley, Francis L., *J. M. Synge and the Irish Dramatic Movement* (London: Constable, 1912).

Bourgeois, Maurice, *John Millington Synge and the Irish Theatre* (London: Constable, 1913)

Burke, Mary, *'Tinkers': Synge and the Cultural History of the Irish Traveller* (Oxford University Press, 2009).

Corkery, Daniel, *Synge and Anglo-Irish Literature* (Cork: Mercier Press, 1966).

Gerstenberger, Donna, *John Millington Synge* (New York: Twayne, 1964).

Greene, David H. and Stephens, Edward M., *J. M. Synge: 1871–1909* (New York: Macmillan, 1959).

Grene, Nicholas, *Synge: A Critical Study of the Plays* (London: Macmillan, 1975).

Hart, William E., *Synge's First Symphony: The Aran Islands* (New Britain, CT: Mariel Publications, 1993).

Henn, T. R., *The Plays and Poems of J. M. Synge* (London: Methuen, 1963).

Howe, P. P., *J. M. Synge: A Critical Study* (New York: Greenwood Press, 1965).

Johnson, Toni O'Brien, *Synge: The Medieval and the Grotesque* (Gerrards Cross: Colin Smythe, 1982).

Johnston, Denis, *John Millington Synge* (New York: Columbia University Press, 1965).

Jones, Nesta, *File on Synge* (London: Methuen, 1994).

Kiberd, Declan, *Synge and the Irish Language* (London: Macmillan, 1993).

Kilroy, James, *The 'Playboy' Riots* (Dublin: Dolmen Press, 1971).

King, Mary C., *The Drama of J. M. Synge* (Syracuse University Press, 1985).

Lucas, F. L. *The Drama of Chekhov, Synge, Yeats and Pirandello* (London: Cassell, 1963).

McDonald, Ronan, *Tragedy and Irish Literature: Synge, O'Casey, Beckett* (Basingstoke: Palgrave, 2001).

O'Ceallaigh Ritschel, Nelson, *Synge and Irish Nationalism: The Precursor to Revolution* (Westport CT: Greenwood Press, 2002).

Price, Alan, *Synge and Anglo-Irish Drama* (New York: Russell & Russell, 1972).
  The Writings of J. M. Synge (London: Thames & Hudson, 1971).

Saddlemyer, Ann, *J. M. Synge and Modern Comedy* (Chester Springs, PA: Dolmen Press, 1968).

Skelton, Robin, *The Writings of J. M. Synge* (London: Thames & Hudson, 1971).

Sanchez, Ramón Sainero, *Lorca y Synge: ¿un mundo maldito?* (Madrid: Edítorial de la Universidad Complutense, 1983).

Smoot, Jean J., *A Comparison of Plays by J. M. Synge and Federico García Lorca* (Madrid: Turanzas, 1978).

Strong, L. A. G., *John Millington Synge* (London: Allen & Unwin, 1941).

Thornton, Weldon, *J. M. Synge and the Western Mind* (Gerrards Cross: Colin Smythe, 1979).

Books Relevant to Synge Studies

Burke, Helen, *Riotous Performances: The Struggle for Hegemony in the Irish Theater, 1712–1784* (University of Notre Dame Press, 2003).

Cairns, David and Richards, Shaun, *Writing Ireland: Colonialism, Nationalism and Culture* (Manchester University Press, 1988).

186

Castle, Gregory, *Modernism and the Celtic Revival* (Cambridge University Press, 2001).

Clarke, Brenna Katz, *The Emergence of the Irish Peasant Play at the Abbey Theatre* (Essex: Bowker Publishing, 1982).

Cleary, Joe, *Outrageous Fortune: Capital and Culture in Modern Ireland* (Dublin: Field Day, 2006).

Flannery, James, *W. B. Yeats and the Idea of a Theatre: The Early Abbey Theatre in Theory and Practice* (New Haven: Yale University Press, 1976).

Frazier, Adrian, *Behind the Scenes: Yeats, Horniman and the Struggle for the Abbey Theatre* (Berkeley: University of California Press, 1990).

Grene, Nicholas, *The Politics of Irish Drama: Plays in Context from Boucicault to Friel* (Cambridge University Press, 1999).

Grene, Nicholas (ed.), *J. M. Synge Travelling Ireland: Essays 1898–1908* (Dublin: Lilliput Press, 2009).

Harris, Susan Cannon, *Gender and Modern Irish Drama* (Bloomington, IN: Indiana University Press, 2002).

Innes, C. L., *The Devils Own Mirror: the Irishman and the African in Modern Literature* (Washington, DC: 3 Continents Press, 1990).

Kiberd, Declan, *Inventing Ireland* (London: Jonathan Cape, 1995).
  Irish Classics (London: Granta, 2000).

Levitas, Ben, *The Theatre of Nation: Irish Drama and Cultural Nationalism 1890–1916* (Oxford: Clarendon Press, 2002).

Mathews, P. J., *Revival: The Abbey Theatre, Sinn Féin, the Gaelic League and the Co-operative Movement* (Cork: Field Day / Cork University Press, 2003).

Matter, Sinead, *Garrigan, Primitivism, Science and the Irish Revival* (Oxford: Clarendon Press, 2004).

Maxwell, D. E. S., *A Critical History of Modern Irish Drama 1891–1980* (Cambridge University Press, 1984).

Morash, Christopher, *A History of Irish Theatre 1601–2000* (Cambridge University Press, 2002).

Murray, Christopher, *Twentieth-Century Irish Drama: Mirror up to Nation* (Manchester University Press, 2002).

O'Leary, Philip, *The Prose Literature of the Gaelic Revival 1881–1921: Ideology and Innovation* (Pennsylvania, PA: Pennsylvania State University, 1994).

Pilkington, Lionel, *Theatre and the State in Twentieth Century Ireland: Cultivating the People* (London: Routledge, 2001).

Reynolds, Paige, *Modernism, Drama, and the Audience for Irish Spectacle* (Cambridge University Press, 2007).

Roche, Anthony, *Contemporary Irish Drama: From Beckett to McGuinness* (Dublin: Gill & Macmillan, 1994).

Saddlemyer Ann (ed.), *Theatre Business: The Correspondence of the First Abbey Directors* (Gerrards Cross: Colin Smythe, 1982).

Sisson, Elaine, *Pearse's Patriots: St Enda's and the Cult of Boyhood* (Cork: Cork University Press, 2004).

Steele, Karen, *Women, Press, and Politics During the Irish Revival* (Syracuse University Press, 2007).

Trotter, Mary, *Ireland's National Theaters: Political Performance and the Origins of the Irish Dramatic Movement* (Syracuse University Press, 2001).

Watt, Stephen, *Joyce, O'Casey, and the Irish Popular Theatre* (Syracuse University Press, 1991).

Welch Robert, *The Abbey Theatre 1899–1999: Form and Pressure* (Oxford University Press, 1999).

White, Harry. *Music and the Irish Literary Imagination* (Oxford University Press, 2008).

Worth, Katharine, *The Irish Drama of Europe from Yeats to Beckett* (London: Athlone Press, 1978).

Edited Collections of Essays on J. M. Synge

Bloom, Harold (ed.), *John Millington Synge's 'The Playboy of the Western World'* (New York: Chelsea House Publishers, 1988).

Bushrui, S. B. (ed.), *A Centenary Tribute to J. M. Synge: 'Sunshine and the Moon's Delight'* (Gerrards Cross: Colin Smythe, 1979).

Casey, Daniel J. (ed.), *Critical Essays on John Millington Synge* (New York: G. K. Hall & Co., 1994).

Clark, David R. (ed.), *John Millington Synge: 'Riders to the Sea'* (Columbus, OH: Charles E. Merrill, 1970).

Frazier, Adrian (ed.), *Playboys of the Western World: Production Histories* (Dublin: Carysfort Press, 2004).

Gonzalez, Alexander G. (ed.), *Assessing the Achievement of J. M. Synge* (Westport, CT: Greenwood Press, 1996).

Grene, Nicholas (ed.), *Interpreting Synge: Essays from the Synge Summer School 1991–2000* (Dublin: Lilliput Press, 2000).

Harmon, Maurice (ed.), *J. M. Synge: Centenary Papers, 1971* (Dublin: Dolmen Press, 1972).

Kopper, Edward A. (ed.), *A J. M. Synge Literary Companion* (New York: Greenwood Press, 1988).

Whitaker, Thomas R. (ed), *Twentieth Century Interpretations of 'The Playboy of the Western World'* (Englewood Cliffs, NJ: Prentice-Hall, 1969).

Selected Essays on J. M. Synge

Arnold, Bruce, 'John M. Synge 1905–1909', in *Jack Yeats* (New Haven, CT: Yale University Press, 1998) pp. 133–51.

Bretherton, George, 'A Carnival Christy and a Playboy for all Ages', *Twentieth Century Literature*, 37.3 (1991), pp. 322–34.

Carville, Justin, '"My Wallet of Photographs": Photography, Ethnography and Visual Hegemony in John Millington Synge's *The Aran Islands*', *Irish Journal of Anthropology*, 10.1 (2007), pp. 5–11.

Castle, Gregory, 'Staging Ethnography: John M. Synge's *Playboy of the Western World* and the Problem of Cultural Translation', *Theater Journal*, 49.3 (1997), pp. 265–8.

Dalsimer, Adele M., '"The Irish Peasant had all his Heart": J. M. Synge in the Country Shop', *Visualising Ireland: National Identity and the Pictorial Tradition* (London: Faber & Faber, 1993), pp. 201–30.

Davy, Daniel, 'Tragic Self-Referral in *Riders to the Sea*', *Éire-Ireland*, 29.2 (Summer 1994), pp. 77–91.

Deane, Seamus, 'Synge and Heroism', *Celtic Revivals* (London: Faber & Faber, 1985), pp. 51–62.

Dobbins, Gregory, 'Whenever Green is Red: James Connolly and Postcolonial Theory', *Nepantla: Views from South*, 1.3 (2000), pp. 605–48.

Doggett, Rob, 'In the Shadow of the Glen: Gender, Nationalism, and "A Woman Only"', *English Literary History*, 67.4 (2000), pp. 1011–34.

Döring, Tobias, 'Dislocating Stages: Mustapha Matura's Caribbean Rewriting of Synge and Chekhov', *European Journal of English Studies*, 2.1 (1998), pp. 89–92.

Eckley, Grace, 'Truth at the Bottom of a Well: Synge's *The Well of the Saints*', *Modern Drama*, 16 (1973), pp. 193–8.

Elkins, Jane Duke, '"Cute Thinking Women": The Language of Synge's Female Vagrants', *Éire-Ireland*, 28.4 (1993), pp. 86–99.

Frawley, Oona, 'Synge, *The Aran Islands*, and the Movement towards Realism', *Irish Pastoral: Nostalgia and Twentieth Century Irish Literature* (Dublin: Irish Academic Press, 2005), pp. 81–103.

Gibbons, Luke, 'Synge, Country and Western: The Myth of the West in Irish and American Culture', *Transformations in Irish Culture* (Cork: Field Day / Cork University Press, 1996) pp. 23–36.

Grene, Nicholas, 'Two London Playboys: Before and After Druid', in Adrian Frazier (ed.), *Playboys of the Western World: Production Histories* (Dublin: Carysfort Press, 2004), pp. 74–86.

Harrington, John P., 'Synge's *Playboy*, the Irish Players, and the Anti-Irish Players', *The Irish Play on the New York Stage 1874–1966* (Lexington, KY: University Press of Kentucky, 1997), pp. 55–74.

Hirsch, Edward, 'The Imaginary Irish Peasant', *PMLA*, 106.5 (1991), pp. 1116–33.

Johnson, Toni O'Brien, 'Interrogating Boundaries: Fantasy in the plays of J. M. Synge', in Donald E. Morse and Csilla Bertha (eds.), *More Real than Reality: The Fantastic in Irish Literature and the Arts* (New York: Greenwood Press, 1991), pp. 137–50.

Kiberd, Declan, 'Synge, Yeats and Bardic Poetry', in *The Irish Writer and the World* (Cambridge University Press, 2005), pp. 70–90.

Knapp, James F., 'Primitivism and Empire: John Synge and Paul Gauguin', *Comparative Literature* 41.1 (Winter 1989), pp. 53–68.

Kurdri, Maria, 'Transplanting the Work of "that rooted man": The Reception of John Millington Synge's Drama in Hungary', *Comparative Drama*, 41.2 (2007), pp. 219–40.

Leder, Judith Remy, 'Synge's *Riders to the Sea*: Island as Cultural Battleground', *Twentieth Century Literature*, 36.2 (Summer 1990), pp. 207–25.

Levitas, Ben, 'Censorship and Self-Censure in the Plays of J. M. Synge', *Princeton University Library Chronicle*, 68.1–2 (2006–7), pp. 271–94.

McDiarmid, Lucy, 'The Abbey and the Theatrics of Controversy, 1909–1915', in Stephen Watt et al. (eds.), *A Century of Irish Drama: Widening the Stage* (Bloomington, IN: Indiana University Press, 2000).

McMahon, Seán, '"Leave Troubling the Lord God": A Note on Synge and Religion', *Éire-Ireland*, 11.1 (1976), pp. 132–41.

Martin, Augustine, 'Christy Mahon and the Apotheosis of Loneliness', in Anthony Roche (ed.) *Bearing Witness: Essays on Anglo-Irish Literature* (Dublin: University College Dublin Press, 1996), pp. 32–43.

Murphy, Brenda, 'Stoicism, Asceticism, and Ecstasy: Synge's *Deirdre of the Sorrows*', *Modern Drama*, 17 (June 1974), pp. 155–63.

Murphy, Paul, 'J. M. Synge and the Pitfalls of National Consciousness', *Theatre Research International*, 28.2 (2003), pp. 125–42.

Ní Dhuibhne, Éilis, 'Synge's Use of Popular Material in *The Shadow of the Glen*', *Béaloides: The Journal of the Folklore of Ireland Society*, 58 (1990), pp. 141–67.

Pollock, Jonathan, 'The Aran Islands, One by One: John Millington Synge and Antonin Artaud', in Pascale Amiot-Jouenne (ed.), *Irlande: Insularité, Singularité?: Actes du Colloque de la Société Française d'Études Irlandaises* (Presses Universitaires de Perpignan, 2001),

Powers, Kate, 'Myth and the Journey in *The Well of the Saints*', *Colby Quarterly*, 26.4 (December 1990), pp. 231–40.

Richards, Shaun, '"The Outpouring of a Morbid, Unhealthy Mind": The Critical Condition of Synge and McDonagh', *Irish University Review*, 33.1 (Spring/Summer 2003), pp. 201–14.

Roche, Anthony, 'Woman on the Threshold: J. M. Synge's *The Shadow of the Glen*, Teresa Deevy's *Katie Roche* and Marina Carr's *The Maï*', *Irish University Review*, 25.1 (Spring/Summer 1995), pp. 143–62.

'Synge, Brecht, and the Hiberno-German Connection, *Hungarian Journal of English and American Studies*, 10.1–2 (2004), pp. 9–32.

Rose, Mary S., 'Synge, Sophocles, and the Un-making of Myth', *Modern Drama*, 12 (1969), pp. 242–53.

Spangler, Ellen, 'Synge's *Deirdre of the Sorrows* as Feminine Tragedy', *Éire-Ireland*, 12.4 (1977), pp. 97–108.

Sprayberry, Sandra, 'Sea Changes: Post-Colonialism in Synge and Walcott', *South Carolina Review*, 33 (Spring, 2001) pp. 115–20.

Tifft, Stephen, 'The Parricidal Phantasm: Irish Nationalism and the *Playboy* Riots', in Andrew Parker et al. (eds.), *Nationalisms and Sexualities* (New York: Routledge, 1992).

Upton, Carole-Anne, 'Visions of the Sightless in Friel's *Molly Sweeney* and Synge's *The Well of the Saints*', *Modern Drama*, 40.3 (1997), pp. 47–58.

Yeats, W. B., 'J. M. Synge and the Ireland of his Time', *Essays and Introductions* (London: Macmillan, 1961) pp. 311–42.

INDEX

INDEX

Flaherty, Robert
Man of Aran 3, 94
flâneur 11, 53
Flaubert, Gustave, 53
Flower, Robin 99
folk traditions 9, 11, 16, 18–19, 25, 45, 58, 59, 93, 94
keen 17–18, 38, 60, 94
folktale 22, 44, 97, 100
wake 25, 34
French literature, 81
Freud, Sigmund
Civilization and Its Discontents 66
Friel, Brian 4, 127, 173
Dancing at Lughnasa 175–6
Faith Healer 72, 73, 174
Molly Sweeney 176
Translations 174

Gaelic League 9, 29–31, 36, 57, 65, 70, 95–6
Geertz, Clifford 58
gender 104–14
Gibbons, Luke 32
globalisation 50, 128
gombeenism 32–3
Gonne, Maud 10, 21, 28, 82, 107, 118, 149
Gregory, Lady Augusta 44, 52, 53, 59, 151, 162–4
Cuchulain of Muirthemne 98
Grene, Nicholas 183
Griffith, Arthur 20–1, 28, 48, 106–8, 149

Harlem Renaissance, 125, 129
Hegel, Georg Wilhelm Friedrich 133
Hiberno-English 21–2, 66, 81, 88, 98, 174
Huysmans, Joris-Karl 11
Hyde, Douglas 30, 52, 57, 97
Casadh an tSúgáin 37
The Love Songs of Connaught 38
Hynes, Garry 155, 171, 173

Ibsen, Henrik 12, 16, 79–80
A Doll's House 22, 39
international reputation, of J. M. Synge 4
Irish language 9, 52, 92–102
Irish Literary Theatre 15–16, 20, 118
Irish nationalism 6, 47
Irish Revivalism 7–9, 28, 39, 41, 44, 52, 68, 71, 86, 119, 125
Irish Studies 13

Jameson, Fredric 137
Jarry Alfred
Ubu Roi 35–6
Johnson, James Weldon 125–6
Johnston, Denis
The Old Lady Says 'No!' 7–8
Joyce, James 6, 7, 12, 17, 133
Exiles 65, 73
Finnegans Wake 144
Ulysses 72, 73, 119, 123, 144

Kavanagh, Patrick 7–8, 23
Keane, John B. 102
Kearney, Richard 174
Keating, Geoffrey 97
Kiberd, Declan 36, 38, 59, 60, 92, 94, 117, 121, 174

Lafargue, Paul 10, 82
Lawrence, D. H. 159
Leerssen, Joep 136
Lorca, Federico García 87, 88–9
Loti, Pierre 53, 84

Mc Cormack, W.J. 5, 136
McDonagh, Martin 4, 102, 173, 182–3
McDonald, Ronan 17
McGuinness, Frank 4
MacNeill, Eóin 44
McPherson, Conor 4, 102, 173
The Weir 179–80
Maeterlinck, Maurice 84–5, 87
Mamet, David 182
marriage 49, 69, 80, 108, 113, 114, 181
Martin, Augustine 181
Marx, Karl, 10, 82, 88, 133
Mathews, P. J. 117
Matura, Mustapha
The Playboy of the West Indies 127–8, 171
medieval literature 81
Meyer, Kuno 44, 84
modernism 12–13, 52, 56, 70, 133–44
modernity 45, 52, 77, 135, 136
Moore, George 67, 98, 150
Moran, D. P.
The Philosophy of Irish Ireland 57
Morris, William 134
Murphy, Tom 4, 155, 173, 174, 177–9

192

Cambridge Companions to ...

AUTHORS

Edward Albee edited by Stephen J. Bottoms

Margaret Atwood edited by Coral Ann Howells

W. H. Auden edited by Stan Smith

Jane Austen edited by Edward Copeland
and Juliet McMaster

Beckett edited by John Pilling

Aphra Behn edited by
Derek Hughes and Janet Todd

Walter Benjamin edited by David S. Ferris

William Blake edited by Morris Eaves

Brecht edited by Peter Thomson and
Glendyr Sacks (second edition)

The Brontës edited by Heather Glen

Frances Burney edited by Peter Sabor

Byron edited by Drummond Bone

Albert Camus edited by Edward J. Hughes

Willa Cather edited by Marilee Lindemann

Cervantes edited by Anthony J. Cascardi

Chaucer, second edition *edited by* Piero Boitani
and Jill Mann

Chekhov edited by Vera Gottlieb and Paul Allain

Kate Chopin edited by Janet Beer

Coleridge edited by Lucy Newlyn

Wilkie Collins edited by Jenny Bourne Taylor

Joseph Conrad edited by J. H. Stape

Dante edited by Rachel Jacoff
(second edition)

Daniel Defoe edited by John Richetti

Don DeLillo edited by John N. Duvall

Charles Dickens edited by John O. Jordan

Emily Dickinson edited by Wendy Martin

John Donne edited by Achsah Guibbory

Dostoevskii edited by W. J. Leatherbarrow

Theodore Dreiser edited by Leonard Cassuto
and Claire Virginia Eby

John Dryden edited by Steven N. Zwicker

W. E. B. Du Bois edited by Shamoon Zamir

George Eliot edited by George Levine

T. S. Eliot edited by A. David Moody

Ralph Ellison edited by Ross Posnock

Ralph Waldo Emerson edited by Joel Porte
and Saundra Morris

William Faulkner edited by Philip M. Weinstein

Henry Fielding edited by Claude Rawson

F. Scott Fitzgerald edited by Ruth Prigozy

Flaubert edited by Timothy Unwin

E. M. Forster edited by David Bradshaw

Benjamin Franklin edited by Carla Mulford

Brian Friel edited by Anthony Roche

Robert Frost edited by Robert Faggen

Elizabeth Gaskell edited by Jill L. Matus

Goethe edited by Lesley Sharpe

Günter Grass edited by Stuart Taberner

Thomas Hardy edited by Dale Kramer

David Hare edited by Richard Boon

Nathaniel Hawthorne edited by
Richard Millington

Seamus Heaney edited by Bernard O'Donoghue

Ernest Hemingway edited by Scott Donaldson

Homer edited by Robert Fowler

Ibsen edited by James McFarlane

Henry James edited by Jonathan Freedman

Samuel Johnson edited by Greg Clingham

Ben Jonson edited by Richard Harp and
Stanley Stewart

James Joyce edited by Derek Attridge
(second edition)

Kafka edited by Julian Preece

Keats edited by Susan J. Wolfson

Lacan edited by Jean-Michel Rabaté

D. H. Lawrence edited by Anne Fernihough

Primo Levi edited by Robert Gordon

Lucretius edited by Stuart Gillespie
and Philip Hardie

David Mamet edited by Christopher Bigsby

Thomas Mann edited by Ritchie Robertson

Christopher Marlowe edited by Patrick Cheney

Herman Melville edited by Robert S. Levine

Arthur Miller edited by Christopher Bigsby

Milton edited by Dennis Danielson
(second edition)

Molière edited by David Bradby and
Andrew Calder

Toni Morrison edited by Justine Tally

Nabokov edited by Julian W. Connolly

Eugene O'Neill edited by Michael Manheim

George Orwell edited by John Rodden

Ovid edited by Philip Hardie

TOPICS